T0322224

New Methods for Women:
A Manifesto

Sharmadean Reid is a British-Jamaican entrepreneur and businesswoman who received an MBE in 2015 for her services to the nail and beauty industry. Reid is the founder of Wah Nails and Beautystack – a networking platform for influential beauty professionals – and is a founding member of the women's co-working space The Wing. A member of the British Beauty Council, Sharmadean is an ambassador for Futuregirlcorp, a business boot-camp for female entrepreneurs.

New Methods for Women: A Manifesto

A Manifesto for Independence

SHARMADEAN REID

PENGUIN LIFE

AN IMPRINT OF

PENGUIN BOOKS

PENGUIN LIFE

UK | USA | Canada | Ireland | Australia
India | New Zealand | South Africa

Penguin Life is part of the Penguin Random House group of companies
whose addresses can be found at global.penguinrandomhouse.com.

First published 2024

001

Copyright © Sharmadean Reid, 2024
The References on p. 373 constitute an extension of this copyright page

The moral right of the author has been asserted

Set in 13.5/16pt Garamond MT Std
Typeset by Jouve (UK), Milton Keynes
Printed and bound in Great Britain by Clays Ltd, Elcograf S.p.A.

The authorized representative in the EEA is Penguin Random House Ireland,
Morrison Chambers, 32 Nassau Street, Dublin D02 YH68

A CIP catalogue record for this book is available from the British Library

ISBN: 978–0–241–46175–4

www.greenpenguin.co.uk

MIX
Paper | Supporting
responsible forestry
FSC® C018179

Penguin Random House is committed to a
sustainable future for our business, our readers
and our planet. This book is made from Forest
Stewardship Council® certified paper.

Contents

Introduction   1

Part 1 Understanding   15
Part 2 Absorbing   83
Part 3 Applying   163
Part 4 Accumulating   211
Part 5 Trimming   291

References   373
Acknowledgements   375

Introduction

The book you are holding in your hands is the result of over ten years of reflections and experimentations in order to deal with my chronic low-level stress and anxiety. I started this work in my head at around twenty-five years old; I started writing things down at twenty-eight; and I finally closed this arc of my life at thirty-eight, with most of the old feelings gone, but new ones arising, because, in reality, the work is never really done.

For me, it was not one person, or one big incident or one big moment, that made me determined to make a change within. It was lots and lots of little choices that slowly broke my spirit. Since I was twelve, I had always held a vision of my future, but for some reason my choices in early adulthood started to veer away from that plan. The choices did not seem like a big deal at the time – I made them casually and without consideration. I would go forth excitedly but randomly, following along with what was expected of me, instead of where my heart lay.

The problem was that each little choice was like a small incision. A nick that you wouldn't even really notice. None of my life choices seemed particularly wrong – in fact, they looked enviable. So I didn't bleed out all at once, it was more like death by a thousand paper cuts. Throughout this period of my life, I felt like the very essence of who I was, was dying. My body tried to tell me that something wasn't working, and in my late twenties I started getting a crushing pain in my chest. I ignored it for months, until one morning, while doing my usual mental checklist of the endless tasks I had that day, an episode of chest pain came over me that was so terrifying I lay on the floor and called an ambulance.

After eight hours of tests which all revealed nothing, the doctor sat me down in a small room and asked, 'Are you stressed?' I answered without hesitation, 'No, of course I'm not stressed. I'm fine.' She looked at me pityingly and said, 'Well, your body is.'

I believe the information that one can turn into an action is a delicate combination of messenger, message and moment. Prior to that moment, there had been many messengers telling me that I should slow down, relax. Be less busy. But either the message was indecipherable or the messenger didn't seem believable or – more commonly – I was not ready to hear it. After all, I had been working twelve-hour days since I was eleven years old. I had a paying job from the age of fourteen. I had high productivity output and whatever I was doing was always well received. In addition, I felt that I did not have the privilege to rest. If I didn't work, I didn't earn, and there was no one else to support me.

But there was something about that particular combination of tests, doctor and pain along with being a new mother that made me take notice this time, so I decided to try something new. Or as essayist Anaïs Nin wrote, 'The day came when the risk to remain tight in a bud was more painful than the risk it took to blossom.' Literally painful. So I looked for the logic. The mental discomfort I had always felt had now developed into anxiety. The anxiety formed a physical manifestation in my chest as a panic attack. My mind was hiding the stress of my body. With this new information I made a very small but life-changing decision. If this pain was a result of stress, it would seem rational that I would just meditate and calm myself down. It was as simple as that. I didn't have another panic attack for a decade, as I now had the ability to catch it at the earliest signal. I had tried a New Method, and with focus, and it worked.

But even though I had figured out how to turn off the warning light, the real work was under the hood. In 2013, I decided to move to my home town in the middle of England and began the slow process of rebuilding myself after having my first debilitating episode. But I carried on my work as normal. During this time, I even launched a new beauty product line and designed a clothing range. When necessary, I showed up and looked good. No one was ever really to know. Home was so healing, and it was there that I experimented with more Methods. Nature, whole foods, yoga. I also learned negotiation, and with all the free time I had, planned how to begin a start-up and play a game I could win. As I gained new strength, I felt that if I wanted to continue my career growth I must move back to the big city. I didn't want to leave Wolverhampton, but I returned to London in 2015 aged thirty-two, ready to turn things around.

There were a few years of bliss with the return of my London life. I was focused, with a plan, and I executed on it all. I opened an innovative new salon space, WAH Soho, developed an amazing VR experience and eventually raised millions in venture capital funding. Tick, tick, tick. But that old feeling of discomfort came back with a vengeance. Between the ages of thirty-five and thirty-eight, I required more intense work. Each year meant a different immersion in my self-development process, but the additional trauma of the pandemic and the impact it had on my business meant I was working harder and giving up more of myself than ever. It was during my last year of Methods that I became stronger in my Self. I grew less concerned with being romantically partnered and everything that comes with that longing, until finally things shifted in a deeper way and I could close this chapter of my life. On my thirty-ninth birthday, for the first birthday ever, I woke up feeling peaceful.

For those who know me, this seems remarkable, because during the period I am referring to I had achieved many things to be proud of. I had a cool business with a global influence. I had an adorable baby that I took everywhere. I was featured positively in the press. I won awards for my work. Tick, tick, tick. Like an undulating line, there were periods of incredible happiness and contentment, especially in my early thirties. But it was never going to last until I really, really did the work. Each time my line was rising, I would somehow step backwards so that it would fall. *New Methods for Women* was necessary for me to maintain an upwards trajectory by working on the things that were holding me back. Not for money or success, but for me to be able to do Important Work. I hated the idea that the anxiety I was carrying would mean that I would not be able to fulfil my mission. If I didn't do the work, I wouldn't be able to do Important Work. So I did.

What is *the work*? *New Methods for Women* was conceived while lazily reading the seminal book *A Room of One's Own* by Virginia Woolf. After just a few pages, the author's exacting internal monologue was like a scratching inside me. It felt so relevant and timely, and with each page I felt as if I was privy to secret knowledge. I flipped to the front of the book to find out when it was written . . . 1928. My heart sank. This book is almost a hundred years old! How can it be that I am still feeling the same discomfort that women felt a century ago? Reading Christine de Pizan's *The Book of the City of Ladies* was even worse. It was written 600 years ago, and I can still identify with the author's questioning of why the men of the day had the power and the women continued to suffer, and her attempt to visualize a world built by and for the ladies. 'This city has been founded and built to accommodate all deserving women.'

Like every new generation of women, I thought, well, all those old feminists must have been doing something wrong. There must be a New Method that will change gender inequities and quell my feelings of anger and my anxieties once and for all! And with my brazen youthful naïveté, I started writing down the things that I felt were my personal experiments in regaining my power. To maintain momentum, I wrote these essays as a series of newsletters during the pandemic, sending them to my Stack World community. I would email the newsletter on a Friday, and then on Monday, like clockwork, we would gather on Zoom to discuss the topic. Writing in public was important to me, to get live and ongoing feedback on these Methods. I always like to work equally with theory and practice, letting them inform each other. I needed to understand where the essays resonated, where they did not, and hear actual experiences of women who had been through the same issues I had. Eventually that community has grown to number several thousand women all over the world, who understand that their personal development is key to their professional development. They have reported better relationships, more confidence and, significantly, more salary increases. Little by little, the Methods work.

All waves of feminism have been born within rapidly changing times, but during all this progress and hypergrowth there is one thing that seems to be pervasive – a system that keeps women as second-class citizens. The American writer and social critic bell hooks describes it as 'the interlocking systems of domination that define our reality', and I reflected heavily on how this system has impacted *my reality*, including my panic attacks and burnout. I retreated inwards while cataloguing my Methods, believing that if I could somehow control myself, it would all be OK.

So were all the old feminists just doing something wrong? Absolutely not. I have mentored, worked with and talked to thousands of women, and my biggest and most disheartening realization is that the issues women are facing today are ones we have been facing for thousands of years, but especially for the few hundred years since the Industrial Revolution, where work started to move away from the home and the gender pay gap widened. Harvard professor Claudia Goldin won the 2023 Nobel Prize for Economics by confirming that women's choices have often been, and remain, limited by marriage and responsibility for the home and family, and urged business leaders and policymakers to create a plan for how we balance children and work if we truly seek gender equity. Having this solid and comprehensive research adds data to an intuitively felt argument. Feminists and scholars have for years been making recommendations for how to improve the lives of women, primarily around childcare and economic independence, but who is willing to change the system?

It was Laura Bates, feminist writer and founder of the Everyday Sexism Project, who helped me untangle that relationship between my personal reality and the patriarchy. After reading hundreds and thousands of submissions of sexism from members of the public, she states: 'We'd all been thinking of these stories as individual problems – our own personal, coincidental lists. But they weren't. They were connected. And that meant that the problem wasn't with us; it was with the system.' In her book *Fix the System, Not the Women*, she uncovers the five pillars of Education, Politics, Media, Policing and Criminal Justice as seats of sexism. These areas are the deep-rooted cause of the hypervigilance required by women just to move through the world. It demanded *my* hypervigilance and my exhaustion. It results in the violence we experience all the way to the simple lack of access to education. It's why women don't get funded or mentored. It includes no access to leadership roles, poor policy-making and actual laws against women. It wasn't just me feeling this way and it wasn't my fault. So if it's not my fault, why bother doing the work? I was sure that the system would continue down this course unless we shifted it one degree in another direction, and that shift had to come from us, the oppressed. While I agree with the sentiment in the title of her brilliant book, I believe that the only way this system will be fixed is by having more women as active participants within it.

New Methods is a personal manifesto, written for me, to regain my power and become an active participant in the society I live in, but I also would like it to be an inspiration for you to find ideas that resonate or the impetus to write your own. During my twenty-year career, I feel that there have been tactics and strategies that granted me the autonomy and economic freedom to be able to fulfil my Important Work, but my greatest satisfaction is when others are able to, too. I want to see women changing laws, rewriting the education system, owning the media. I want investment in women's health research. I want women politicians and world leaders. Since Sirimavo Bandaranaike was first elected Prime Minister of Sri Lanka in 1960, just seventy-seven women have held the most powerful positions of leadership in their respective countries. I want to see a female Democrat president in real life, not just in political TV dramas.

The system won't change unless we have more women in decision-making roles at the highest levels of power in our societies, but how can we devote ourselves to collective action at these highest levels if we haven't yet done the work on an individual level? For me, I followed the capitalist dream, thinking individual success was the answer, and tick-tick-ticked all the boxes, but surprise surprise, it wasn't enough. Working hard on my external success was pointless until I felt secure and safe within. I needed to do the work on myself in order to be able to do the work for others. My starting point wasn't zero because the system put me at −10. *New Methods for Women* was my playbook to get myself from −10 to zero, just to enable me to move forward on a level playing field and fulfil my purpose and scale my work. By doing the Methods, you will hopefully reach a point where you have got to zero and you no longer have to be in constant hypervigilance to protect yourself − you can now free up your mental load to look outwards and change this system from zero to 1.

The book is designed to be read in chronological order, as with each essay I found myself getting closer and closer to understanding myself and the world around me. Some of the essays are practical and actionable, and some reflective. Ideally I would love you to read it all through and then go back and actually do the work, experimenting and writing your own personal Methods as you go. What worked for me might not work for you, but I hope my own self-direction informs yours.

9

I would love for you to read the beginning of each chapter aloud, as an affirmation or call to arms. I wrote it as a shortcut or a reminder for you that you have the ability to make choices within this system.

This book is not a memoir, and I've taken pains to get my decision-making and thought process across with as little personal detail as possible so that you can see what is possible for you. You'll find many references to ideas and thoughts taken from writers, largely male, and squeezed into a framework that fits for me. In my start-up journey, I found some incredible business books that would offer sharp advice, forgetting that as a Black woman, I would not be able to apply that advice so swiftly and easily, given the systemic challenges I face just to get inside the door. Of course I believe that everything is possible and attainable to you, but I had to think personally about my approach and I would urge you to log and document your approach for the next woman.

Documenting it for the next woman means that we are not learning from scratch. I feel there are not enough books outside of fiction or memoirs that outline women's thinking or mental models to create a framework that we might use to achieve self-actualization. The blessing and curse of fiction is that it's hyper-dramatized and sometimes at the extreme end of what a woman might do in any given situation. I instead want to find the mundane journaling of what a woman has done in order to get to her version of the top, and the innermost working of her mind, to know what she was thinking about the times in which she lived. In the eighteenth century, discussing the nature of genius, French mathematician Émilie du Châtelet wrote: 'One must know what one wants to be', along with many other *bon mots* on talent, education and self-comparison. In 1934 the British psychoanalyst and writer Marion Milner published her seven-year experiment in living, to discover what it was that made her happy. It is one of the greatest experiments in female autonomy, where she analyses moments of everyday life in order to find her highest consciousness.

While writing this book, someone gave me the game-changing *The Revolution from Within* by eminent feminist Gloria Steinem, and I almost stopped writing, thinking, well, everything that needs to be said has been said. She writes in her introduction that 'The "inner" books rarely talked about politics and the roles of race, gender and class bias in stealing self-esteem, and the "outer" ones celebrated women's success without addressing the dilemma of those who . . . became addicted to ever more success because they felt there was a vacuum inside.' It was pure genius. But I continued writing to illustrate what it might be like to put this self-direction into action and what it might be like for me, a Black woman living in England in this new century. Abolitionist and women's rights advocate Maria W. Stewart wrote in 1831: 'How long shall the fair daughters of Africa be compelled to bury their minds and talents beneath a load of iron pots and kettles?' I certainly aim to make her proud. I encourage you to do the same and to write your brain processes on the page so that we have a wider body of modern writing by women thinkers and intellectuals.

At this point, I also feel compelled to tell you that the title of this book is misleading. There aren't many new things in *New Methods for Women* because so much of this wisdom has been shared by feminists before me, and it's likely that there is much you already instinctively know. I've included quotes and references so you can do deeper research on anything that speaks to you. I am indebted to all the writers and thinkers who have shared their knowledge past and present, people of all genders who believe in equality for all. I am so privileged to have access to literature spanning thousands of years across many cultures, informing me of what it means to live a good life. I have turned these insights into my personal actions, and I would love to have an open dialogue by continuing to build on each other's work.

Every generation of young women is slowly but surely inching towards a world that is becoming more equal. I just want it to happen faster, and for them not to have to wait until they enter a biased workplace or completely burn out before they decide they need to find a women's community like ours, just in order to survive. I may be putting myself out of a job, but I don't want anyone to pick up this book in 256 years' time (when the gender pay gap is due to close) and think: 'Wow, this resonates!' just as I did with *A Room of One's Own*. I want this book to be put into action, making the content redundant in my lifetime and absurd in a century. And to do that we must ride the infinite loop of self-reflection to citizenship until we achieve personal and collective power. Are you with me?

Some key terms I use throughout this book

Vision: Your life's work, a broad utopian statement. How you imagine the future to be.

Mission: The current iteration of your life's work. Could be a business or project.

Values: Your internal rules that guide your behaviour. Usually adopted from family. Necessary to define your own.

Principles: Values translated to external actions. The list you return to when you are most lost.

Important Work: Anything you do that contributes to your vision and mission.

Self-design: The way to construct your identity and environment based on your own Vision.

Brainspace: The percentage makeup of your various thoughts.

Domestic cognitive load: The amount of brainspace taken up by unpaid labour such as childcare, family appointments and school chores.

True Self: The most authentic version of you that is not defined by what other people think.

Higher Self: Your True Self at work, developing your best.

Lower Self: Your Ego at work, bringing out your worst.

Muscle memory: Repetitive tasks and thoughts that eventually become intuitive. Necessary for autonomy.

Vibration: A constantly shifting energy, mood or feeling.

Autonomy: Your ability to make informed decisions for yourself, free from coercion or external control.

PART ONE

Understanding

The journey usually begins with a bubbling dissatisfaction. A longing and a seeking for something, but you're not sure what. You want something external to 'fix' you. It doesn't really matter if it's a partner, a baby, a career or a drug, because the outcome you want is the same. Despite this intense desire to search outside yourself for comfort, the foundation for New Methods is to look within. All the answers you need are within you, you just need to listen quietly so that those answers find the confidence to come out. *New Methods* is here to be your guide on this Persephonean journey. This section is about *knowing yourself*. If I were to be more extreme, it's about becoming obsessed with yourself, about what makes you you. Understanding is about devoting the same amount of time and energy to learning about yourself as you might give to a romantic fantasy, social media or self-criticism. Reclaim your brainspace. Learning about your essence will give you the confidence you need to move forward. By looking at your past and indeed your present, we can draw a through-line towards your future: your True Self.

Understanding how you operate, how humans operate and how the world operates will help you make sense of your dissatisfaction. It's not your fault and it never was. I can prove it to you.

New Method 1
Self-reflect to Self-design

We question every element of our person to determine which part of our being is prescribed or self-designed. There is much discussion on what is natural or unnatural when it comes to the application of womanhood, and let it be known that 'natural' is merely customary to those who hold the power. Since the day you were born (possibly even while you were in the womb), there has been a narrative impressed upon you about who you are and what you want. Today is the day you start turning over every single physical and mental trait, every fancy and folly, every ideological belief in your mind, prodding a finger at it to check for the firmness of truth. Through self-reflection, we aim to peel back our layers and analyse whether our assigned character traits and beliefs represent our True Self, or if we are simply feeding into the narrative we were assigned by others. Today is the day we can choose whether we want the weight of our predetermined narrative to continue to crush us or if we want to move consciously and awake through the world, knowing we have the power to write our own story, line by line.

According to legend, 'Know Thyself' was carved into stone at the entrance to Apollo's temple at Delphi in Greece. Scholars, philosophers and civilizations have debated who the phrase was first attributed to, but regardless of its origin, I believe that knowing who you truly are is the critical foundation of knowing what you want.

You may already have an idea of who you are. Or it may seem like too vast a question to address, but it's likely that the version of you that exists right now is the one that your society, your upbringing and your close community have impressed upon you.

Even before you were born, there was a narrative waiting for you. Your parents may have told you of their excitement before you arrived. They had high hopes for you and for what you might represent to the family. They had a vision of you before your very existence. Your mother may have shared what you were like in the womb, interpreting every movement, kick and turn of your foetal mass as a formation of your personality.

'She's so active.'
'She loves this music.'
'She's a night owl.'
'She likes it when I eat carrots.'

When you're born it continues with fervour. Compounded by the echo of wider family and friends.

'She's very tired.'
'She wants that.'
'She doesn't like that.'
'She loves the colour purple.'

The first way you begin to make sense of yourself is through the stimulus you receive from your family as a baby. I remember that on the day my son, Roman, was born, I proclaimed him to be wonderfully observant. Imagine that! I didn't even have ten minutes' worth of data from his existence. He was a brand-new human being, and I had already assigned a personality trait to him. I believed he was observant simply because he looked right at me with his big brown eyes, then he looked at his father and back to me again. The reality is that at the time of birth, a typical newborn's eyesight is weak; the best they can see is blurry shapes. He wasn't showing observance – he was simply focusing on the only movement in front of him. He had no idea who or what I was.

Sometimes this story about ourselves can be negative. For example, if you were told you weren't wanted or that you were unplanned. Or even that you were a 'miracle baby'. (Imagine the pressure of that responsibility!) If you were estranged, abandoned or separated from your caregivers, as I was, the story deep in your subconscious may actually be a hurtful one: That you were defective, not good enough, not wanted.

When we embody the character traits people think we have – such as Roman and his observation – we receive praise for it, along with a healthy hit of dopamine (our feel-good hormones), and we crave more of that encouragement. Roman could barely see, but the exclamation in my voice, the soft cooing, and the positive reinforcement meant that I encouraged him to develop this trait of 'being observant' over the years. Now he notices everything. Nature or nurture? We can never really know, because we get stuck in this cycle. We think to ourselves consciously or otherwise: 'I'm [insert character trait here]. How can I bring it to the forefront and get more of that delicious positive reinforcement?' We develop this habit, without ever questioning whether the trait actually represents us or not. Eventually, it becomes us.

This continues throughout childhood, when we are constantly tested against societal checkboxes through various grading systems. School reports telling us about ourselves. 'Sharmadean can often be overenthusiastic.' 'Sharmadean knows what she wants and how she intends to achieve it.' 'Sharmadean now has a less selfish approach to group situations.' Grades herding us into pens, closing the gate and deciding that one facet of our personality warrants a label for our entire being.

As adults, we're no longer validated by grades but these formative years have already done their work. They've told us who we are. Psychologist Jane Loevinger argues in *Measuring Ego Development* that it's not until around twenty-five years old that we start to turn inward, become more self-aware, and think about what we inherently do and don't like, as opposed to what society has told us we should like. When you look internally, is a pat on the back for that grade really what you want? Are you still looking for acceptance, measuring yourself against a system forced on you by your surroundings? Who we are isn't discovered by simply following the patterns of our environment or by following the assigned track we were put on in school. Instead of measuring yourself against society, now is the time to define what it is that truly makes you, you.

The first New Method, the one you may need to return to over and over again, is about self-reflection and analysis so that you can begin the work of self-design.

Start to ask yourself, 'When did this become me?' When you discover a trait whose origins you are unsure of, try to get to the root of it. Take the trait you want to evaluate and start playing with it, pulling it apart like play-dough and turning it over in your mind. It could be as simple as 'I like to go on holiday to Italy', or something more internal such as 'Having straight hair makes me feel good.'

Then ask yourself. Who decided this was you? When was this decided? What is the evidence you have to prove that this is really you? Is that evidence still relevant today?

Sometimes it's easier to keep travelling down a designated road than it is to turn back and have a go at writing your own map, but to me that's like sleepwalking through life. If you've been unconscious about your True Self, now is the time to wake up.

There's something powerful about asking why. To do this effectively we must set aside judgement and bring forward curiosity. When you want to challenge something, drill down by using the 'Five Whys' technique, which literally means asking 'Why?' five times to get to the origin of a problem. It's so simple, but you will discover how something came to be and, in our case, our assigned narratives. The Five Whys technique was originally developed by Sakichi Toyoda and was used within the Toyota Motor Corporation during the evolution of its manufacturing methodologies. It is a critical component of problem-solving training, delivered as part of the induction into the Toyota Production System. Toyota developed several manufacturing techniques after the Second World War that are interesting to research. Many of the Methods in this book apply business frameworks to the self. Why should corporations alone get the value of reflection and analysis?

Here is how you can apply the Five Whys to move closer towards Self-reflect to Self-design.

An example of a character trait: 'Sharmadean is competitive and anxious to succeed.' (Actually written by my wonderful teacher Mrs Foster when I was seven years old.)

Why?

1. Winning is important – Why is winning important?
2. Because I get a reward – Why do you need the reward?
3. Rewards (especially financial) are the only way I'll get ahead in life – Why are the rewards the only way you'll get ahead in life?
4. Because I can only rely on myself – Why can you only rely on yourself?
5. I don't come from a wealthy family – Fifth Why – The Root Cause.

Thus you see that the root cause of financial insecurity has shown up in my personality as being competitive and anxious to succeed. But is this still relevant today? Now that I have created financial security for myself, do I still need to be competitive? As a functioning adult with a community and close friends, do I still need to hold on to the fear of only being able to rely on myself?

There's a great fable for this that I heard recently, implying how culture gets set. There was a woman who would cut the ends off a ham before cooking it every Sunday. She didn't know why she did it, though, so one day she asked her mother. Her mother thought. 'Hmmm, I'm not sure why I do it. I've always done it this way. Your grandma taught me.' So they both went to ask grandma why she did it. After questioning, the response was, 'I've always done it this way. Your great-grandma taught me.' But why? 'Well, she had to – it wouldn't fit in the tray otherwise!'

This story demonstrates just how easily we can reinforce actions that no longer serve us. The fact is that you are your own woman and you can just get a bigger tray.

The Five Whys model is a useful reminder to pause, unpack and reflect, giving you a chance to recognize and reprogramme behaviours that aren't authentically you. However, it's worth being aware that criticism of this model points out that it relies on the investigator's knowledge of the situation. So in short, you need to gather more evidence before you feel comfortable with your whys. But in a classic case of chicken and egg, your traits might be self-fulfilling impositions and may direct the way you gather the evidence in order to prove yourself right. Don't let the notion of right and wrong hinder your exploration. Just work on gathering as many data points from as wide a variety of sources as possible. Start with the Five Whys, and use personality tests, natal charts, freeform writing, interviews with peers, or whatever tool you prefer to kick-start the process of self-discovery. Experiment with what brings forward your character and then ask yourself – is this real?

When I first started doing this work on myself, the work you are now holding in your hands, I found it incredibly challenging. The work of understanding yourself shakes your identity to its very core. I spent weeks, maybe months, in a daze. I started to question everything I had ever done in life, and why. My whole reason for existing started to fall apart. Why had I been so desperate to be successful all my life? For a pat on the head from the invisible hand of my absent father? And the patriarchal society that represented him? If I wasn't working for the pat on the head, who was I working for? Were the drivers for my success pure and true? I began to lose hope.

The walls of my internal house started to crumble. As I was doing the work to improve myself, I was terrified that without having low self-worth I would have no motivation to succeed. I would just fade away into nothing. If I didn't self-sabotage in order to keep myself in a place of insecurity so that I might then work like a maniac to build financial security, what else would I do?

But then I discovered that growth isn't born from being in a state of perpetual pain. By understanding myself and the things that are truly me, I can be motivated by my mission. I can be motivated by being of service. It was at that harmonious point that I started to build the house of my mind back up, brick by brick, with intention and purpose. This time, using my own design.

New Method 2
Know Your Body

We take control of our bodies by managing the level of toxicity, both physically and energetically, acknowledging that for a long time we have had our senses dulled by various marketing aspirations to keep us subdued. Part of knowing ourselves is knowing the glorious miracle which is the human body, and using data to track and analyse what works and does not work for us. Where possible, we use this information to biohack ourselves to ensure that we have the energy and disposition to achieve the things we set out to do. Sometimes we do bad things to our bodies because bad things can temporarily feel good, but we do them with open eyes and do not dumbfoundedly question the results. We know what we did and how it happened and we accept responsibility.

'It's just like magic!' I exclaimed, looking at the constantly refreshing screen of our app, while our engineers tweaked the code in real time. 'Um, no,' he said through the screen, 'it's just a command. I tell it what to do, and the computer just does it.'

Input, output. What I love about most technology is that it historically has been fairly predictable. You give it commands, and the machine executes them. Even artificial intelligence today requires a starting input. But to me, the most interesting part of an artificial neural network is what is known as 'hidden layers'. A hidden layer is the layer between input layers and output layers. That is where the 'intelligence' happens.

To me, our bodies and minds are just like machines: they process whatever we give them. New Method 1 showed you that many of our early inputs come from external influences outside our control. The output is the way we see ourselves, the limits we set for ourselves and the way we talk about ourselves. These inputs affect us both psychologically and physiologically, and recognizing the various inputs for your whole body and mind can help you fine-tune it (just like when we tweak code in real-time) to get the best and most optimum output. The hidden layers are a mystery. You could eat the exact same meal as a friend and digest it differently, you could watch the same movie and it could make one of you sweat and the other laugh.

Understanding what elicits responses from your body and mind is a key New Method. Abolitionist author Harriet Beecher Stowe once said, 'A woman's health is her capital,' and as I age, I understand that this is essential to achieve our Important Work. To understand our bodies, we need to be conscious of the whole flow – the data that you are feeding your machine, the hidden layers that determine the processing and the output.

This may be a mental input. If your inner voice is constantly negative, you're putting low-grade fuel into your system. If you surround yourself with negative people, that verbal and energy transference also counts as mental input. How can you be expected to perform optimally with low-grade fuel? Managing toxic thoughts and people will come up a lot in this book, so for this New Method I want to bring your attention to your body.

On the physiological side, the data is somewhat easier to capture. Biologically, it's time to learn about yourself. Blood, DNA and food intolerance tests can all illuminate your hidden layers and the way your body will process and provide outputs. Science is more forthcoming with data than therapy.

It was during my pregnancy when I was twenty-six that I started to actually pay attention to my body. I desperately wanted a home birth and a blood test showed that I had an iron deficiency, which put me at risk. As I was early in my New Methods journey, I brushed it off as a temporary imbalance. I took iron pills and ate spinach with orange juice to get my levels up to the safe zone, and had a successful home birth. What I wasn't thinking about was the hidden layer of genetics that makes me, and many other women of colour, susceptible to anaemia. In fact, it was years later, when I did a nutrition-based blood test, that I started to take my iron levels seriously.

So, let's look at the data.

Input
Low iron meals
General unconscious eating

Hidden layer
Genetic disposition to anaemia

Output

A constant state of low-level tiredness, especially
around my period

Moody with loved ones

Unable to deliver my best work through exhaustion

If you know what makes your body process your
inputs, you can make changes to operate at your highest
level. This is the start of data-driven decision-making.
You might be unknowingly holding yourself back on so
many levels by giving your body inputs that it's not best
equipped to deal with.

Here's how my New Method works now:

Input

Two portions of red meat per week (but not while
menstruating)

Daily iron and vitamin C supplements

A non-heme iron source while menstruating, such
as spinach, red beans, oats, with vitamin C to
enhance that absorption

Cook with cast-iron skillets

Hidden layer

Genetic disposition to anaemia

Output

High energy

Positive mood

While the obvious change is around food, this New Method runs much deeper, to urge you to learn more about your whole body, inside and out. While ultimately what you put into your body affects everything, now is the time to also uncover your hidden layers. We all know that drinking alcohol can give you a hangover, but have you explored how your genes may affect this? Do you know if you have a severe alcohol allergy? Which type of alcohol gives you a hangover? Grain-based or potato-based? Beer or wine? Have you experimented with your mixers and managed the sugar level spike? There are so many variables you can play with to work out what's best for you.

Here are some inputs to reflect on:

Some inputs
Friends
Family
Food
Sleep
Medication
Meditation
Music
Weather
Exercise
Environment
Air quality
Media

Some hidden layers
Genes

Blood type
Repressed trauma
Hormones
Menstruation

Some outputs
Abnormal weight gain
Skin conditions
Low mood
Anxiety
Pain
Loneliness
Fear

Pick one thing from each section and analyse the journey. For example, how does your exercise regime – affecting an underactive thyroid gland you may have – result in fatigue and joint pain? Uncover your hidden layers by getting tested. Home genetics testing has revolutionized the market and can provide you with a starting point for your research. Blood tests can be acquired through your doctor or privately, and will give you raw data to work with. Begin to live consciously and notice the micro changes that happen to you throughout your day, and list the things that provide quality outputs. If you don't want to submit your DNA, or if blood tests aren't available to you, you can begin by tracking your mood. I have the simplest list on my phone, entitled 'Things that Make Me Happy', covering Self, Family, Relationships, Work and

Health. If something isn't on the list, I minimize my exposure to it.

Nature is critical to my mental health. There is something about woods and forests that makes me feel relaxed, satisfied and whole. I need to live near green space or water so that when my machine starts to overload, I can update my inputs. The same goes for music. Driving while playing UK Garage music from 1997 to 2013 means that upon arrival at my destination, I am in the best mood ever, fully energized and on good form with my friends. Whereas, constantly listening to nothing but the news can cause me fear, stress and anxiety, meaning I arrive at dinner with worry and concern.

I know what I need in order to perform, giving me the freedom of choice to decide my input. Sometimes I might choose a negative input because things that are bad for you – like alcohol, sugar and fats – can often feel good temporarily. But then I can't feign ignorance as to what the output might be. I can't exclaim repetitively after eating pasta for lunch, 'I have no idea why I'm so tired!' I'm doing it with my eyes open. There is so little research into how inputs work in the female body (women are often underrepresented in clinical trials, meaning we don't always know how certain medications work on our systems) that we need to advocate for our health and get to know our own bodies.

The more methodical and aware you are about each of your inputs, the better your outputs. By listening closely to what you need, you begin to take a more productive, data-driven approach to your life. Adjust your routines and behaviours to those that serve you well and become more aware of why your body and mind respond to what you're giving them. Your body is the ultimate intelligent machine, so service it well.

New Method 3
You Are a Work in Progress

We give ourselves permission to be ever-evolving. As humans, we are living, breathing organisms that are constantly in motion, and the work has to start somewhere. The process is just as important as the outcome, and there is no such thing as the perfect partner, mother or woman. The perfection presented to us in the media is simply a colage of the male gaze. We accept that striving for this perfection is an impossible task, and one that will only serve to waste time and energy, as well as sacrifice our mental health. We embrace all the freedom and power that comes from accepting ourselves as a work in progress. We are not broken or flawed – we are simply human. Changing our minds, evolving our personalities, making mistakes and learning new things about ourselves are all part of the journey to get to know who we are and what we like. This self-acceptance will no doubt attract critics. Society is afraid of the self-accepting woman, because this woman is difficult to control. We know that everyone has critics, and there will always be people who like to have an opinion despite not knowing anything about our individual journey. We practise loving disengagement. We can hear and acknowledge what people say, but work so it has little effect on us. Our journey is ours alone.

If we judged the *Mona Lisa* on the first layer, there's no way she would have made it to the Louvre. She started as a dark green sludge on a plank of wood before building up to the legendary final work we know today. While it is generally believed that it took Leonardo da Vinci four years to paint the portrait, some say it took another three years to complete, right up to the year the painter died. Its creation was a process and one that didn't end with the death of da Vinci. Even after the last paint stroke of the *Mona Lisa* was applied, its impact continued, influencing other artists for centuries as well as being a mainstay of popular culture. The work is never done.

As you start to look within, you may feel like a green sludge. I know I did. As I started to begin the work of understanding myself, there was so much that felt invisible and unobtainable to me. Would I ever feel relaxed and comfortable in my own skin? The very idea of not being stressed or feeling loved seemed quite remote. I have learned over the last decade of reflection that contentment is a forever journey, and as I understood myself better it was like adding layers to the painting until I could see myself clearly. My legacy will be decided long after me, but the work will never stop evolving.

If you are successful at this, you will continue to evolve until the day you die, so get comfortable with the ongoing change and if you are brave, you can create systems to encourage it. So if you are feeling like you may never 'get there', remember that there is no finish line. The process is just as important as the outcome.

One of the seven principles I created for my company is 'Launch and Learn', which is centred around the theory of *kaizen* – a term that refers to ongoing or continuous improvement. *Kaizen* comes from two Japanese words: '*kai*' meaning 'change' and '*zen*' meaning 'good'. *Kaizen* isn't a specific set of actions as much as it is a philosophy, and I take this method to most areas of my life, whereby I make an assumption that nothing is fixed, but instead is the starting point for something that is ever-evolving. The only thing I can be certain of is change. And even when it is at its most painful, as the word *kaizen* denotes, change is good.

Growing up, I loved chopping and changing through different identities as I worked to find myself and my style. Even today, when I get into something, I completely immerse myself in it, wearing the clothes, listening to the music, hanging around in the locations and reading the books. In my early teens, I loved punk and indie; the DIY attitude matched my creative ambitions. I would make flyers and zines and be right there in the mosh pit. In my late teens I got into UK Garage – I loved the energy, the carefree vibe and the club culture. In my early twenties, I was obsessed with hip-hop. I loved the hustle, the glamour and the lyrical intelligence. It was at this point that a boyfriend casually accused me of being inauthentic, that I was just absorbing a subculture until I was bored. While I can accept that as a purist he would see my methodology as blasphemous, in hindsight I don't believe I was being inauthentic. I saw it as a building of layers, just like the *Mona Lisa*. With each new interest, I was adding to my understanding of culture and the world, creating new synapses, not switching them out. I would follow trails of information and learn that my favourite filmmaker worked with this artist. This artist was inspired by this writer and so on, until the trail would eventually take a turn that didn't chime with me and I would move on to the next thing.

Some people are static, and have a finite view of what they allow themselves to experience. I believe in the dynamic and infinite. I see myself as a collector of ideas, and as I gather, my bucket becomes Tardis-like and bottomless. I see this curiosity as a superpower, giving me range and an edge, not as something to be chided for.

Your teens and twenties are your prime data-gathering years. You're still determining who you are and what you like. Everything is fluid and constantly evolving. That's half the fun of growing up. When people and society apply the predetermined narratives we spoke about in New Method 1 to you, they are undoubtedly going to try to keep you there. That boyfriend didn't seem to like my ever-evolving identity and it was crushing for me. I never felt like I was the 'right type of girl' for him, or for anyone, for that matter.

The New Method here is to understand that you're a work in progress and embrace all that means for you and your personal development. Just because those around you have a belief that you should settle into one singular identity doesn't mean you should. By accepting that you're a WIP, you go easier on yourself. Understand that you can and will make mistakes. Take each experience and lesson in your stride, acknowledging that they are helping you get closer to a fuller understanding of who you are.

There will always be people offering criticism and feedback, whether or not you ask for it. Take the opportunity to thank your unpaid critics and use it as another lens to help you develop even further, instead of taking it personally. My then boyfriend's accusations did make me reflect on whether or not I was a phoney, and they forced me to ask questions about my behaviour. Upon that reflection, I found and trusted my own truth, which was that every part of the culture I absorb pushes my thinking further in some way. I didn't need to be the right girl for him, because eventually, I became the right kind of woman for myself.

New Method 4
Reflect on the Role of Your Emotions

We commit to understanding what drives our emotions, knowing that some are reflexes to our past traumas and some are cavewoman responses to survive and are out of our control. Neuroscience tells us that our brains are ancient, with three distinct areas that govern us. The brain is so old that sometimes it still thinks we are hunter-gatherers and at risk of being eaten by predators. It becomes hypervigilant to keep ourselves safe against forces that are no longer threatening. In order not to be completely consumed by these ancient responses, we endeavour to create breathing room between our emotions and our decisions, understanding that they reside in completely different areas of our brain. When we experience an extremely negative emotional response, we take pause and ask ourselves where it's coming from, and if it serves us right now.

Neuroscience is the study of the nervous system – from structure to function, development to degeneration, in health and in disease. It covers the whole nervous system, with a primary focus on the brain. Let's consider the different parts of your brain. There's your hypothalamus, responsible for your autonomic functions, temperature regulation, blood pressure and blood glucose. It is the oldest part of your brain, developed many millions of years ago to ensure you stay alive. Your limbic system

39

deals with emotions and memory and is the one we are most concerned with here. Finally, your neo-cortex, the youngest part of your brain and where your decisions and reasoning come from.

The hormones and nervous signals in your limbic system – the centre of your brain – are stronger than both your hypothalamus and neo-cortex. When you're not consciously aware of all the chemical reactions happening within yourself, it's often your limbic system that will win out. Your emotions will steal the show and can wreak havoc on your mindset if you fail to catch yourself. When it comes to your brain, there is a big gap between emotion, reason and reality.

In your path to understanding yourself, I urge you to take an interest in the growing field of neuroscience. We need more women in STEM subjects (science, technology, engineering and mathematics) to prevent continual bias – remember, women were diagnosed by men as 'hysterical' as far back as Ancient Egypt and as recently as the current century, and there are so few studies on women's health. But right now, there's only one part of the brain that I really want you to remember: the amygdala. This collection of cells near the base of the brain is where emotions are given meaning, remembered, and attached to associations and responses to them (emotional memories). There are two, one in each hemisphere of the brain. Parts of your brain become activated by the two stress hormones: cortisol and adrenaline, impairing function and your ability to reason. Both hormones are released from your adrenal glands to prepare your body to flee or fight. The amygdala is considered to be part of the brain's limbic system. It's key to how you process strong emotions like fear and pleasure, and it was designed to protect you. As a cavewoman. But you're not a cavewoman any more.

Because of the complexity of your limbic system, it's often hard to put your emotions into words. You may feel triggered in some way, but fail to pinpoint exactly why. There are so many stimuli running through your brain and body every second of every day that trying to unpack each and every feeling would make us overload, like a smartphone with no storage left. For our own protection, our brain packages up the root of our emotions into the most basic story possible, to help us process things quickly. Think of it like a low-resolution graphic taking up less computer memory than a 4D movie.

Have you ever been at a store and been really angry or rude to an innocent cashier? You'll feel that the current situation is triggering the anger. That the person opposite you is offending you somehow. Your brain will be developing a really simple story in a lo-res graphic, to make it easier for you to understand this feeling of anger. Your eyes trick you by sending visuals of the scene, convincing you that it's all about the person in front of you. Epinephrine, also known as adrenaline, is among the chemicals that are released by the adrenal gland, sending signals to the brain's frontal lobe, which then allows neurotransmitters to speed up your heart rate and display other signs of anger. Your whole body is working to make you angry because you might need all those chemicals and all that strength to fight.

But is it real or is it ancient? Are you angry because that person is really insulting you? Or do you actually feel lonely and separated from your community? Does the cashier subconsciously remind you of someone who harmed you in the past, someone you might not be aware of, triggering hostility? Are you angry because your current home situation makes you feel powerless and out of control? And are you angry because you're repressed? Did the cashier say something rude and undermining which reminded you of how small and insignificant you are in the world? Reminded you of how you were spoken to as a child?

Think of emotions as an elegant fuel for evolution. When you are in real danger and you don't fight, you die. And so your line of the human race stops with you. Emotions are designed to avoid that. They're a subtle, beautiful piece of code that helps you create rapid (albeit lo-res) responses to experiences in your life, to nudge you towards positive ones that create connection (and ultimately procreation) and away from negative ones that cause you to interrupt the evolutionary process and die out as a species.

The idea that my emotions were just cavewoman responses developed over millions of years seemed totally basic to the overwhelming impact they had on my life. Of course, I had New Methods in my tool kit. I can edit my diet, design my environment and I can recognize my triggers, but the very idea that this reptilian brain from a million years ago was controlling me today made it easier for me to accept that this is just how nature made me.

I now take the view that emotions are ancient signals, set in motion millions of years ago to ensure our species' survival, but not always needed today. In fact, the excess cortisol, adrenaline and other hormones released during the negative emotional experience can create long-term disruption to your endocrine system. The endocrine system is a complex network of glands and organs. Think of it as your body's messenger system. It uses hormones to control and coordinate your body's metabolism, energy level, reproduction, growth and development. When your endocrine system is out of balance it can lead to intestinal problems, anxiety or depression, weight gain and increased blood pressure. Holding on to my negative emotions was literally bad for my long-term health. Not to mention passing that genetic code on to future children, as explored in the field of epigenetics.

Remember the two sides of you: your Higher and Lower Self. When you're operating as your lowest self, your amygdala and fight-or-flight mode are constantly triggered, the hormones are pumping through your veins and you're more susceptible to falling victim to your emotions. When scrolling through Instagram and seeing your friends eating dinner without you, your Lower Self might quickly start feeling low, and left out, and create a narrative that they are all plotting against you. Your Higher Self would simply celebrate their fun and move on.

Try to pause. Create space between your emotion and

your reasoning, to give yourself time to catch up and make the connection. The next time you feel any visceral emotion rising, take a step back, pause, and question it.

The New Method here is to stop trying to control your emotions. They're part of you, and bigger and older and mightier than you. Instead, turn your attention to the circumstances that lead you to a stressful or highly emotional situation and pull apart what they might stand for. Bring greater awareness to how you respond in the moment. This takes a lot of practice and self-awareness, as you're trying to self-reflect for why your emotions surface while you are living through them.

To better understand how your emotions are affecting you, keep an emotional diary. Use a mood tracker app, or simply get a notepad and start logging how you feel. Every time your emotions change, for better or worse, write down what you were doing at the time. Question how your emotions might be holding you back, dragging you to your Lower Self. Building an arsenal of information and insight into what makes you you.

I felt so in control the first time I was able to verbalize why somebody's simple action (asking me: 'What do you want for dinner tonight?') sent me completely spiralling (the normalcy of a relationship that I subconsciously felt I didn't deserve gave me a mild panic attack), which then made me clam up entirely (preparing for self-sabotage). My old self would have just made my excuses and left what would have been a nice evening. But now, I have the knowledge to communicate what is going on, and I do so for the benefit of myself and those around me.

Becoming a New Method woman encourages you to take ownership of the situations you're in and how they affect your mental state and behaviours. Greater awareness will allow you to identify when your emotions are overshadowing logic. It will slowly begin to reduce the number of fight-or-flight situations your body goes through, as you're early to catch yourself slipping.

Above all else, consider the amount of energy you expend being stressed, angry or fearful. Is that really where you want to use your greatness?

New Method 5
Label Your Trauma

Self-loathing is the disease of the modern woman and we must find compassion in ourselves and our own experiences. We know that doing the work of uncovering and naming our traumas is painful, but it is only through this work that we can begin self-acceptance. Naming our traumas allows us to identify the problem, and it is upon identification that we can begin to work to solve it. This work is critical because it forms the foundation of how we move through the world and breaks the intergenerational trauma cycle, the genetic imprint of our trauma that lives on in future generations. We chart the root cause of the behaviours that keep us from accessing our full power and from building deep relations with ourselves and others. Once we know our trauma triggers, we create systems to manage them from within rather than project them externally. The work starts with acknowledgement and acceptance.

Dominic wasn't someone who I spent much time with. We had moved in the same social circles for the last decade or so, but he was the type of person in my life that I saw at parties and fashion shows and had a stop-and-chat with. But for some reason (and in my belief a divine reason) he was on the end of the phone as I was hyperventilating and slipping into a deep sadness about being dumped. The only time in my life that I have ever been properly dumped. After four hours of late-night talking, Dom gently said . . .

'Have you ever thought that you might be codependent?'

Codependency.

I knew so many big words. So many specialist words were nestled within my vocabulary, but for thirty-two years the term 'codependency' had evaded me. Dom seemed hesitant to explain it fully but just urged me to explore it more. As I searched on the internet through my tears, I entered a trauma-filled rabbit hole.

I discovered that a codependent is someone who cannot function on their own and whose thinking and behaviour are instead organized around another person. Many codependents don't listen to their own needs and become excessively preoccupied with the needs of their partner.

The articles that surfaced were filled with headings like '10 Symptoms You're in a Codependent Relationship!' and 'Warning Signs! How to spot the red flags of a codependent!' It was an eye-opening discovery of a world that I had previously never known existed.

Many of my friends, especially in the USA, went to 12-Step meetings. Every time I went to New York or LA, it seemed like the whole of the city would pause for the meetings, and therapy language was a normal part of their vocabulary. I didn't ask about it or question it. I would just patiently wait outside with a coffee until my friends were done. Addiction seemed so far removed from who I was.

It turned out that codependency is an addiction. The addiction is my partner. Dominic was kind enough to take me to a meeting. More new words started to enter my vocabulary, such as avoidant behaviour, love anorexia, anxious attachment and the key one, narcissistic personality disorder. Our conversations went sort of like this . . .

'So essentially what you're saying is that because I never received the love I needed as a child from my parents, I resorted to being obsessed with finding a partner to fill that love-shaped hole?'

'Yes.'

'And this is called codependency or love addiction?'

'Yes.'

'And it means my whole life revolves around my partner, even though I'm a super independent woman?'

'Yes.'

'And I tend to attract avoidant or narcissistic partners who won't truly love me, thus proving my own theory that I'm unlovable?'

'Yep.'

'And also work really, really hard and be a high achiever to prove myself to this absent father.'

'Yes, that too.'

'And my real trauma is fear of abandonment caused by the father who I have never known.'

'YES!'

'Oh, OK.'

I was shell-shocked. These revelations made me question everything. In that summer of 2017, millennial girl self-help hadn't yet made it on to my social media feed. Mental health was at around 50 per cent on Google Search trends globally, and the Narcissistic Personality Disorder (NPD) memes hadn't made it to my phone. I felt incredibly alone. All I remember of that summer is eating a lot of takeouts on the sofa and watching documentaries while trying to numb out.

The labelling of my trauma – abandonment – was a turning point for me to chart how my behaviours had been driven by a fear that I had made part of me since the day I was born. I had named the thing.

Naming the world, naming the thing and labelling your trauma, gives you the power to do the work. *Pedagogy of the Oppressed*, written by Brazilian educator Paulo Freire in 1968, is a book I've returned to often. In it, Freire proposes a new relationship between teacher, student and society. He argues that we should instead treat the learner as a co-creator of knowledge, and as the illiterate start to name the world around them, they can use this language as part of their liberation. He says, 'To exist, humanly, is to name the world, to change it. Once named, the world in its turn reappears to the namers as a problem and requires of them a new naming. Human beings are not built in silence, but in word, in work, in action-reflection.'

So as a historically oppressed gender and race, I can be a co-creator of my own knowledge? My oppressor cannot liberate me? No man is coming to save me? I can only liberate myself? This notion was powerful to me.

Freire is intentional in his order:

Word
Work
Action
Reflection

I had the words – 'Fear of Abandonment'. I continued my work of attending meetings, reading books, and talking to others. I took the action of seeking professional help to support me on my way to recovery. I reflected constantly about what got me to this place. Whenever I started a new relationship, I felt able to speak completely and freely about what I was feeling internally, in real-time. I didn't have to lie in bed next to someone and feel silenced. I didn't have to hold anything in, because I wasn't confused. Instead I was just trying to retrain my mind to focus on the root of the problem that would cause my anxiety, not the inconsequential event that triggered it. I would say confidently to myself – *yes, I have a fear of abandonment because my father wasn't around and it shows up in these ways, and it makes me act like this and I'm triggered by this, and so on and so on*. I now had the vocabulary to describe my behaviours and actions. It felt liberating.

I used to always feel like people were having fun without me. I grew up building thick defences to protect myself. I would sabotage a relationship before they had the chance to abandon me. I believed that people didn't want me, and the slightest glimmer of behaviour that indicated this set off alarm bells. For example, if a group of friends had serendipitously met in the street and then all went for lunch, I would assume they had planned the whole event purposely to exclude me. But it's not real. It's a 'truth' I've convinced myself of since I was a child.

Being ruled by previous trauma can be exhausting and frustrating for the people around you, but mostly for yourself. Punishing other people is another indicator that you're acting from a place of trauma. When my friends or current partner would go away for long periods of time, like a summer trip, upon their return I'd find myself being rude or cold for no reason. I would give them the silent treatment for days and stop being as forthcoming and loving as I normally would be. Withholding love was a way I protected myself. Working through my traumas, I realized it was related to the feelings of abandonment that had been with me since a young age. But that wasn't the case today. No one abandoned me; they were just living their normal lives and their absence was not an indicator of their affection.

Labelling your trauma is critical to your recovery. Not so that you can use it as an excuse or a shield, but so that you can build up the knowledge, experience and research of so many others who have been in your shoes. Every part of the human condition has been experienced by someone else before, and we are lucky that many of them document and share their journey to recovery.

For me, a key part of my recovery was labelling the traumas and recognizing my triggers. A trauma trigger is something that transports you back to an unpleasant experience. These triggers can be set off by any of your senses in inexplicable ways. Seeing something on TV, hearing a piece of music, smelling a certain perfume, people's behaviour, can all take us on an unwelcome journey to the past. It's time to understand which traumas – perhaps some you aren't even aware of – are holding you back.

Trauma is labelled differently by various industry bodies, but they roughly fall into the following categories:

Type 1 Trauma: refers to single-incident traumas which are unexpected and come out of the blue, such as being mugged, sexual violence, losing a loved one, an accident, a natural disaster and many more. They can be referred to as big T trauma, shock or acute trauma.

Type 2 Trauma: Complex trauma describes trauma which may have been experienced as part of childhood or early stages of development. It goes beyond a one-time incident and is usually repeated over a certain period of time. It can be part of an interpersonal relationship where someone might feel trapped emotionally or physically. Examples are prolonged sexual abuse, emotional abuse, neglect and more. Those experiencing complex trauma may also feel as if they have been coerced or were powerless to prevent the trauma.

I have also felt the heavy weight of ancestral, historical and intergenerational trauma. As an empath, I feel things deeply and when I read of the women being force-fed with tubes so that I could have the right to vote, or what Black slave women experienced at the hands of their colonizers, I feel that trauma. If you have grown up in a country that has experienced war and heard the whispers of your parents and family discussing it, or there was a dark family secret of sexual violence that you weren't part of, but you knew about, this is all secondary trauma that we experience. This is the effect of hearing and seeing it even if it didn't happen to us. It could even be that someone you love dearly has experienced trauma and you know all about it and feel powerless to protect them. You knowing about it is painful too.

Mirror neurons are an interesting phenomenon. Mirror neurons are a type of brain cell that respond equally when we perform an action and when we *witness* someone else perform the same action. It's why your heart beats faster when you are watching something particularly emotive in a film. It could also be why you flinch when you see your parents fighting with each other. It is another way that you may feel trauma that isn't quite yours.

In addition to labelling my traumas, I found schema therapy eye-opening. Schemas are unhelpful patterns that some people develop if their emotional needs aren't met as a child and combine elements of cognitive behavioural therapy (CBT), psychoanalysis, attachment theory and emotion-focused therapy, among others. Practitioners have identified eighteen distinct schemas, but they all fall into one of five categories or domains:

- Domain I, disconnection and rejection, includes schemas that make it difficult to develop healthy relationships – *the codependents*.
- Domain II, impaired autonomy and performance, includes schemas that make it

difficult to develop a strong sense of self and function in the world as an adult – *the learned helplessness.*

- Domain III, impaired limits, includes schemas that affect self-control and the ability to respect boundaries and limits – *the narcissists.*
- Domain IV, other-directedness, includes schemas that lead you to prioritize the needs of others above your own – *the people pleasers.*
- Domain V, over-vigilance and inhibition, includes schemas that prioritize avoiding failure or mistakes through alertness, rules and disregarding desires or emotions – *the hypercritical.*

You may find schemas useful in the process of labelling your experience, and in the first instance, the preceding sections of this book will help stir your memories of the roots of the trauma. Knowing yourself is where it starts, but then I recommend you seek professional help that has specific expertise in the area you want to work on. Labelling is just the beginning.

Even after years of work, while I intellectually understood the concepts and origins of my trauma, I could not shift my emotional responses to them. I was hard-wired. I didn't yet know about brain plasticity or how to reprogramme my neural pathways. The last piece of work which marked the end of this section of my life journey was hypnotherapy. In my initial consultation with my hypnotherapist, he said quite simply and bluntly: 'Almost everyone I meet suffers from either loneliness, abandonment or rejection.' Four years later, now aged thirty-six, there were my words again. I had come full circle. With him, I managed to look at my traumatic memories differently. By the end of our sessions, I felt . . . light.

For me it was hypnotherapy, but for you, it may be something else. How exciting for you to start the journey, and go easy on yourself while you do. However painful it may feel at first, work to name the thing. Until you learn to recognize the chains of your past, you're stopping yourself being free and having the future you deserve.

New Method 6
Know Your Attachment Style

We understand that in their most simplistic terms, there are three attachment styles: secure, anxious and avoidant, which can determine our behaviour towards others. We work to understand where we sit on the spectrum and analyse the behaviours that come with that self-diagnosis. What was the trauma that activated our attachment alarm system, and how do we cope with it? From here, we start to make choices. We no longer mindlessly attract partners that create low self-worth and we work to reprogramme the protest behaviours that stop us building deep connections with ourselves and others.

Humans are social animals, requiring connection for survival, but it is important to recognize the connections that aren't helping you step into your power. When it comes to relationships – romantic or otherwise – there are many 'attachment styles' at play, affecting the way we behave and the difference between healthy relationships and addiction.

In *Attached: The New Science of Adult Attachment and How It Can Help You Find – and Keep – Love* by Dr Amir Levine and Rachel S. F. Heller, the authors aptly describe the core three styles of attachment: the secure, the anxious and the avoidant. They say secure styles are the easiest to spot. It's the couples who got married in their early twenties to their absolute 'soulmate'. They're genuinely happy, nice people. It's never in your face, it just seems to come so naturally to both of them. People with secure attachment styles tend to partner off with each other sooner, which means as you approach and enter your thirties, what tends to be left in the dating swamp are the anxious and avoidant types.

The anxious type worry constantly about their relationships. Negative self-questioning such as 'Do they really like me?' and 'Are they about to break up with me?' is constantly playing on the anxiously attached mind. They're on alert for any signs of rejection and are likely to throw tantrums and create drama through protest behaviour when their needs are not met. Protest behaviour is what the authors of *Attached* refer to as a form of punishing your partner. It could be withholding sex, or not returning calls immediately. Think of it as the actions of a sulky child. Anxious types require constant reassurance and typically fall in 'love' very quickly.

With an avoidant style, the opposite occurs, but not right away. They'll dive in headfirst and, for the first few weeks, the excitement of a new person will be euphoric. As feelings develop and things get a little too real, the avoidant starts to cool off. For whatever reason, they start to keep the other person at arm's length – and from there, they detach more and more. The avoidant is the one who never wants to label the relationship and fails to create security and safety for their partner.

If you recognize yourself in these styles and don't like

what you see, don't worry, your attachment style isn't fixed forever. It's merely how your personality and past experiences have influenced the way you respond to relationships. Once you recognize where you sit on the spectrum, you can take greater control over how you approach and behave in relationships. You can begin to identify and catch any destructive behaviours you're putting yourself and the relationship(s) through.

To understand your attachment style more, it's a good idea to look at your trauma labels. A big part of how you behave today has been imprinted on you since childhood. If you grew up in a household showered with praise and love, encouraged to talk openly about your feelings and surrounded by positive relationships, you're more likely to form secure attachments later in life. On the reverse, if you were physically abandoned, had a parent that was mentally absent, showed no affection, or had toxic examples of love and relationships surrounding you, it wouldn't be unusual to exhibit anxious or avoidant attachments. Regardless of which category your childhood falls into, the environment in which you were raised is going to inform how you now believe love should be shown. Remember what got you here.

Anyone can move into – and just as easily out of – being securely attached. It's up to you to stay aware, catch yourself, and work to uphold the attachments you want. I had an anxious attachment style and I would always centre others in my mind. With both lovers and friends, I would be on high alert that they were going to leave me and always assume I was not a high priority for my partner and friend circle. Once I understood what was happening, I tried to decentre others and swung to the other extreme, developing an avoidant style and sabotaging relationships early because I was terrified I would become attached to someone again and become engulfed. I could easily go a year without talking to a good friend out of fear that they didn't want to be around me. Between relationships, I would be celibate for long periods because I didn't trust my judgement and I didn't want my anxious attachment consuming me again. Whether I was anxious or avoidant, it didn't matter. I couldn't get on the secure ground and the entire relationship would take up my brainspace.

I would exhibit protest behaviour actions to justify my internal alarms and feelings of discomfort. I had one particularly avoidant partner that I would protest by ignoring his calls – not because I wanted to, as I wanted to talk to him all the time, but as an attempt to wield power and control. It was hurtful to both of us.

The problem with this style of friendship or romantic relationship is that it halts your self-development. When I look back and consider the HOURS and DAYS I wasted in my anxiously attached frame of mind, thinking, 'Do they like me?' or 'Are they going to leave me too?' I am actually repulsed with myself. When I try to show compassion instead of judgement to myself, I remember my traumas and lack of parental affection and understand that my anxious attachment is just an output of that.

The anxious/avoidant cycle holds so many women

back, as they become intensely fixated on their relationships and neglect their own success and economic future in the process. They then go into their next relationship even more insecure or more avoidant than before and it becomes a vicious cycle.

I've also noticed attachment styles popping up in the workplace, shaping how people relate to their colleagues and superiors. It can be a key indicator of whether you're going to be in a working relationship that will help you thrive, or if you are displaying protest behaviours to your colleagues.

Individuals with a secure attachment style tend to exhibit a positive approach to work. You can just feel the calm optimism oozing from them. They feel comfortable both giving and receiving support and fostering a collaborative and cooperative work environment. Securely attached individuals tend to be self-assured, trusting, and open to feedback. They don't immediately get defensive and they aren't constantly seeking praise from their peers. Their performance is directly related to their own self-satisfaction, and when they get things wrong they don't immediately jump to, 'Well, I must be a loser and my boss hates me.'

Those with an anxious attachment style often seek constant reassurance and validation in the workplace. They always want to make sure you know exactly how they contributed to a project. They have a strong desire for approval from superiors and colleagues, constantly. They want a gold star and a pat on the head! I also find that anxiously attached individuals struggle with setting boundaries, which means they end up burning out. It can be a mental burnout and they are overly sensitive to criticism or rejection, experiencing heightened stress in work-related situations. I am prone to displaying signs of this type when dealing with my investors and mentors. I want them to think I did good!

Individuals with an avoidant attachment style tend to prioritize independence and self-reliance, and have a tendency to distance themselves from colleagues and avoid close relationships at work. They never turn their cams on for the Zoom calls. They often prefer working alone and can downplay the importance of teamwork or collaboration. Avoidant individuals may appear self-sufficient and detached, struggling with trust and vulnerability in professional relationships. They always think you might screw them over. Sometimes it includes a big dash of ego – I work better alone. Avoidant types are difficult to manage but it is important to do so to ensure a strong company culture and to stay up to date on their progress.

Those with a fearful-avoidant attachment style often exhibit a combination of anxious and avoidant behaviours in the workplace. They may desire closeness and connection with colleagues but simultaneously fear rejection or abandonment. Fearfully attached individuals may oscillate between seeking approval and distancing themselves from others, often experiencing internal conflict and difficulty navigating professional relationships. I can see how I used to get very close and vulnerable with my team members, only to think – oh no, I've taken it too far, they're going to reject me! So then I would immediately pull back and create distance. Maintaining consistent and clear communication is key. In an unequal power dynamic, the leader has the responsibility of setting the tone of professionalism. Work towards a secure and relaxed style.

For this New Method, your goal is simply to understand where you sit on the spectrum: what is your attachment style? Awareness is the first step. Then later you can analyse the behaviours that come with that. What triggers activate your attachment alarm system and how do you cope with them? From here, you can start to make choices. You can choose to exhibit protest behaviour in a desperate attempt to hold on to a relationship. You can choose to remain detached and never feel the warmth of true intimacy.

Or you can choose to build stronger, healthier relationships and make better decisions about the people you keep close to you. You can stop gravitating towards the attachment styles that don't suit you and better handle the relationships you're already in.

In comparison, a secure/secure relationship might appear boring once you've lived a life of dramatics, but relationships aren't supposed to be soul-destroying. They're not always easy but they most certainly should not be hurtful.

You'll find there are a lot of people in your life that fall into the various attachment categories. I would love for them all to be secure for you, but the chances are they won't be. It's important not to berate yourself for falling into these traps. Remember, you're a WIP and you can't possibly look out for the red flags that you didn't realize were there yet. I believe every red flag or toxic relationship is capable of positive change provided you're prepared to both be open and do the work together.

As you practise observing secure, anxious and avoidant behaviours, you can more readily recognize them in your budding relationships. Next time you find yourself constantly checking your phone for the text-backs, or creating barriers between you and your relationships, try to understand whether or not they are a healthy choice in your life. Only then can you ensure that you're forging secure and equal relationships.

New Method 7
Identify Numbing Behaviours

Existing as a human can be emotionally painful and we find ourselves practising numbing behaviours in order to self-soothe in the face of our daily trauma. It is difficult to determine the difference between activities for pleasure and activities for numbing, so our first job is to understand them. We aim not to engage in these numbing behaviours to the detriment of our Important Work. We list out our modes of being in Study, Service, Consumption and Rest modes, maintaining moderation and never remaining in the one mode for too long. Consumption is the warning sign for potential numbing behaviours and is the slippery slope towards self-loathing.

It was a constant pattern. I'd be so busy at work that I would catch up on the day's news and social media while lying in bed just before I went to sleep. I would scroll, scroll, and then I would close the app and open a shopping app and purchase a new dress or top. The packages would come to the office and pile up around my desk. It was things I sometimes didn't even remember ordering. What's my problem?

And then I realized, I was numbing out. Late-night internet shopping was one of my comforting and numbing behaviours when I felt FOMO. I was working all the time, not hanging out with friends and not getting the nourishment of their company. Or of my own company.

My mind wasn't scrolling on social media and thinking, 'Oh, I love her outfit, I want a dress like that, let me find something similar.' It wasn't even thinking, 'Ugh, I'm so terrible, let me buy a dress to feel better.' I was not consciously connecting the feelings of loneliness with compulsive spending. It was a series of actions that I did subconsciously in order to make myself fill the void.

It's all too easy to avoid situations that make us feel sad, stressed, or negative. Instead of tackling the matter directly, we mask it with a different task and numb ourselves. There's a big difference between engaging in a task – whether that's spending money, watching TV, dating – because you actually want to do it, and doing it as a coping mechanism or a comforter for something else.

Numbing behaviours are not full-blown addictions or even acts of self-care, they're ways you self-soothe when you're feeling stressed or low, and they keep you hovering just at the threshold of your Lowest Self.

There's also a distinct difference between numbing out and zoning out. In today's hyper-busy world, we all need respite. Sometimes I get back home, lie on the sofa, and put on a good TV show because my day has been so packed and I need to just space out. I'm not covering anything up, my intent is just to relax. I've decided I'm doing this because my body and mind need downtime. This is my form of self-care.

Compare that to my internet shopping. I would sometimes buy without purpose, with the completion of the act making me satisfied that I could go to sleep. I took no pleasure in the process.

There are seven key numbing behaviours we can all slip into:

Eating: Food is a common numbing behaviour. Who hasn't turned to a takeout or ice cream when they're feeling low? This doesn't mean you can't enjoy a good meal or a nice glass of wine; it becomes a numbing behaviour when we do it as a bandaid. Eating is a numbing behaviour I still turn to, where I use food to self-soothe when I'm stressed. I'm not just self-soothing with food, I'm also feeling validated that I have the financial ability to buy whatever fancy meal I like. The whole process is like a big cushion against whatever issue I might be facing at that moment.

Watching: On-demand has made TV even easier to consume. While we all love diving into the latest series, you can easily end up wasting days of your life finishing a seven-season show or just channel-surfing. If you're flopped in front of the TV barely even taking in what you're watching, you might be wasting time to avoid dealing with something else. Are you using TV to hide away from the world or because you're enjoying it?

Overspending: I know that when I'm spending a lot, I'm in a numbing phase. Are you shopping because you need something or just because the action of digitally swiping your card is making you happier in the moment? Does acquiring more stuff make you feel safe? Do you feel protected by the amount of possessions you have? Does spending make you feel temporarily more powerful?

Overthinking: Getting lost in your thoughts is a great way to lose a large chunk of your day. There's a difference between thinking about something productive, such as your plan in life, and obsessing over something that doesn't matter. Sometimes I can lose several hours in bed just thinking about nothing, the internal chatter just masking the focused thinking on the things I actually need to do.

Social media: We can spend hours each day on social media. You're spending a good chunk of your time just looking at other people's lives. Why?

Overworking: Work is a serious numbing behaviour for me. When my personal relationships are challenging, I dive into my work because it's a safe, orderly and predictable world there. In the same way some people might say, I feel sad, I'm going to call a friend, I would think – I feel sad, I'm going to my laptop to send some emails.

'U up?': The cliché 'u up' text that haunted our twenties is textbook numbing behaviour. You have zero intention of actually meeting these hookups or exes, you just want some attention. You want the message back: your temporary dopamine hit. You may be scrolling on dating apps for the same feeling. Self-soothing at its finest.

I started to identify primary modes of being that I have: consuming, studying, service and rest and looked at where my numbing behaviours sit.

- Being of service is what I can do to help others. If I'm helping my family or a team member out with something, I am being of service. If I'm doing a talk or writing, I'm being of service.
- Studying is what I can do to help myself. If I'm listening to a podcast, watching a documentary or reading, I'm studying. I'm widening my knowledge and awareness of the world in some way.
- Consumption is me at my lowest self. Consuming social media, consuming empty gossip, buying things, materialism and so on. If I'm in the mood to consume I will try to do so ethically by shopping women-only or I'll donate to some of my favourite causes instead. It surprisingly gives me the same satisfaction.
- Rest is a new addition for me, after realizing that being in any of these modes would result in a circuit overload. My mind and body need rest, whether that's a spa or just simply sleep.

Numbing behaviours can sit in all these modes, but I define it as sitting in any one of them, mindlessly, for too long. I manage mine by diverting my energies to a more purposeful task in a different mode of being. I would make an exaggerated point of putting down my phone and reading a book, because for me, it was far easier to switch my behaviour to something else than to stop them entirely.

The New Method is to move through your modes of being with moderation and try not to get stuck in your numbing behaviours. Be clear with yourself when an activity is for the purpose of self-soothing, and act with intent. It can be easy to blame the external factors. Yes, advertisers prey on insecurity, and algorithms make bingeing effortless, but the person choosing to engage in these behaviours is you. No one can make you do or feel anything you don't want to. Once you know what triggers your insecurities and anxieties, you can stop the numbing habits at the source.

By simply noticing what you're doing, you've taken the first step to stopping it. The next time you spot yourself slipping into a numbing behaviour, you can shift your focus to something that leaves you feeling happy, satisfied, and content instead.

New Method 8
Trust Your Intuition

We are naturally intuitive. Our innate understanding is stronger than we think. We have a protectionary power to pick up on subtle cues and signals from the face and body and make quick and accurate judgements about people and their behaviour. And often we ignore it. We ignore it to our peril, and sometimes to our death. From now on, we listen intently and unequivocally to our intuition. When we feel uncomfortable, we exit. With immediacy. We do not let our desire to be liked block actions guided by our intuition. Our intuition is evolutionary, honed over millions of years of having to detect danger, deception and hidden agendas. We listen to it.

Everything you need to know is within you – as long as you are listening. It is essential to trust your intuition. Your intuition is your inner compass, and it will always guide you in the right direction. It's that little voice inside you that knows what's best for you, even when your logical mind is telling you something different. Trusting your intuition can help you navigate life's challenges with confidence, grace and resilience. Every time you choose to trust your intuition, you are validating yourself and backing yourself. Every time you ignore it, you are quietly telling yourself that what you think doesn't matter. You are abandoning your self.

Unfortunately, society often encourages women to second-guess themselves and ignore their intuition, which is to be expected when we have been told over and over again that we are less than. We are taught to be logical, to look at the facts, and to make decisions based on what we think is rational. Anything outside of westernized science (a mere few hundred years old in its conception) is disregarded. But I believe that intuition is just as valuable as logic, and sometimes even more so. Your intuition is based on your experiences, your emotions, and your instincts. It's a combination of your conscious and subconscious mind, and it can give you insights that your rational mind could never come up with. In this regard, your intuition is indeed a data-driven tool.

Every interaction, experience or event you've witnessed or heard – whether directly or indirectly – will have been logged inside your mind. You might not remember a nasty fight between your parents that happened two decades ago, but if a similar situation (let's say two friends you respect) were to happen right now, your body would remember the motions it went through, and your response would likely feel the same as it did all those years ago. Your body latches on to these familiar events, as it can guess the outcome and therefore copy a previous response. Maybe it didn't even happen to you. It might be secondary trauma you experienced. Or a news story you read. If you are especially empathetic, your body still responds in a low-level similar way as if you experienced it. These emotional skills are closely linked to intuition because intuition is all about understanding your own emotions and the emotions of others.

However, trusting your intuition can be difficult. It requires you to be vulnerable and open to the possibility that you might be wrong. It can be scary to make decisions based on something that is quite intangible, especially when other people are telling you that you're making a mistake. But the truth is, your intuition is always there, waiting for you to listen.

I have ignored many red flags in my life. Flags I could not quite explain. My body would know what's best for me and start to walk out of the door and my head would say – that red flag looks fine! Take it! Wrap yourself in it! It's safe! Only it wasn't. Time and time again I replayed events in my mind, reliving the exact point I decided to disregard myself.

When I have ignored my intuition, it has usually come from a place of not wanting to appear impolite, or inexperienced. I don't want to seem like I don't know what I am doing, even when my senses are telling me that something is not quite right. I once had a term sheet from an investor, who I felt uncomfortable with. I didn't want to appear biased, as some of the ways he acted could be perceived as cultural, but he didn't make me feel entirely at ease about taking his money. At the last minute he lowered the valuation of my company, despite me filling the funding round and hitting some key product milestones during the fundraising process. As a person, he had already flashed many red flags. Things that don't work for me in my partners. When he got on the phone and said, 'It's not my fault you don't know what you are doing,' I laughed, grateful for a red flag so big that a bull could see it, and cancelled the deal. Later on I discovered he was an aggressive bully to another founder, and that confirmed that I had made the right decision. When you feel something in your bones, listen the first time.

What happens when you repeatedly ignore your intuition? If you lean too far into your 'logic' and ignore your gut, your body quietens your instincts because you're falsely training it that those hunches don't serve you. By telling yourself, 'I don't trust you,' you'll lose touch with this powerful tool over time. Your intuitions become harder to recognize the more they're suppressed. As we distance ourselves from our intuition, we cut ourselves off from powerful energy. But without these instincts, how can we be our real, authentic selves?

To practise this New Method and trust your intuition, you need to start by tuning in to your body. Your body is a powerful tool for tapping into your intuition because it gives you physical signals when something is right or wrong. You might feel a tightness in your chest when you're faced with a decision that doesn't feel right, or you might feel a sense of excitement and joy when you're on the right track. Pay attention to these physical signals and use them to guide your decisions. When something is off for me, it shows up in the tightness of my throat and I know it's a signal to recalibrate my position.

An important part of tuning in to your intuition is to practise self-care. When you're stressed, tired or overwhelmed, it can be difficult to hear your inner voice. Take time to quiet your mind. When you meditate, go to therapy, journal, or practise other forms of self-reflection, you are sending yourself into a state of consciousness that allows you to hear your intuition and make decisions that align with your values and goals.

Remember that your intuition is unique to you. It's based on your experiences, your emotions, and your instincts. Your intuition is your superpower, and you should begin collecting these data points with journalling and mood monitoring. These help you create a tangible and verbal description of what is happening inside you.

Trusting your intuition is essential for your safety and growth. Your gut instinct should never be ignored. Whether you call it vibes, mood, aura or energy, it doesn't matter. When you feel something from deep within you, telling you to do or avoid something, that's the real you dialling in. Don't ignore the call.

New Method 9
Have Compassion for Your Fellow Woman

Divide and Conquer has been one of the most basic strategies to keep women disunited in their plight. While it can be easy to utter the words, 'I'm not like other women', all women are alike in their subjugation regardless of race, class, sex, socio-economic status, intelligence and so on. We cut out the internalized misogyny which forms like cataracts on our lens when we view other women. We recognize everyone's path is their own and we have compassion for the diverse needs of women across the world. When we speak for women, we speak for all women or we speak for none at all, otherwise our advocacy remains incomplete. Only through solidarity and intersectional feminism can we hope to dismantle the systemic barriers that hinder women's progress and foster a world where gender equity prevails.

Not only have I witnessed some of the most insidious violence against women perpetrated by women themselves, but in my youth I was also petty and critical of other women. It took me a long time to understand how division within a sex was a key component of keeping us distracted and powerless. We must seek to understand the perspective of other women, those who at first may seem to be your enemy, or those that you have not even included in your fight for equality.

Patriarchy has clever tools at its disposal to slow attempts to challenge and dismantle the systems of oppression that have historically marginalized and disadvantaged women. One of the most pervasive: turning women against each other. Why do the hard work of attacking the movement if you can make us agents to do it ourselves? This is often done by making us feel we are all competing for the same scarce resource – power – instead of standing shoulder to shoulder in a united movement.

So what does this look like in practice? In my experience, the divisiveness begins small. It begins with gossip and chatter. Calling women you may know (or think you know because you follow them on the internet) derogatory terms. Judgemental terms. I don't need to write them here because you know what they are. You may have said these things to your friends about your other friends. You may have heard them said to you by your new partner about their ex-partner. Maybe the person you are having an affair with says these things about their wife. Words are the first weapon against women, and the words we use against women hurt us all.

I am lucky to have had friends who can keep me in check. I remember absentmindedly trash-talking another girl I was mildly envious of, only for my friend to say, 'She's really nice and I think that if you would get to know her you would actually be friends.' She stopped me in my tracks and made me question my vindictiveness. I did end up becoming friends with said girl and she is indeed now one of my inner circle. These behaviours are entrenched in our culture, and even the most ardent supporters of women can be prone to relapse. We can start by reframing how we view other women.

We need to hold each other to account in the way that these words are used to maintain the myths of women as second-class. These seemingly minor ways in which women deride women just set the stage for bigger divisions when the personal becomes political.

As patriarchy grows, it uses those with more relative power to hurt those with less. Often the founding voices and thinkers of the feminist movement – those in the most marginalized positions – are forgotten. Black trans women were at the heart of creating so much of the gender equality movement many of us support now yet they are often excluded in the media.

In her powerful and thought-provoking book *White Tears, Brown Scars*, journalist Ruby Hamad describes the notion of white tears: 'This weaponization of White Womanhood continues to be the centerpiece of an arsenal used to maintain the status quo and punish anyone who dares challenge it.' She calls for white women to 'do what they expect of men: to separate the act from the person and look at racism as they look at sexism, as a structural problem that can only begin to be solved when they stop putting their hurt feelings ahead of our material harm. It is not enough for white women to have their hearts in the right place or to claim they don't see color and treat everyone equally. Feminism must commit to an explicitly anti-racist platform. And that means severing themselves from their historical and emotional attachment to inherent innocence and goodness.'

White women must actively engage in dismantling systemic racism. This involves not weaponizing their privileged proximity to the patriarchy. It means supporting women of colour in leadership positions, and working to create an inclusive and welcoming feminist movement. The role of white women in the feminist movement is pivotal. They have the power and privilege to influence the direction of change. The words of Ruby Hamad serve as a timely reminder that change is not just about good intentions, but about concrete actions and structural transformation. Violence against women of colour is still a systemic issue that needs urgent attention. The stories of women of colour have long been scrubbed from the history books, and it is imperative that white women actively challenge and change this narrative.

In her book outlining the experiences of trans people, Shon Faye eloquently highlights why this intense desire to maintain a binary system is enforced. 'The oppression of trans people is specifically rooted in capitalism. In short, capitalism across the world still relies heavily on the idea of different categories of men's work and women's work, in which "women's work" (such as housework, child-rearing, and emotional labour) is either poorly paid or not paid at all. In order for this categorization to function, it needs to rest on a clear idea of how to divide men and women.' By being trans-exclusionary, cisgendered women may unknowingly be working to maintain a system that also limits them. It can sometimes feel as though we are crabs in a barrel.

These elements of white feminism and anti-trans sentiment collide when we look at the heightened vulnerability faced by transgender women of colour, particularly Black transgender women. They are at the intersection of racial discrimination, gender bias and transphobia, resulting in alarming rates of violence and discrimination. Transmisogynoir, a term coined by writer Trudy, is the specific experience of Black trans people where anti-Blackness, sexism and misogyny form a unique system of oppression. The term comes from 'misogynoir', coined by Black Queer feminist Moya Bailey, who created the term to address the misogyny directed toward Black cisgender women in American visual and popular culture. Every year there are many gender non-conforming and transgender people whose lives have been inhumanely and tragically taken through intentional means, including through gun violence. Who is protecting these women?

For feminism to succeed, it must be intersectional. Intersectional feminism, a term coined by Kimberlé Crenshaw, is a way that we can understand the diversity of women's needs. This perspective recognizes the intricate interplay of various social identities and systems of oppression. To grasp the realities of social inequality, we must acknowledge that an individual can confront multiple layers of discrimination simultaneously. Factors like race, gender, class, sexual orientation and disability, among others, can converge to shape one's experience. I myself am a working-class, Black woman from a town that is consistently voted one of the worst places to live in Britain. In the same vein, I am educated, living in a developed country, with access to human rights. All these facets shape the way people see me, and the way I see the world.

Feminism must be global in its breadth. The challenges faced by women in the West always seem to take precedence over women from other parts of the world in our media. The women fleeing wars, migrating with children tied to their backs, the young women wearing the abaya (a long, robe-like garment often worn by Muslim women which is now banned in French schools), the children who experience female genital mutilation, a practice that, according to the World Health Organization, has affected 200 million women and girls alive today and more. While there are women working for justice to end the subjugation of all women, there are many women still who are actively patronizing or pointing fingers at other women who we believe unworthy in our goal for justice. There are many more marginalized groups I could highlight here, and I also acknowledge that I am looking at this through my own Western lens. These global issues around women's equality are a challenge, because they are big, complex and entwined in a history of culture, religion and tradition. While I'm not urging you all to become activists or abandon your culture, I am urging for compassion and understanding through a humanist lens.

If we want to remain united, we also need to understand that we will not all make the same choices on that journey. The ways in which feminism has shifted and evolved across the past decades shows the ways in which different generations interpret equality – and often don't agree on how it should look. The current rise of the 'trad wife' or stay at home girlfriend movement reflects a segment of women who consciously choose to embrace traditional gender roles within their relationships. The choices made by women to embrace particular values can be influenced by a multitude of factors, including cultural or religious influences, economic circumstances and family experiences. It is crucial to approach these choices with nuance and avoid sweeping generalizations or judgements that may overlook the intricacy of a person's decision-making processes. A mantra I often repeat silently in my head is that 'you never know what people are going through'.

Feminism is not a static concept but a dynamic and evolving movement. It encompasses a multitude of perspectives, including liberal feminism, radical feminism, intersectional feminism and more. These various strands of feminism often have differing and antagonistic views on issues such as gender roles and personal choices. For bell hooks, confronting this self-hatred is key. 'Without confronting internalized sexism, women who picked up the feminist banner often betrayed the cause in their interactions with other women.'

Intersectional feminism is not merely an academic exercise but a call to action. It urges us to advocate for equal rights, access to healthcare, legal protection, and social acceptance for all women, especially those at the margins. Intersectional feminism seeks to broaden the feminist movement's scope, making it more inclusive and attuned to the diverse needs of all women everywhere. It acknowledges that a one-size-fits-all feminism is inadequate, emphasizing that the movement must adapt to consider the rich tapestry of experiences among women in its quest for gender equality. Audre Lorde's powerful words are something I refer to often. She says, 'I am not free while any woman is unfree, even when her shackles are very different from my own.'

So what is the answer to taking a progressive, inclusive feminist movement forward, one where we can support each other instead of succumbing to being divided? First, understand that women are not a monolith. The most progressive in humanity are those who have the ability to foster independent thought. Then, I would urge empathy. Rather than finger-pointing, or aggression, work to have compassion for the experience of your fellow women and how their unique experience may shape their beliefs. Finally, remember that one of the principal tenets of feminism is respect for individual autonomy and the agency of all individuals, including women, to make their own choices. Respect for autonomy means acknowledging that people have the right to make choices that align with their own beliefs, even if they differ from yours. They are still to be included in your fight for equality. They still deserve their rights.

PART TWO
Absorbing

For too long in knowledge there has been a singular voice, dominating history, science, language, culture and more. The singular voice has pierced us, giving us opinion presented as fact, small studies based as absolute science, and a Eurocentric view on a global world. The results are often harmful: self-loathing on an individual level and systemic inequality at a citizen level. So what can we do to change that? Sharing ideas and information is how humans have accelerated in evolution. A powerful tool and also a dangerous one. What ideas have you adopted to rule your life, without question? Are they working for you right now? This section on Absorbing is about reflecting on how you process information and what you define as the authoritative voice. Whether you're at a dinner party or in a hospital, there will be a beam of white light through which information comes at you. We might act like a prism and separate all the colours, and all the facts, to determine which information is most relevant for us in that moment. Truth is never absolute. You can cut the data however you want to make it serve you. If you are going to be a sponge for information and hone your curiosity, you had better be aware of the biases involved in the current modes of production and distribution of that knowledge. Work to get access to the full picture, so that you can unpick the narratives that harm you and go into all situations with your eyes wide open.

New Method 10
Start Actually Listening

We have so much to say after years of silence. When we find communion with others on our vibration it can be easy to unload everything on our mind. But we listen. We actively listen to build trust. To do this we stay present; check our understanding of the conversation with clarifying questions: encourage the conversation; validate their emotions; question deeper; give feedback IF they ask for it; embrace the silent moments; try to avoid killing the conversation. If talking to someone we do not vibe with, embrace every conversation as an opportunity to work on our listening and communication skills and learn about new types of humans. Those dead-end conversations with people you'll never see again are perfect for practising.

You are now a data-gathering machine – but how can you possibly gather data if you're truly not open to absorbing information from the person sitting opposite you? This is where active listening becomes crucial.

I can sometimes struggle with active listening, especially when I'm excited. Often when someone's talking to me, I'm so busy thinking about a hundred solutions to their problem that I forget to listen to what they're saying. Because my own brain is so full of suggestions, I tend to interrupt whoever is speaking to blurt out my own advice without giving them a chance to speak first. I can be so focused on replying with my own thoughts before I forget them that I end up not listening to what the other person has just told me. I'm aware that this isn't an ideal mode of communication, nor is it a healthy way to build trust with someone. Active listening is something I have to constantly work at, but when I practise it, the results are incredible.

When I was twenty-four, I took a break from work while I moved house. I made a decision that while I was house-hunting during the day, I would spend the evenings going out and meeting new people, and would act as interested as possible in what they had to say. I would be curious and questioning. I would make it clear that they were the most important person in the room to me at that moment and I wanted to hear all about them.

At that point, I hadn't even read the famous book *How to Win Friends and Influence People* by Dale Carnegie, but I was practising Fisher and Ury's tips on perception, emotion and communication and on how to 'listen actively and acknowledge what is being said'. I just did it as a fun personal challenge and it was one of the best few months of my life, socially. Many of the friends I made in that single month I still maintain to this day.

So how to do it? There's a big difference between listening and truly being present in a conversation. Active listening is a shortcut to presence and is essential for effective communication. That said, the fast-paced nature of our current world can cause us to rush through interactions without maintaining that presence. Active listening, however, allows me to hear what another person is really saying. Basically, it's closing my mouth and opening my ears. Not only does this strengthen relationships with others, as they feel heard, but I might stand to learn something (which is my favourite mode of being).

Active listening is about recognizing that my voice is not the only important one in the room. If I assume that the person I'm talking to might know something I don't, I'm far more likely to ask thoughtful questions and engage in a way that takes the conversation to a deeper level. Active listening is not quite as simple as staying silent, it's about taking a genuine interest in what the other person is saying, in an empathetic, non-judgemental way.

The New Method here is to perfect the skill of active listening. There are hundreds of techniques you can use to achieve this but, to keep it simple, here are a few of my favourites:

Stay present

If I want someone to open up and share information with me, I need to be present and sincerely engaged in the conversation, rather than appearing distracted, thinking about what to make for dinner or which museum to visit this weekend.

Put away your devices

I want to show awareness for the person standing in front of me by closing my laptop and putting away my devices. Would you open up to someone if they were constantly looking around the room or kept checking their phone? Probably not.

Mirroring

Sometimes, checking into a conversation can be as subtle as maintaining eye contact or nodding. Other times, I might repeat a certain word or phrase they have said. Not repeating like a parrot, but to check in and show I'm still actively following what they're telling me.

Clarifying questions

To be an excellent communicator, it's important to be on the same page as the other person. I want to confirm that I'm following the narrative and not barking up the wrong tree. So I might say: 'To make sure I've understood correctly, do you mean . . .', 'Just to be clear . . .', or paraphrase what they've expressed in my own words as ways of checking my understanding.

It's important to be aligned on their perspective before

adding any of your own opinions to the mix. Otherwise, you risk muddying the waters.

Encourage the conversation

When people give me very little information to work with, I can feel at a loss about how to respond. Short answers could stem from a worry that they're oversharing. Simple displays of acknowledgement and acceptance of what they're saying are a good way to keep the conversation flowing. A little nod or a genuine 'mmm' can help. 'That sounds interesting – tell me more about that' will directly give them permission to open up further. I'm proving that I'm engaged and want to hear more of what they have to say.

Validate their emotions

I want to show people I'm on their side by creating a safe space in which they can speak freely without fear of judgement. Listening with an open mind and empathy is crucial. Try putting yourself in their position and think about their circumstances before formulating your thoughts. You can show this in your responses: 'I know this can't be easy to talk about . . .' or 'I can understand why this might have been stressful for you.' It's about doing what you can to show you hear them and see them.

Labelling their emotions

Show you're hearing this person on a much deeper level by labelling the emotion behind their words. For example, 'This seems really important to you . . .' or 'It seems as if it's making you feel this way . . .' encourages them to look deeper within themselves. You're relating what they're saying to a more tangible emotion and encouraging them to explore it further. Labelling emotions is like calling out the elephant in the room. You help the other person see things more objectively. As a communicator, this shows you're not only listening to what's explicitly said, but you're also aware of the bigger picture. If you are labelling incorrectly, go back to clarifying questions.

Question deeper

Asking the right questions is an obvious tool for deep diving in your interactions. 'How does that feel?', 'What was that like?', 'What do you think would happen if . . . ?' are some examples of questions I love to use in conversation, especially if it's something I've not got a lot of experience with myself. These questions should always come from a supportive place – I'll wait for a natural pause or lull in the conversation to introduce them. I want to allow the other person to continue their train of thought before stepping in.

Remove bias

I try to keep my questions open-ended and unbiased. It's not about interrogating someone, but about trying to paint a richer picture of their circumstances. The person I'm talking to will be very involved in their own story, but I won't be. I'm simply gathering more information to better serve them as a listener or confidant. It's also important to pay attention to the other person's comfort level. If a topic or question comes up that they'd rather leave alone, it's important to be receptive to that and respect their boundaries.

Give feedback IF they ask for it

Not everyone initiates a conversation in search of advice or an answer. Ask your companion which version of you they want during that conversation. They may want a full solution offer or they just might want a friendly ear. Only if someone makes it clear that they want to hear your feedback or suggestions should you take your chance to add value to the conversation. By sharing your observations on their situation, you're hopefully bringing a fresh perspective on the matter from a new angle with different insight.

If you don't know where to start when offering advice, say so. This will be better than half-heartedly shoving some thoughts together that don't really offer any value. Be upfront and say, 'This isn't something I've experienced myself, but however I can help, whatever you need, know that I'm here.' With this, you're allowing them to set the pace for what they need from you.

Embrace the silent moments

There's this strange notion that silence in a conversation is bad. People can find it awkward, perhaps worried that you've run out of things to say. I love a silent pause. When I'm talking to people, I'll say what I have to say, then stop, giving the room a minute to process the information before I carry on. The reason is threefold:

1. It gives people a break from my chatter.
2. It gives me a minute to gather my thoughts.
3. It's a good way to make sure the person is still listening.

When pauses happen, don't be in a rush to fill the silence. Let the person speaking take that moment for themselves. Allow for comfortable silences to slow down the exchange, enabling both parties to think deeper and be more intentional in their communication.

Try to avoid killing the conversation

On the other end of the spectrum, there are certain things that might not help move the conversation in a meaningful way, such as:

'Why?'

Keep the question 'why' to your internal reflections. In a conversation, these make the person you're talking to feel like they have to defend themselves, and matters quickly become confrontational. Nothing's more frustrating than hearing 'why?' for the 5,000th time. It's brilliant to be inquisitive, but 'why' can be a closing-down question that doesn't help get to the heart of matters.

Avoid telling people what to do

I try to avoid telling someone whether they should or shouldn't do something, as no one likes to be preached to. Instead of telling people what to do, I'll offer more gentle suggestions. 'Have you tried or considered X?' is a softer way to move towards a positive conclusion.

'I know how you feel'

When it comes to conversation – unless you have the exact same experience and are of the same race, age, and gender – be wary of trying to 'relate'. Telling someone that you know how they feel sometimes does more harm than good. We can never truly know how another person feels. And it can sometimes feel reductive that someone presumes to know. Instead, you can ask: 'I have some idea what that's like, what impact did that have on you?' Acknowledge that this is their situation, not yours, but position yourself as a willing listener and person of support.

*

Listening isn't actually that easy to do. Before you even consider the person standing in front of you, think about what's going on internally. Our bodies are doing so much at any given time. You have about 3,000 thoughts an hour. At the same time, the human body is processing 11 million pieces of information every second, yet your brain can only process about fifty at a time. So your body is under tremendous pressure to compress all the vital information. And then, you approach a conversation and the other distractions turn up. Your phone is ringing, the people chattering nearby are making a ruckus, the music in the background is loud, there are people moving all over the place, and it can be hard to focus. None of these are conducive to an intimate conversation.

As well as considering your external environment, there's your internal one to think about too. Do you like this person, and do you even believe what they're telling you? If the answer is no, take the opportunity to practise your listening skills. If I'm at a business event and it becomes obvious I'm never going to see someone again, rather than sit bored I focus on my skills and explore how I can be a better listener. It's amazing how much easier it is to practise with the pressure off.

By honing your active listening skills, you'll find that not only will your relationships improve, but the data you gather will become richer too. You are collecting samples of human nature and experiences which will be fruitful as you begin to apply your knowledge in the wider world.

New Method 11
Think Macro

We discard our obsession with self and seek a more humble mode by remembering our insignificance but also our tiny power. We seek an outward expression of community purpose with macro thinking, reflecting on the interconnectedness of all things. We know that 'me' is immediately followed by 'we' and a 'me, me, me' mentality harms us all in the long term. Positive change is possible during the limited time we have on this planet. The collective economy is key to sustainable growth and we use our choices and voting power for the benefit of the whole and for future generations.

Macro or systems thinking requires you to understand who you are as part of a whole. It asks you to consider interrelations, multiple dynamics and the bigger picture. It relies on an acknowledgement that as an individual, you're contributing to a much larger cosmos. The purpose of this technique is to quell the loneliness and anxiety that comes from micro-thinking and to leave our world better than when you entered it.

Today we are living in the age of the Self. Everything is about me, me, me. We talk at length about our own lives, problems and dramas without considering our own role and responsibility in our issues or the macro environment that might be affecting them.

Sometimes I'm astounded by how irrelevant an individual life can be. When we zoom out and look at the entire world history, are we as one entity so important? I don't see myself as important. I think the collective work I do is important, otherwise I wouldn't do it. But for the blink-and-you'll-miss-me time I am on this planet, I'm indispensable. All I can do is keep edging closer to the success of the greater good.

The individualistic world we live in now means that you see this inward attitude everywhere. In her book *The Lonely Century*, Noreena Hertz charts the roots and causes of the worldwide loneliness epidemic and the age of the self. While she covers the front and centre causes such as social media and technology, she also reflects on the breakdown of civic institutions, open-plan offices, city growth and urban development, and decades of neoliberal policies that have placed self-interest above the collective good.

Self-interest is good for capitalism but bad for the community, and especially bad for the long-term future of the planet. Individualism makes the world a little bit worse for generations to come. Those who feel isolated, lonely and left behind are easy targets for extreme right thinking. The powerless are often more dangerous than the powerful.

Why are we like this? We view ourselves as the most important thing in the world, because, in some respects, we are. Our existence is a miracle. Life is an astounding experience. But I urge you to consider yourself in the grand scheme of things. You and I are both just one in billions of people breathing the same air. And we are just one of a trillion species. And that's just our planet. If we consider how many planets are in our galaxy, galaxies in our solar system, and beyond, we realize just how insignificant we are as individuals.

The New Method here is to make more of a conscious effort to be humble in your role on this earth. Consider your impact as a global citizen and as just one actor in the drama of life. I am obsessed with the idea of cosmopolis and citizenship. I enjoy knowing that I play a role within a larger structure, however minute that may be. I see myself as just one little body in the service of the wider community. If we can rebuild the idea of the civic activity, maybe we will be less lonely?

When applying systems thinking – the act of looking at the whole rather than the individual parts – start by reflecting on your day-to-day activities. Are you making conscious decisions considering the wider impact? For example, as fewer people work in offices, your local lunch-time sandwich and coffee shop may end up closing as the trade dries up. This knock-on effect isn't factored in when we are creating employee policies, but has a detrimental effect on the economy in the long term. Similarly, when you are choosing to shop at small businesses, are you buying from a marginalized community? By putting dollars directly into the pockets of those who are typically excluded from wealth creation, you are playing a small part in changing the makeup of those in power. It's the tiny powerful little actions that help you find your place in the world.

When you choose not to vote, or not to have a say in how your company, city or world is built, you're missing the opportunity to redefine the status quo and tip the scales in your favour. Get involved in the decision-making in your world and represent for the many.

If you regularly only consider yourself in your actions, you're not practising systems thinking. Of course you should still prioritize yourself – oxygen mask on first, etc. – but let's strive to inject macro thinking into your mindset. The result is a deep sense of purpose by being part of a movement. There are many ways to play your role as a global citizen, and if our little pinprick of existence can do anything to improve the state of the world or develop our species in some small way, then we are experiencing a life well-lived.

New Method 12
Control Your Media Diet

The entire media industry, and in particular magazines, have for hundreds of years done extensive harm to our self-worth. They create false and misleading images of what it means to be a woman. Advertising – which pays for media – creates even more potent images, inciting women to shop, diet and drug ourselves. Social media initially democratized media by allowing us to take control of the messages we consumed, and turned every individual into a media machine. But sadly, the algorithms then took over, serving advertisers and ensuring our attention is on the content they want us to see, which has been proved to be especially harmful to young girls and women. It's our mission to break their hold over us and our decisions. We approach all media with a certain level of distance and wariness, and use ad-blockers and online anonymity where possible. We pay attention to how we interact with the advertisements themselves. We read a wider breadth of sources to create a more informed picture of the world and news. Finally, we read news and consume media produced by diverse voices.

We are all exposed to some form of media almost all the time. Are you the type to scroll through social media with the TV on in the background? Or are you more of a newspaper and magazine kind of person? Regardless of the channels you prefer, the simple truth is that all mainstream media will be influenced by money. The 'truth' you buy into will always be slightly skewed. Whoever is creating the content of your chosen channel has a biased influence over the information being shared, and the media you absorb will have a direct impact on your well-being.

Editorial integrity vs profitability is an issue that has proved difficult to balance. A journalist's mission may be to enrich lives through the content they report on and ultimately unite us in knowledge. In turn, it is the media publication's prerogative to pay that journalist's salary and create profit. The issue is that many media platforms rely on advertisers to make money, and advertisers make money when readers buy from them. As a result, they lean on both our conscious and unconscious spending habits to make sales. I don't believe a women's magazine can talk authentically about loving the skin you are in and then have an advert for a $300 face cream on the next page.

I believe so much of capitalism relies on the anxieties and insecurities of women. How do we consume content that helps us step into our power, as opposed to limiting our potential with content that encourages us to buy more and speak out less?

Much of this aggressive media energy came about after the Second World War. In an effort to reboot the economy and raise morale, consumer culture began to dominate. On top of this, women who had previously been working while men were at war were gaining independence, and the prevailing thought was: how can we get them back into the home and out of our jobs?

The first step was to glorify domesticity, suburbanism and being a good homemaker. TV shows, adverts, magazines all directed their content in this way. Dieting became a hot topic, and any good feminist knows the history of 1950s advertising. It was, and still is, *a complete distraction*. A fabrication of a feminine ideal that you have to keep up with in order to be accepted by society. From *I Love Lucy* to *The Real Housewives* franchise, the media you consume has largely been designed by men and designed to keep you out of industry.

Well, not all industries.

Women then controlled the household purchasing decisions (as they do today), so it became essential to market to women. Advertising to women has become big business, and when I think back to my younger years of self-loathing, it was reinforced by the media and advertising industries' portrayal of women.

Why am I not thin or white enough like the
    women in magazines?
Am I a bad mom like the women in movies?
Did I deserve it? Like the women in the headlines
    of the newspapers?
Which dress should I buy to keep up with the
    Joneses?
Maybe I need to look younger. Everyone
    successful looks young.

And so on . . .

The thing about all of this is that it's rarely women who are controlling the narrative and the media. Even the editors of the world's top magazines are still beholden to a male publisher who may be the one signing off the cover. The New Method here is to understand that the media can be the devil and it's not your fault. Someone who looks like you hasn't had the power in its creation. This devil is a presence that has an influence over you and doesn't operate in your best interest. They operate to keep you consuming and to keep you distracted. Biased headlines about women keep us down.

Media can prey on your insecurities and lead you away from self-acceptance, wealth creation and career advancement. Keep that in mind next time you read something on your chosen form of media. When you feel like you're not good enough, or you feel anger or other strong emotions, remember that this is what it was designed to do. Extreme emotion means more engagement. More engagement means more advertising revenue.

Things are slowly changing. We are seeing more and more content written and designed by diverse voices that can craft their messages through the lens of their history. We are seeing more incredible TV being produced, written and directed by actresses who would formerly have had no say in the characters and stereotypes they are portraying. We are just now giving women directors the autonomy to choose the 'gaze' by which we consume media, and we have seen a spate of top-grossing movies and TV shows that are women-led. If you are working in the media and advertising industry, now is your time to think consciously about the power you hold to shape how women see themselves for generations to come. I hope you make good decisions about the words and images you put out.

As a reader, it's your mission to break the media's hold over you and your decisions. We should all be wary of where we're gathering our information and news. Profit inevitably shapes the production and distribution of content. Having an informed, conscious mind when you're absorbing this data can help give you greater ownership over the information you take on board and positively influence your actions. Read local and national newspapers from both sides of the political spectrum. Support small, independent media outlets. Become a paid subscriber to your favourite women writers. Help them break free from the chokehold of advertisers. Women's magazines are a delicious way to access a fantasy world and zone out, but like social media, realize that they are just fantasy and don't make this content your main course. Maybe take a break from reading them consistently. I know when I did, the self-loathing and consumerism took a break too.

New Method 13
Separate Fact, Opinion and Experience

We decide what information is most important to us at that particular moment and understand that context is key when choosing how we absorb information. We create a filter that sorts facts, opinions and experiences in order to weigh the impact and believability of others' words. Some people will pass off their opinion without experience. Some people will share their experiences without facts. We are discerning with what we take as gospel, knowing that false information reinforces both our limiting beliefs as well as the culture of inequality that determines our place in the world. We absorb and process information correctly and prepare to speak up when our instinct tells us that something is not right.

Many arguments with partners in the past have stemmed from their unwavering belief in the random 'facts' they espouse and my refusal to let them get away with it. I've noticed that various levels of entitlement will cause someone to say something and assume it is instantly true.

'This is the most remixed song ever.'
'Babies dance naturally.'
'Women want to be housewives.'

Much to their annoyance, I will be the first to say, 'Is that so? Based on what?'

The reason I find it so frustrating is twofold. First, it is not necessarily remarkable that some people often state their opinion as true, but it is remarkable to me which ones can then relax smugly, knowing they won't be challenged. Usually the most dominant male. Second, I find it frustrating because ideas and misinformation are spread in this way and it's becoming even more deadly to democracy and public trust. When we don't know who to trust, we may end up trusting no one.

While it can be scary to challenge a dominant but incorrect voice, it's important to do so. How many of us have been at dinner or in a room with one person telling a story that we know to be false or exaggerated truth? We sit quietly, knowing that if we propose an alternative we may be ignored or told to shut up. In her seminal book *Men Explain Things to Me*, Rebecca Solnit observes this pointedly: 'Every woman knows what I'm talking about. It's the presumption that makes it hard, at times, for any woman in any field; that keeps women from speaking up and from being heard when they dare; that crushes young women into silence by indicating, the way harassment on the street does, that this is not their world. It trains us in self-doubt and self-limitation just as it exercises men's unsupported overconfidence.'

But I believe it's imperative we speak up because the truth is all we have.

To me, a fact is a truth that can be proved over and

over. An opinion is based on someone's individual beliefs. Experience is a first-person fact, but it may not be a universal truth, more of a subjective one. But experience is still primary information, and I tend to weight this higher than opinion only. Advice is the blend of fact, experience and opinion to give a recommendation. But what do you do when a piece of information awkwardly sits somewhere between all of the above? By asking the right questions and gathering the right data, you minimize the opportunities for you to misconstrue information.

You can practise this challenge with close friends. One day, I was at lunch with Chloe and Paul. Paul was telling us about a plan he had for a social enterprise to help the homeless through physical fitness. To understand more about his idea, I asked him if he would allow people who are homeless by choice to use the service. His goal was to get people off the streets, but I was curious what this meant for those that are happy as they are, just wanting to use the facilities to clean up and stay every once in a while. Chloe then stated that people never really want to be homeless. They just say they do because they have no other choice in the matter.

What Chloe did was to present her statement as fact, when in reality it is her opinion, which, by the way, is also valid.

The reason I had a different view was that I had a number of experiences and anecdotes of people who rejected society and wanted to be homeless. I did believe there was some truth in her root argument that the possibility of low self-worth perhaps contributed to wanting to be homeless, but I also personally know people who just don't like cities and consumerism and all the trappings that go with it. They want to be alone and live off-grid.

Ultimately all experience is some form of data. I knew my small amount of data and had seen both those who wanted to live in a home and those who wanted to stay homeless. I turned to Paul and asked him if he had worked with any homeless people previously, or if his idea was something that came to him from a general social angle. He explained that he had volunteered at homeless charities for a number of years and that previously he would have thought the same as Chloe, but his experience of working with homeless people means that he has also met many who want to stay homeless.

Finally, I asked Chloe how many homeless people she'd met and worked with, and the answer was zero. She had recently been doing some influencer work with a homeless charity but never actually had direct contact.

Opinions are valid, and voicing them is equally so, but take care to separate them from fact. In Chloe's case, where she had no data, it could have been voiced as a personal belief or even as a question.

Why is this important? If her insight had been taken as pure truth she could have influenced Paul into significantly reducing the reach of his project and locking out patrons who didn't adhere to his end goal but would have benefited from the service. She might have swayed the direction of his work.

I tend to preface many of my statements with 'in my opinion . . .' or 'to me . . .' or 'I think . . .' so that there is no confusion that the statements that follow are anything but my opinion.

Try a New Method of questioning others over the source of their words, and also applying the principle to yourself by stating your opinions as opinions and your facts as facts. As a general rule, neither one is more important than the other because the context is essential. All data can be cut and skewed in so many ways to the analyst's intent. The goal is to know the right way to process and absorb the information at that particular moment.

How do we do this practically? When you meet someone on their soapbox, ask clarifying questions to determine the weight of their argument and use your intuition to place them on your trust scale accordingly. One way to do this is through the Socratic method of questioning – a form of enquiry and discussion that involves asking probing questions to stimulate critical thinking. Here's how you can apply it.

First, question assumptions: the Socratic method encourages us to find the underlying beliefs. Why do we believe what we believe? Who is influencing us? When evaluating information, it's important to be aware of personal biases and preconceived notions that may steer the interpretation of facts. By asking (and being open to) thought-provoking questions, we can critically examine beliefs and consider if they are twisting our ideas.

Seek multiple perspectives: my favourite thing to do is

to engage with diverse viewpoints to expand my under-standing and help identify the presence of my opinions or biases. Actively seeking out differing perspectives broadens our intellectual horizons and guards against confirmation bias. Have you ever tried researching and conversing with the opposition in order to learn?

Ask for evidence: in order to differentiate between fact and opinion, it is crucial to assess the evidence and reasoning behind a statement or claim. Ask questions that force us to provide supporting evidence for beliefs. By challenging others to provide logical reasoning and factual evidence, it helps to uncover the basis for their opinions and distinguish them from actual verifiable facts. I will often be heard saying – show me.

Uncover contradictions and inconsistencies: if their argument doesn't hold, you can respond using the other person's own hypocritical beliefs so that they can see internal inconsistencies within their own opinions or recognize contradictions between their beliefs and estab-lished facts. It requires quick thinking and active listening on your part, and is frustrating and deadly to the other person.

By employing the Socratic method, we can develop a more discerning approach to information and enhance our ability to distinguish between facts and opinions. We want to promote critical thinking here and encourage self-reflection, contributing to a more accurate assess-ment of information. The more you do it, the more confidence you will gain in speaking up against misin-formation. Sometimes we don't have the time to engage in a lengthy Ancient Greek style discussion. So here is a simple way to identify the validity of something you're being told. Listen to the language people are using.

Facts

- They use numbers and statistics
- General known truths
- Documentation
- Eyewitnesses involved
- Dates and records are available
- Can be proved
- Demonstrated by

Opinions

- Think
- Feel
- Guess
- Probably
- In my . . .
- Assume
- I . . .

With active listening, we understand how others are defining a subject and their experience of it. We can hear when they are attributing themselves, or even others, as a primary source. Imagine I am in a conversation and someone mentions single mothers. One person might believe that I have personal experience of this. To them, because I'm separated, that's how they might categorize me, but I am a co-parent. I have not had the experience of being a full-time lone parent. I can *imagine* the stress, exhaustion and frustration, but I have not experienced it. I was raised by a single mother, so I have stronger data on the child's point of view, and I personally know many single mothers, but I have never fully been one. That means my opinion has less weight than a true lone parent, and my statements are less relevant in the face of someone who has factual and first-person experience. By asking the right questions, you very quickly establish whether the person spouting their opinion is someone you ought to weigh highly. If someone had asked me, 'Do you consider yourself a single parent?' they could have ruled me out earlier in the conversation.

Many of our assumptions about who holds the knowledge are simply patriarchal. In her book *The Authority Gap: Why women are still taken less seriously than men, and what we can do about it,* Mary Ann Sieghart states: 'When boys grow up to be men, many of them act out that entitlement by interrupting women, talking over them, ignoring them, resisting their influence, discounting what they have to say, and mansplaining to them even when the women are experts.'

This is a direct result of men holding more positions of power globally and the trickle-down effect of their words having more weight. But should your level or gender determine the believability of your words? We don't think so, and one of our company principles, Smartest Idea Wins, reflects this. Regardless of the level or department, whoever has the best ideas can submit them and be heard. Someone may be very senior in the team but have no real experience of the challenge being presented. I will often ask my team, 'Who has the most experience in this?' and then I ask them what they think based on their knowledge. It could be that the most junior person has lived it first-hand. What I'm looking to do is to blend my facts, opinions, experience and knowledge with someone closer to the problem.

We're living in a world of social media where everyone has a say. Everyone thinks they are an expert. But why should someone else's opinions be important to you? If someone has never had their own business and has no experience in business, yet has an opinion on yours, why do you care? If someone doesn't have kids, and never plans to have kids, yet has an opinion on how you should be raising your family, why should you give it a second thought? Dominant people in any society will try to assert their opinions as fact. It's your job to distinguish between the two.

New Method 14
Choose Your Healer

We understand that no personal growth can be achieved without a teacher. Knowledge is passed down from experienced humans to learning humans, and as infinite learners, we seek wisdom from others. Healing is not linear or singular, so we choose a roster of support, from physical to mental and from spiritual to playful. All forms of guidance that can help us on our journey. While we seek out the sages, we remember that no one person is our guru and we strive to maintain a sense of autonomy and faculty of mind. While the healing process will open some wounds and at times be painful, it should not destroy us beyond repair. We seek healers who centre us, lift us up and make us stronger.

Things changed when I decided to heal. They changed at the point when I consciously realized that if I did not work to heal, I would never truly be able to reach my highest potential. I would not be focused on my Important Work if I was drowning in anxiety and anger. I would not be able to be the best leader when I was carrying so much resentment and sadness. I would not be the best mother and partner if I let my fears become insecurities which in turn would become repression.

Healing is a slow and delicate spider web of transformation that occurs physically, emotionally and spiritually.

Over many years, I worked to identify and resolve the wounds and traumas that hindered my overall well-being. Healing in my late twenties and early thirties seemed like an all-consuming activity, and it most definitely was not instantaneous.

Not only do you not have to do this alone, but it is almost impossible to do. Working on healing your whole self requires a plethora of treatments and teachers. I spent my childhood years playing the 80s computer game *Street Fighter*, and now the phrase 'Choose Your Fighter' has reappeared in the internet lexicon. But what if, instead of selecting a character to destroy your opponent, you selected a character to heal yourself? The New Method of Choose Your Healer means finding out who and what you need to regain your contentment and balance. Whose energy and wisdom do you need to absorb?

My own healing journey took a series of false starts. I remember distinctly when healers would try to impart their wisdom, but my eyes and ears were closed. I was too inward-looking and despairing to hear anything. Upon reflection, I know they could see that I was in dire need, but was not ready to learn. Having compassion for myself, I like to believe that it is crucial to honour your own timing and readiness for growth. I was often brought to the water, but was not ready to drink. I had to get really thirsty first.

Taking yourself on an intentional journey is one of the most ancient ways of healing. My healing journey started sincerely on my first-ever trip to Jamaica, aged twenty-eight. I told everyone that I was going because I had never been to my motherland before, and with a two-year-old child who was a mix of four different ethnicities, I wanted him to know this part of his culture. But if I am really truthful, I was broken – it was really about me connecting to myself. When I landed in Montego Bay, I immediately felt at home. The wild nature, the Ital food, the music, all reminded me of who I was. In Jamaica, there are healers everywhere. Everyone from my taxi driver to a herbalist doctor would impart varying forms of wisdom every single day, peppering my trip with new mantras and thought processes. 'Nuh worry yuself' (Don't worry yourself) being my favourite. But I was also ready and open to receiving these messages. I was ready to drink.

I had planned to go to Jamaica and then India that year, connecting with both my ethnicities, but I was so taken with Jamaica that I went six times in two years, each time deepening my relationship with its history and culture. I stayed in different parts of the island, meeting different teachers on the way. This little green jewel in the sea was the first thing that saved me. If my people can survive their violent history, I can survive too.

Back in England, I continued the journey. Using the New Method of Minimizing Toxins, I sought healers and experiences that would help me come to terms with the root causes of my anxiety and pain. I tried everything from Colombian cacao-drinking ceremonies to celebrating the Sikh festival of Vaisakhi and singing devotional prayer songs. I took herbal baths at home in the style of medieval monks and vibrated my internal waters with sound baths in the desert in Joshua Tree. I collected healing experiences like one might collect shoes, trying a bit of everything to see what really made a difference.

After a decade of data collection into what healing works for me, I now know that journeys and travel are really important, especially when I can call on my ancestors. Weekly therapy doesn't have an intense shift in my thinking but an immersive twelve-week executive coaching or self-development bootcamp can help me reach new heights of peace. Hypnotherapy was the most expensive, but game-changing, form of therapy I tried – only recommended when you have done a good deal of healing already and want to reinforce it in your subconscious. The gift that is 12-Step Programs is global, frequent and free, and was absolutely essential to me feeling less anxious on a daily basis. Find the one that works for you. For my body, acupuncture is an instant reliever for when my emotions are bound up in my muscles, resulting in panic attacks and spasms. Jivamukti yoga once a week is like going to church. The combination of singing, chanting and movement leaves me feeling lighter. Daily, I practise transcendental meditation, I read Stoicism, I bathe and I walk.

Choosing Your Healer means knowing what you need to restore yourself in the big moments of angst, as well as the daily practices that keep you balanced. If you are wandering through life, lost and in pain, like I was, now is the time to start a practice to help you maintain your Higher Self.

Some forms of healing you might want to explore:

Acupuncture: Acupuncture is an ancient Chinese practice that involves inserting thin needles into specific points on the body to stimulate energy flow and promote physical and emotional healing. Think of it as unblocking the build-up of stress in your body that can cause pain. It is also used to address stress, anxiety and hormonal imbalances. Find a traditional Chinese medicine practitioner who has studied this healing in depth.

Meditation: Meditation involves training the mind to focus and redirect thoughts, leading to a state of clarity and relaxation. There are many types of meditation, such as mindfulness meditation, loving-kindness meditation, transcendental meditation. Experiment with many and see what is right for you.

Reiki: Reiki is an energy healing technique that originated in Japan. It involves the practitioner placing their hands on or near the recipient's body to channel universal life force energy. Try rubbing your hands vigorously together and placing them over your eyes to get a feeling of what that means. Reiki aims to promote balance, relaxation and healing on physical, emotional and spiritual levels.

Hypnotherapy. Hypnotherapy uses hypnosis as a tool to facilitate healing, personal growth, and behaviour change. It involves guiding individuals into a relaxed and focused state of consciousness, where they can access their subconscious mind and explore and address various issues. You're not completely knocked out, so to speak, you are just in a state that's receptive to seeing what's deep below the surface.

Forest bathing: Forest bathing, also known as shinrin-yoku, is a practice that involves immersing oneself in nature, particularly forests, to promote physical and mental well-being. Call it a conscious and mindful walk in nature, or go one further and lie down in the forest. Feel the moss and get your hands a little dirty. Absorb all that good oxygen.

Sound healing: Sound healing utilizes the vibrations and frequencies of sound to promote relaxation and healing. Practitioners will use singing bowls, tuning forks, or guided sound meditations to help release tension. I prefer doing this 1:1, not in a group setting, so the bowls can really be close to my body.

Herbal remedies: Herbal remedies involve using plants and their extracts for healing purposes. Herbal teas, tinctures and supplements may be utilized to support emotional well-being, reduce anxiety and improve sleep quality. I've found mushrooms to be the ultimate stress reliever when I'm going through it, and I take ashwagandha regularly.

Ancestral healing: Engaging in rituals and ceremonies that honour and connect with ancestors is a powerful way to facilitate healing. This can include setting up ancestral altars, making offerings, lighting candles, saying prayers, or participating in culturally specific ceremonies that recognize and honour ancestral presence.

Breathwork: Breathwork is a practice that involves intentionally and consciously manipulating the breath by using different nostrils and breathing into different parts of the body. I'm still amazed at how effective and free breathing is for the nervous system. When in doubt, breathe.

Yoga: A Hindu spiritual and ascetic discipline, a part of which includes breath control, chanting, meditation, and the adoption of specific bodily postures called asanas. Yoga is widely practised across the globe and this ancient practice has given me so much. There are lots of different types of yoga, ranging in spirituality to fitness – check them all out.

Trauma-specific therapy: This therapy is particularly valuable for addressing and healing trauma. Trauma-focused therapy modalities, such as Cognitive Behavioural Therapy (CBT), Eye Movement Desensitization and

Reprocessing (EMDR), or Trauma-Focused Cognitive Behavioural Therapy (TF-CBT), can help individuals process traumatic experiences, reduce symptoms, and regain a sense of safety and empowerment. I have many friends who have used these techniques successfully to heal.

These are just the start, and there are many more healing practices to discover, but one thing I want to touch on is how healing – an ancient and spiritual practice – has evolved into a multi-billion-dollar wellness industry as well as a space for cult leaders to thrive. When you are at your most broken is when you are most vulnerable. You should never feel pressured to spend a lot of money on your healing journey or to be exclusive to one modality. Heal within your financial means. Most of the best healing is free anyway, and true spiritual guides will take whatever you can afford. If any supposed healer aims to control you, silence you, drain your finances or break you, they are not for you. I have met a surprising number of young women who have been involved in cults, believing that their leaders were the only voice of reason, which is why I urge you to build a roster of healing practices so that no single source is your gospel. Your intuition will start to sound the alarm when something does not feel right. Listen to it. Eventually, your goal is to connect so deeply to yourself that it is your own inner voice that is guiding you when things get difficult. You can begin to heal yourself.

When you are early in your journey, try to remember

that healing is not linear and it shouldn't be lonely. Without falling into the trap of having friendships based purely on your trauma, connect with others who are headed in the same direction as you. Build a small community or group around your journey and support each other on the way. Meet consistently to check in on your progress and don't be disheartened if you are way ahead or way behind others. Remember that healing is a multi-faceted process, unique to each individual. Your paths may intersect, providing opportunities for shared insights and growth. Yet they may also diverge, as you navigate the intricate labyrinth of your personal healing. Despite this, keep putting one foot in front of the other. Through community and collective healing, we can find solace, understanding and strength. We can break intergenerational traumas and be the best humans for ourselves and for others.

New Method 15
Sit with Your Demons

After labelling our trauma we can sometimes see how we can be the ones that stand in our own way. Our intense desire to be liked and respected can be an overpowering force and make us act from our superego rather than from our hearts. We actively confront our demons, facing them and not letting them destroy us. We know that managing our superego is absolutely essential to unlocking personal and professional growth, so we sit with it and invite it to tea. Only through being comfortable with being uncomfortable can we begin to shift our focus from external validation and approval to a deeper sense of self-awareness and self-acceptance. We sit with our demons until we no longer notice they are in the room.

What is the ego? The most prevalent theory was developed by Sigmund Freud in 1923. Freud's psychoanalytic theory was that our minds exist in three parts. The id refers to the rudimentary and instinctive aspect of the psyche that harbours repressed memories. The superego functions as a moral compass, while the ego represents the rational part of the psyche that serves as a mediator between the id's impulses and the superego's standards.

The superego's role as designated as a moral compass can simply go too far. Responsible for internalizing societal standards, it can often strive to uphold these standards through the use of guilt and shame. It can become too rigid and harsh, leading to excessive self-punishment and self-hatred. It's the one that creates binary thinking. Losing your job means that you are an incompetent person. Someone dumping you means that you are worthless, and so on. This can occur when the superego's standards are too high or unrealistic, or when your life circumstances make it difficult to live up to these standards. The superego is like an overbearing parent. They believe they're protecting you, from real or imagined danger, but whatever their intentions, your superego holds you back.

The brilliant Dr Margaret Paul is a psychologist, author, and co-creator of the Inner Bonding self-healing system. Her book *Healing Your Aloneness* was one of the electric shock books that propelled me forward on my journey. According to Dr Paul, the ego develops in childhood as a result of unmet emotional needs and experiences of rejection, abandonment or trauma. She calls it your 'wounded ego' – the tiny but piercing voice that can lead to negative self-talk, self-sabotage, and patterns of codependency and unhealthy relationships.

This is the part of you that is hurting and upset, and so causes you to behave in a way that often has a negative impact on your life. Some people refer to it as your inner critic, but instead of thinking of it as a horrible, nasty part of you, think of it as a small child who is scared and then becomes mean and a bit of a bully to make sure it doesn't get hurt again. I often visualize my superego as petulant Baby Sharma, who really wants a hug, but doesn't know how to communicate it, so lashes out instead.

As a leader, managing your superego is essential to your ability to grow yourself and your business. Management expert Jim Collins's book *Good to Great* talks of Level 5 leadership. Many of us are good leaders, but pushing ourselves from good to great comes down to our ability to be humble while also getting things done. According to Collins, 'Level 5 leaders display a powerful mixture of personal humility and indomitable will. They're incredibly ambitious, but their ambition is first and foremost for the cause, for the organization and its purpose, not themselves. While Level 5 leaders can come in many personality packages, they are often self-effacing, quiet, reserved, and even shy.'

While reading this book a few years ago, I went through the levels, one by one, mentally marking myself. The examples of humility in the book were interesting: leaders who required no praise, who constantly supported their team and refused to accept accolades or any reference to their 'genius'. It was at that point I realized that there was no way I was a Level 5 leader because my ego meant that I was desperate for acknowledgement, a pat on the head and being told – you did good! I always wanted to make sure everyone knew it was MY IDEA that got us results. It is obvious to me now that this absence of humility was down to my inner child, my wounded ego self, seeking praise from the parents who never gave it.

I still have to work to soothe this ego.

The number 1 place my ego shows up is with my need

to make sure that people know and understand what I'm capable of. It is completely illogical, because I don't recall any specific examples where someone has undermined me, and even when they do, I'm not embarrassed because I always love to learn. Despite this lack of evidence that someone might be prejudging me, I still carry this desire to make sure they respect me as a person.

If I go one step further, I could even ask, why am I so busy and constantly consuming information? The fear of being caught out or not ready for a meeting or conversation has meant that I hoard intel as a protective mechanism against a world I always thought was against me. It became difficult for me to know if I had learned something because I am genuinely curious, or if it was because I needed to prove myself in a room of strangers.

With some self-questioning, I determined that I want to know about the world simply because it's interesting. So in order to work with my ego, not feed it, I try to stay on the side of curiosity and humility and not knowledge-hoarding as an armoury to impress others. This in turn helps me stay on a higher frequency.

Let's unpack the idea of humility. When you're humble, you understand that you are no more and no less important than others. It's about acknowledging that we're all different and show up and thrive in our own ways. Humility means you can assert yourself reasonably when appropriate, but let someone else take the reins at the right time too. Humility doesn't mean having a lack of self-esteem or having a low opinion of yourself. Humility isn't batting away praise you earned, talking about how humble you are (otherwise known as the humble brag), putting yourself down, making jokes about yourself, or falsely dialling yourself down. Humility is being gracious and maintaining a state of equilibrium in terms of your opinion of yourself.

My internal ego, desire for praise and inability to be humble was affecting my career and my ability to grow in my work. How does this show up for you? It might mean undermining your team in meetings and making your contributions known loudly. It might be impressing your ideas on how some things should be done, not because you have experience in the task but simply because you are higher up than someone else. It might mean criticizing your team because you are worried they are going to make you look bad to your superiors. You aren't focused on their development and well-being, you are focused on yourself. By feeding your ego, you are only hurting yourself, because in the long run, no one will want to work with you.

Your ego is not your amigo, but they're also not your enemy. Much has been written about the need to quash or kill your ego, but a big fear of mine throughout my career was – if I lose that insecure drive to 'do well', will I do anything at all? Will my ability to heal affect my ambition? Not if we connect to our higher purpose.

Let's go back to that Level 5 leadership. Great people don't just consider themselves, they focus their minds on people and causes outside of themselves. By being mission-driven and having a larger purpose towards gender equity, it seems ridiculous that I might not achieve that purpose for the sake of a Pandora's box of jealousy, insecurity, anger and regret. Imagine that! I couldn't make a difference in the world because I couldn't get out of my own way! The higher purpose can only be achieved by working collaboratively and all pushing in the same direction towards the same thing. When I hire people, I'm looking for people who are obsessively attached to the mission, not to me. Their desire to impress me will impede their ability to achieve the mission and will also feed my ego. You should be at the company because you want gender equity and everything else, including your ego, should fall by the wayside.

When your superego does start to flare, you can neutralize it by thanking it. The Ho'oponopono prayer is a traditional Hawai'ian prayer of forgiveness and reconciliation. It is a powerful tool for managing the ego, as it helps to release the attachment to the situation at hand. The prayer consists of four simple phrases: 'I'm sorry. Please forgive me. Thank you. I love you.' When practising Ho'oponopono, you repeat these phrases either silently or out loud, while focusing on a particular person or situation that is causing you distress.

Whenever I was feeling scared or hurt, I would think of my little child backed into a corner within myself and I would say, 'Thank you, I love you', with the addition of (speaking from my Adult Self), 'But I can take it from here.' I wanted to let my ego know – thank you for alerting me, I'm here, I'm listening, but you're not helping us move forward right now, and I need to do this for us. Having compassion for my superego and the stress or hurt it is feeling allows me to move past it.

I See You is another phrase that has changed my relationships with myself and others. Coach Adrian Green shared with me the story from the Buddist tradition of Mara the Demon as a way of me moving towards feeling uncomfortable and towards the lesson. In her book *Radical Acceptance*, Tara Brach retells the story.

The night before his enlightenment, the Buddha fought a great battle with the Demon God Mara, who attacked the then bodhisattva Siddhartha Guatama with everything he had: lust, greed, anger, doubt, etc. Having failed, Mara left in disarray on the morning of the Buddha's enlightenment. Yet it seems Mara was only temporarily discouraged. Even after the Buddha had become deeply revered throughout India, Mara continued to make unexpected appearances. The Buddha's loyal attendant, Ananda, always on the lookout for any harm that might come to his teacher, would report with dismay that the 'Evil One' had again returned.

Instead of ignoring Mara or driving him away, the Buddha would calmly acknowledge his presence, saying, 'I see you, Mara.' He would then invite him for tea and serve him as an honoured guest. Offering Mara a cushion so that he could sit comfortably, the Buddha would fill two earthen cups with tea, place them on the low table between them, and only then take his own seat. Mara would stay for a while and then go, but throughout the Buddha remained free and undisturbed.

The American Tibetan Buddist nun Pema Chödrön says that through spiritual practice, 'We are learning to make friends with ourselves, our life, at the most profound level possible.' We befriend ourselves when, rather than resisting our experience, we open our hearts and willingly invite our demons to tea.

The easiest way to manage your superego is to nurture your self-worth, security and spirituality. People who are full up with love don't need to draw from others to fill their emptiness. This may mean reconnecting to whatever philosophy or religion you choose to follow. It means surrounding yourself with those who love and support you, or finding new friends if your current crew doesn't. It means knowing that everything you need is on its way to you. It's having an abundant mindset and knowing you are enough.

Sadly your ego doesn't want to be out of a job, so it's going to work hard at its career, just like you are. Start thinking now about how you can put your ego into retirement. Some place you can visit occasionally and drink tea and allow it to moan, gossip and draw you into negative thinking. And then you can quietly get up and go home and back to your Higher Self.

New Method 16
Return to Nature

We are ruthless in carving out time and space to connect with nature. Part of the discrediting of our power is the severance of the relationship between humans and our planet. Nature is cyclical, as we are cyclical. Our bodies are directly in tune with the planetary cycle, evolving a rhythm in accordance with our earth. We stay in tune with our bodies by staying in tune with nature. Whether it's grasping at ten minutes of stillness to watch a bee go from flower to flower or a full-blown forest bathing ritual, we protect our relationship with the earth at all costs.

I grew up in a garden. A big wild garden that was part allotment, part orchard, part herbarium, with a small patch of actual grass. I remember grabbing mud, crunching it up and tenderly adding water to make mud pies. I made insect traps and snail jails and pulled onions out of the ground and strawberries off their stems. As my beloved Grandad planted, I would follow behind him patting down the seeds. But my absolute favourite activity was just watching the white 'Cabbage Patch' butterflies and listening to the grasshoppers while lying in the sun. Nature has always been in my story. I grew up in a garden, and now I live in a concrete block. In this apartment block, I don't notice that I'm being suffocated, because it happens very slowly. My senses become dull, and I can no longer smell the flowers. My skin becomes grey. My breathing becomes shallow. And then I slowly slip into a mild depression. My spirit begins to wither when I am not connected with nature.

Nature of course is all around, even in a big city like London, so it is not so much the lack of nature that I find challenging. Instead, it is the lack of connection and absorption to nature that has a detrimental effect on me. And so I start small – I touch things as I walk past them. I touch leaves and sometimes if they're in abundance I'll grab a few, holding them in my hand as I continue my walk. I smell jasmine flowers on a warm evening. I brush myself against hedges and run my hand along the moss on the walls. In my finest handbags, you may find little shells and pinecones and rocks that I keep as secret amulets. It's not just about collecting these things, but looking at their intricacy and respecting the magic of their existence. Even a rock stores energy that I too can absorb. A rock is a living thing.

But these are just amuse-bouches, and even a plateful cannot satisfy the stomach. So for those of us living in cities, we must make a concerted effort to connect with and absorb nature through exploration and by dedicating time. Reverting back to the elements and feeling the wind on our face reminds us that we are very much alive.

Water is a place I feel especially free, and swimming has changed my relationship with my body and my hair. Swimming has never typically been a home for Black women and many of us cannot swim with confidence.

Previously my consistently straightened hair and my long extensions meant that swimming would have to be carefully scheduled around my beauty routine. Now I shed those trappings and swimming *is* my beauty routine because in the water, I am home.

Forests and walks are where I can declutter my mind. I've had many mild breakdowns at work, only to pack my bag and go off to the countryside, renting a cheap B&B in order to walk. I have walked in the boiling sun and I've walked in freezing rain. But I walk and I breathe deeply and it feels good. Usually after just twenty-four hours, I feel myself again and inspired.

Once a year I like to do something that really pushes my connection to nature by learning how to be at one with it. Years ago, I went to a forest in Kent to learn how to make a fire from scratch. Four of us wandered around the forest collecting all the different types of tree bark necessary, under the guidance of a bushcraft instructor, and after hours of collecting the right wood we then spent hours attempting to light a fire. It took so long and I had so much time alone to think, that I could do nothing but be thankful for my ancestors. All of those before me who invested the time in staying alive, in making fire, so that I could be here today. As dusk approached, I continued to furiously pull my bow drill back and forth. It really felt like it was never going to happen, until the smoke started to billow. The moment the kindling sparked I felt such a joyful achievement! I created fire! I am a wild woman!

Nature is where we meet ourselves, and so it's only natural that we must return there often to honour our wild spirit. *Women Who Run with the Wolves* is a seminal book for all of those who feel that their soul is beginning to fade. Author Clarissa Pinkola Estés beautifully writes directly to those yearning for some visceral experience.

And then there are the cravings. Oh, la! A woman may crave to be near water, or be belly down, her face in the earth, smelling the wild smell. She might have to drive into the wind. She may have to plant something, pull things out of the ground or put them into the ground. She may have to knead and bake, rapt in dough up to her elbows.

She may have to trek into the hills, leaping from rock to rock trying out her voice against the mountain. She may need hours of starry nights where the stars are like face powder spilt on a black marble floor. She may feel she will die if she doesn't dance naked in a thunderstorm, sit in perfect silence, return home ink-stained, paint-stained, tear-stained, moon-stained.

The New Method I want you to implement is to be in communion with nature on a daily basis, however small. Brush your hand across a hedge. Look up and meditate on the sky for a minute or two. Touching and feeling and bathing in nature will remind you of your insignificance to the world as well as your power within it. We, like nature, have a cycle of creation and destruction, and within that cycle there is a movement and transference of energy. Draw your energy from nature and nurture your wild spirit so that you can go forth, boldly.

New Method 17
Filter Your Myths

We confront and dismantle entrenched narratives to challenge the very foundations of a patriarchal system that has endured for millennia. It is a call to re-examine the stories we hold dear and question the values they perpetuate. We remind ourselves that while myths may be timeless, our capacity for critical reflection and change is boundless. In this ongoing struggle for gender equity and justice, it is imperative that we unmask the patriarchal myths that have masqueraded as beloved stories and reshape the narratives that define our collective future.

I have long been obsessed with mythology and fairytales. It didn't matter if it was the Brothers Grimm, Greco-Roman mythology or religious texts, I loved the fantastical storytelling of the past. But it was around the age of thirteen that I started to question some of my beloved myths, as it became clear that the hero of the story would never represent me. Nearly all the world's social storytelling involves the subjugation of women, so I started to abandon the storylaws that are designed to shape me as a functioning member of society and seek out alternative histories that might motivate me to self-actualization. In the early 1990s this was difficult, but today we are currently experiencing a burst of industriousness in the retelling of popular myths to make them more gender equal. This retelling is currently seen most in classical history, which has defined so much of how the West designs its systems, from government to media. One might trace today's 'decriminalization' of rape and its horrifyingly low conviction rate as a direct line from the long list of rape victims of Zeus in Greek mythology. What will the next few thousand years look like if we have women in the centre of our mythologies instead of being mere accessories or playthings for the male protagonists?

Myths create a framework for living that is necessary for humans, at different points in history, to survive by contributing to the dominant agenda. Early on in the life of homo sapiens, this may have been simply to live past the age of fifty, but today there is a complex set of cultural frameworks that ensure the human race lives on. The eminent writer on myth Joseph Campbell lays out the four functions of myth in his book, *Pathways to Bliss*:

1. . . . the first function of mythology [is] to evoke in the individual a sense of grateful, affirmative awe before the monstrous mystery that is existence.

2. The second function of mythology is to present an image of the cosmos, an image of the universe round about, that will maintain and elicit this experience of awe. [or] . . . to present an image of the cosmos that will maintain your sense of mystical awe and explain everything that you come into contact with in the universe around you.

3. The third function of a mythological order is to validate and maintain a certain sociological system: a shared set of rights and wrongs, proprieties or improprieties, on which your particular social unit depends for its existence.

4. . . . the fourth function of myth is psychological. That myth must carry the individual through the stages of his life, from birth through maturity through senility to death. The mythology must do so in accords with the social order of his group, the cosmos as understood by his group, and the monstrous mystery.

With the bounty of nature being essential for life, we would first mythologize the sky, sun, moon, earth and water, but as it became clear that the female played an essential role in growing the next generation of humanity, her image became a narrative to maintain the social order. Over millennia that image has been twisted and warped and become a key pawn in male dominance.

In her quest for the source of this accepted dominance, science journalist and author Angela Saini wrote *The Patriarchs: The Origins of Inequality* – deconstructing the argument that male power is natural. Weaving through the history of societies, it is during the analysis of the gender fluidity of Greek heroes that she also acknowledges that, 'The state couldn't function without its suffocatingly narrow set of rules . . . that maintained the population, its productivity and the dominance of the elites.' When I interviewed her for our Stack World book club, I was awakened by this. Is the patriarchy really just about population growth? We go through all this oppression just to ensure we have babies to supply for fighting wars and paying taxes (to fight wars)? The patriarchy maintains procreation, capitalism and inequality, to benefit a minority of elites?

To maintain this trio, myths have played a profound role in shaping social structures and power dynamics. Patriarchal myths, those tales and stories that perpetuate and reinforce this hierarchical system of male dominance, have been instrumental in justifying and perpetuating the oppression of women. Our most popular stories throughout history often serving as conduits for the transmission of deeply ingrained gender biases. Disguised as timeless tales they continue to wield considerable influence in contemporary society, moulding our perceptions and guiding our actions.

Patriarchal myths are foundational in constructing and maintaining rigid gender roles. They depict women as submissive, nurturing and reliant on men for guidance and protection. Such narratives, embedded in cultures across the globe, serve as the cornerstones upon which societies build their expectations and norms. For example, the biblical myth of Adam and Eve has been interpreted to justify women's subordination, with Eve portrayed as the instigator of mankind's fall from grace. It is a recurring theme in these myths that blame and shame are attributed to women. They often hold women responsible for the world's societal problems or their own suffering. Eve biting the apple is a story of the danger of women's desire for knowledge, and Pandora's box lays the blame for all the world's evils at the feet of a curious woman. By propagating these tales, societies have a ready-made mechanism for further limiting our freedom for fear of retribution.

Many myths are structured around the premise that women require male guidance or protection, curbing their autonomy. These stories, with their damsel-in-distress motifs, reinforce the notion that women are incapable of self-reliance and decision-making. This underpins the restriction of women's autonomy, leading to paternalistic and controlling attitudes. Women become delicate flowers that need protecting. Fathers, brothers and husbands must look after us! Which in turn becomes owning us. This in turn leads to the normalization of violence in order to protect. It is a disturbing aspect of these myths to endorse violence as a means of control and protection. Stories of heroic men 'rescuing' women from perceived threats subtly indicate that when it comes to women, violence is OK. This normalization frames violence as a form of chivalry rather than as the oppression it truly represents.

Patriarchal myths frequently reduce women to objects of desire or commodities to be owned. This objectification dehumanizes us and fuels a culture of sexism and sexual harassment. Myths that depict women as rewards or trophies for male achievement commodify their bodies and reduce their worth to mere objects. Women are often held up as the prize for the most masculine of endeavours. If you do X task, you'll win the hand of my daughter, and so on.

Central to many patriarchal myths is the notion of male superiority. Heroes, leaders, and gods are overwhelmingly portrayed as male, reinforcing the idea that men are inherently superior and deserving of power. This representation justifies the exclusion of women from positions of leadership and decision-making authority. It trickles down. Economic disparities between men and women are often rationalized through patriarchal myths also. Women are portrayed as less capable, or as those who should prioritize family over career, thereby justifying the wage gap and unequal economic opportunities.

Patriarchal myths play a pivotal role in policing female sexuality, prescribing how women should behave sexually and who they should marry. Myths perpetuate notions of virginity and purity, which are used to control women's bodies and choices. Virginity testing, abortion bans and honour killings are among the grim consequences of such narratives. All genders can succumb to these stereotypes, with women themselves internalizing this policing and attacking each other. This is not surprising when many patriarchal myths promote competition and jealousy among women, undermining solidarity among them. There are always some ugly sisters or jealous friends in the mix. This division hinders collective efforts to challenge the systems that perpetuate gender inequality.

I feel that one cannot overstate the significance of myths in shaping social structures and power dynamics. Stories are how we learn to be human. Myths are the distilled essence of cultural values, aspirations and fears, and they function as powerful instruments for the maintenance of societal norms. Patriarchal myths are key agents in this enduring saga of inequality. These myths are carefully crafted stories that endorse and validate the supremacy of men and the subjugation of women.

Consider this Inuit fairytale. Sedna is a giant and her father tells her that she must marry. He sends prospective suitors to her from many different lands, and she rejects them all. She doesn't want to be married. Her father continues to insist and so in an act of defiance, she marries her dog. 'Well, I'm married now,' she says smugly. 'Aren't you happy?' Her father is not happy, and in a fit of rage, he drags her out to sea in his fishing boat and throws her over the side. She clings to the edge but he grabs an axe, brutally cutting off her fingers one by one. His own daughter. Sedna falls into the waves and her fingers transform into the seals and whales of the ocean, and she grows up to be a goddess of the deep sea.

The elements of women as property to be married off and violence against women, against your own daughter, are not unique to this story, and there are thousands of other tales that support these harmful myths. So what is an alternative image to change this? Lithuanian archaeologist and anthropologist Marija Gimbutas researched Neolithic and Bronze Age cultures and ignited a feminist wave of goddess worship when she published several books on goddesses in the 1970s and 1980s. She found icons and statues in Europe that she interpreted as historical proof of female divinity. Gimbutas's theory that we once worshipped women was derided by the academic community, and although times are changing and she has since been held as a pioneer in her field, we are still not certain of the historical truth. Did we once worship women?

As a science journalist, Angela Saini will always seek pure truth, but I asked her, does it hurt for us to create a new narrative – like Marija Gimbutas did – that decentres male power? Especially when history has long been one-sided? There have been many beliefs throughout history that have been proved to be incorrect and yet still have devastating effects on the treatment of women and people of colour today. I think about the historical inaccuracy of eugenics and female hysteria. I think about how in Ancient Greece, Hippocrates, the so-called father of modern medicine, shared the idea of the 'Wandering Womb', the theory that the uterus moved round a woman's body and was responsible for her health problems, which for centuries was seen as scientifically accurate. Who decides what is true? If I was to invent a history that powers me instead of squashes me, would that be so bad?

I don't think so, and so the following chapter is my version of events. My own story, my own personal myth. It's a flexible version of a truth, based on what lifts me up and makes me whole. Haven't men been doing that for centuries? After all, even Napoleon Bonaparte said, 'History is a set of lies agreed upon.'

New Method 18
Call on Your Ancestors

As part of understanding ourselves, we create and design our own mythologies. To do this, we build intergenerational relationships with women in each decade of life and hear their stories. Not merely as 'mentors', but as friends and chosen family, so that we may see first-hand the self-assurance, freedom and wealth that can come with age. We need our elders around us to pass down the legends of our people. Using this knowledge from our family or our DNA, we connect to the divine source. We can, if we choose to, research the history of our ancestry and anoint ourselves with the confidence of knowing we have come from a very long line of intelligent, resourceful and powerful women. It is our birthright to own that power. Whether it's Viking, Nubian, Ancient Briton, Amazon, Persian, Indian and others, dig deep into your history to find your taliswoman to remind you of nobility. Our existence is a miracle – one that started with Mitochondrial Eve, and our matrilineal human right is worth living and fighting for.

'In the beginning, there was only ocean. Until the Mother Island emerged: Te Fiti! Her heart held the greatest power ever known! It could create life itself. And Te Fiti shared it with the world.' The opening lines of the movie *Moana* read like much of our human history, both mythically and genetically. Tens of thousands of years before humanity popularized the monotheistic father god, we worshipped the Primordial, Great Mother Goddess, the divine feminine. We worshipped women.

Symbolic representations of the Primordial Goddess have been around since the Paleolithic era, which spans from 2.5 million to 10,000 years BCE. Frequently these images portray a fertile, rounded woman, often having a vulva with an eye or seed inside it as a symbol of new life emerging from her creative power. Through the image of the seed, the female body was linked to Mother Nature's reproductive capacity, leading to matrilinear practices of governance by women. Scientific reproduction was still a mystery, so the woman was seen as the magic and mysterious creator of life. As the creator of life, mothers were held responsible for leading the community.

In the Upper Paleolithic era, reverence of the Primordial Goddess was widespread and many theorists suggest that she was used to explain natural events. Using her body as a model for comprehending what prehistoric people experienced in their environment created an intimate connection with nature. I have long been emboldened by the fact that it is the female sex that is so deeply and cyclically connected to the planet we live on and beyond. Only our bodies are connected to our earth and the moon.

The goddess is reflected in woman. Her power was felt by early humans and manifested through seasonal changes, wild animal behaviour, and a plethora of observed cosmological patterns. The natural world – animal reproduction, the growth and flowering of plants, the cycles of the moon – echoes the regular changes in most women's bodies, from the menstrual cycle to pregnancy and childbirth, to lactation and eventually death.

Our ecological and psychological systems ran on principles related to the adoration of goddesses long before those based on male deities became dominant. It all ended with the notion of the one supreme god, who across all major world religions happens to be male. How bizarre. For almost 30,000 years and possibly beyond, women are revered, and then for just the last 10,000 years, it's all about the father god, who of course passes his power through the male in the household, through law and through violence. Instead of stories of women's divine power, we are fed with the story of the original sin that Eve – woman – sent humanity to shame with her thirst for knowledge.

Patriarchy was not an instant shift but a wave that slowly swept over the world as we moved towards agrarian societies. Women were now open vessels instead of fountains of knowledge and wisdom. Men ruled the plough and hence from them came the new power over life, death and taxes. As the nomadic lifestyle drew to a close, there was an enormous transformation in thinking and beliefs. The Industrial Revolution followed, accelerating the exaltation of machines. We moved from worshipping nurturers to worshipping conquerors. And now our planet is dying. We are dying.

I am skipping through millennia, of course, but I firmly believe that in order to keep the current generation of women under duress, it has been necessary for the West to break the cultural bonds between ancient women and modern women, preventing the wisdom of our divine power from being passed down from generation to generation and refusing us self-security and contentment. This division can easily be created by closing the portal to the prehistoric past and instead defining the past through a singular lens, ridiculing any attributes of womanhood in order to make us shameful to ourselves.

The myth of Eve may have been the beginning of this shame, so let us move towards the concept of Mitochondrial Eve. When it comes to human genetics, Mitochondrial Eve is a vital concept. She holds the title of matrilineal Most Recent Common Ancestor (MRCA) for all living humans. She's the most recent woman in an unbroken line that has descended purely through mothers and their mother's maternal ancestors – all human females can trace back to one single individual: Mitochondrial Eve. In her book *The Women's History of the World,* Rosalind Miles writes, 'The story of the human race begins with the female. Woman carried the original human chromosome as she does to this day.' Miles continues: 'In human cell structure, woman's is the basic "X" chromosome; a female baby simply collects another "X" at the moment of conception, while the creation of a male requires the branching of a divergent "Y" chromosome, seen by some as a genetic error.'

This idea that the female chromosome was the source of all life and the male chromosome simply an addition felt both revolutionary and conspiratorial as I read it. A conspiracy because I had grown up with the Freudian idea that girls had penis envy. That woman was born from the rib of Adam. That I, as a woman, was the defect.

Of course, this is a simplified take, but the simplicity of this premise was startling to me. That is because so many of the reasons for patriarchal dominance seem also very simple. Just simple and not in our favour. When we zoom out, further than the mere few thousand years of monotheism, further than the millennia of patriarchy, one can find solace in that there was indeed a time when things were more equal. If we can zoom backward, to find equality, I can imagine a zoom forward to bypass the current era of oppression. We might land on a mutual agreement that all genders and races can exist without one feeling the need to dominate the other. I feel positive knowing that inequality is a young concept and that the tenets of this oppression are crumbling with each year that passes.

I was keen to learn more about my own DNA, so I submitted my saliva to learn about precisely where my people came from. I am 47.6 per cent South Asian and 47.4 per cent West African via Jamaica. While my know-ledge of my Jamaican culture and family is fairly strong, I knew little of my Indian heritage or African ancestry, so I have taken measures to learn more about the culture of where I come from.

It was illuminating to know that I am specifically Pun-jabi, and while I don't know if my family was Sikh or Hindu, both religions have deeply ecological roots. I find a lot of comfort in practising yoga, chanting and listening to Indian prayer music. Ayurvedic principles and chakras make sense to me.

For my African heritage, I read about Oshun, an orisha (deity) of the Yoruba people of south-western Nigeria. Oshun is commonly called the river orisha, or river goddess, in the Yoruba religion and is typically associated with water, purity, fertility, love and sensuality. She was the only female of seventeen deities sent to restore Earth after an attack. None of the male deities could complete the task, but she brought forth her sweet and powerful waters, bringing life back to Earth.

Artist and businesswoman Beyoncé regularly channels Oshun in her yellow dresses, especially in the music video for *Hold Up*. I have enjoyed watching Beyoncé move into her Goddess Era, becoming a mother, retreating inwards, seeking solace in her power. 'I am Beyoncé Giselle Knowles-Carter,' sings Beyoncé in 'Mood 4 Eva', one of the tracks on her visual album *Black Is King*. But that's not all she is: 'I am the Nala, sister of Naruba, Osun, Queen Sheba, I am the mother.'

While I am planning a healing trip to India, and I loved the energy of Lagos, I am still most comfortable in Jamaica. With each visit I learn more about my people. I met an older woman in Treasure Beach – Sharon – who had left London to live permanently in Jamaica. She had glistening skin and a greying afro. Her body was strong and firm. She and her partner taught me about Rastafarian culture and Ital food. They served me soup – 'sip' – while teaching me about Nanny and the Maroons. Nanny was a hero, leading a community of formerly enslaved Africans called the Windward Maroons, fighting a guerrilla war against British authorities to battle for, and subsequently win, their freedom. She is the only female national hero of Jamaica. She is part of my history. Connecting with Sharon brought me closer to that history.

I want to interject on what I see as the difference between ancestry, culture and tradition, as I believe they are three parts of the same animal. Ancestry is the heart, it is the life force. It is the essence. It's from the beginning of time, before the fiction of country borders and religions. A time when our ancestors roamed the Earth and followed a beat, a cadence of nature. Calling on your ancestors goes beyond the last few hundred years of what you know. Culture is the skin, it envelops us. It's taken for granted as the largest organ, but one that bears witness and carries scars and ages over time. Culture is ever present, and before you know it, it is just who we become. And tradition? That is the hand. When it is good, it is a limb that guides us and holds us. It's the hand that reaches out in peace. When it is bad, it is destructive – it's a violent pounding fist.

Tradition is not the same as ancestry, in my opinion, and it has been used time and time again to justify global male violence against women, from female genital mutilation to bride burning. Tradition can be an excuse.

From the original patriarchal myth of Eve, our lineage has been packaged as the weaker, oppressed sex, created merely for the service of the male. What does that do to a young mind? To be told that you have been born from a perceived degenerate, shameful sex? That to be born a female is to be 'less than', viewed as so worthless that being killed by your own father or mother upon birth was routine?

But what would it do if you knew the true origin of your peoples and their goddesses, queens and noble ladies? What would it do to go all the way back mythically to the Great Mother Goddess, but also genetically to Mitochondrial Eve? To uncover the women in your history from ancient times and learn their stories of resilience? Had I known the true source of my power earlier, I don't think it would have taken me so long to feel the strength of my divine feminine. To feel proud and strong.

So call on your ancestors and dig deep into your cultural history. Connect with your elders and ask them for stories of female hope. I implore you to expand your knowledge of your ancestry by going deeper and further into your past until you can find a story or myth that speaks to you and inspires you. Regardless of whether it is fact or fiction, find the part of your past that helps you walk with your head held high.

Start at 39BC and beyond. Go back as far as you can and then turn around and work forward to your present day. Ask your family, check your DNA, and if you are estranged from your family, just use your name origin for inspiration. You can even make up your own name! Walk barefoot on the earth of your land. Go to the museums and see your stolen artefacts. Read your books. Get yourself a goddess statue. Visit the ancient temples.

Research the culinary history of your people, and cook and eat your food. Eat it with your hands. Communal meals are the cornerstone of our human survival. Meet with other women of your ancestry for supper and talk about your experiences.

Or simply sit quietly in your room, breathe deeply and call on your ancestors. Imagine yourself on an infinity plane, looking to the past, the present and then to the future. You are the beginning and the end of time.

In the 1972 documentary *Goddess Remembered,* Luisah Teish states, 'It helps me a lot to remember that I am an ancestress of tomorrow and that what I say and do today, a thousand years from now may be coded into the symbolism of what they believe then.' The way we exist today is just a few millennia old. The next thousand years will be different.

So after you've called upon your ancestors, remember to also be a good one.

New Method 19
Develop Adult Friendships

We actively seek new friends that we have chosen for their qualities. There comes a turning point when we start to shed the friends we made that were arbitrary and default. We went to the same school. We grew up next door to each other. Our parents were friends. And so on. Some of these friends will grow with you and some of them will not. We build new relationships on the basis of shared beliefs and ideals so that we do not feel alone in our New Methods journey. Even though it can be weird and hard and embarrassing to make new friends as a grown-up, we know that healthy social bonds are key to our survival and so we push through.

Now is the time to stop assuming that you're always going to be alone. Or that you can only rely on yourself. Or that no one understands you. Or whatever warped schema you use to avoid making new friends. Know that this feeling is both endemic (so you really aren't alone in your thoughts) and an indirect result of our current capitalist methods of human progression.

Why are we so lonely? Neoliberalism insists that we remove obstacles to free markets and allow capitalism to generate development. The argument that prevails is that if only everyone is allowed to work freely, capitalism will generate wealth which will trickle down to everyone. Neoliberalism gained traction with Reaganism and Thatcherism, and experienced a growth trajectory with the 1980s cult of individual money-making before peaking with the era of GirlBoss personal development. We are well into the Age of I.

To power this incredible personal and economic growth, the world had to physically change. Like taking a reliable and safe car and souping it up with high-performance modifications to allow it to run faster, our planet had to gear up. We call these improvements 'cities', and they allow neoliberalism to thrive. They beckon us with their opportunities to earn as much money as we like and obviously give us places to spend it. They separate us from our families. They force us to live on top of each other, buttressing up with perfect strangers. Globally, over 50 per cent of the population lives in urban areas today, and by 2045, the world's urban population will increase by 1.5 times, to 6 billion.

We move to the cities for a better life, only to realize that we are anxious, exhausted and lonely. And women feel this more than men. According to ONS data, UK women reported feeling lonely more frequently than men. They were significantly more likely than men to report feeling lonely 'often/always', and in a poll conducted by the Angus Reid Institute in Canada, women under thirty-five tended to express greater feelings of loneliness than other age groups, despite having social lives. Never before in our entire human history have we lived with such global urbanization. It's only natural that you might feel a bit lonely in your tower block apartment in the middle of millions of people who don't know your name. The feelings are natural, but the situation is not.

Despite this, cities also give us so much. Technology, culture and ideas are all born from cities. They come from the cross-pollination of people and experiences that spring forth innovation. Cities create diverse communities around shared interests, and I mean your actual interests. Not the ones you're forced to pretend to be into just because your family is. Because cities generate such incredible human progress, how can we learn to make them work for us, rather than the other way around? City developments ballooned to generate economic growth, but we don't have to spend all our time being productive in them. The obsession with individualism and self-development has resulted in a capitalist calendar filled with work and networking, and many of us are approaching breaking point.

I find no irony in the fact that famed actor Michael Douglas played both Gordon Gekko – the exemplary capitalist in the 1987 movie *Wall Street* – and William Foster, the unemployed, divorced man having a breakdown in the 1993 movie *Falling Down*. Gekko's most famous line – 'greed is good' – is the sentiment that turned up the dial on our desire for more and created the pressurized environment that six years later led to the second character, Foster, stating: 'I lost my job. Actually, I didn't lose it. It lost me. I'm overeducated, underskilled – maybe it's the other way around. I forget – but I'm obsolete. I'm not economically viable. I can't even support my own kid.' He then lets loose on a violent warpath of simply trying to get home in the city. It can often feel like an either/or situation. Work for the man and for the money and lose your soul, or give it all up, have a life crisis and shoot down the city. Both of these feelings can be the direct result of urban isolation.

One of the ways I work to combat this is by finding my Family 2.0. Many of us moved from our provincial towns to seek work in the big city, from Baltimore to NYC, from Wolverhampton to London, and immediately expected to find new families to replace the ones we had left behind. We didn't understand why these new urbanized friends didn't get our banter, our cultural references and our penchant for deep-fried Mars bars, so we stuck out our bottom lip and said, 'No one understands me!' and decided to stay in instead. As Sunday comes around, the scaries tell us, 'You are going to die alone!' and then Monday comes, and we trudge from home tower to work tower and the cycle starts again.

In an attempt to break this cycle we need to think differently about our relationship to our work, money and the city. In their book *Rebuild: The Economy, Leadership and You*, Graham Boyd and Jack Reardon make a call to arms for a world that creates an economy that works for the planet, for people, and for profit. And it starts very simply – with the way we make meaning: 'The reality you experience is inside you, triggered by what actually happens and shaped by your lenses and meaning-making stories. You grow your capacity to use better lenses, and so experience a better reality, because you can reinvent the lenses and meaning-making stories you use.'

To develop meaningful relationships, we need to look through a new lens. Maybe it's not the cities themselves that are to blame, but the way we spend our time in them and who we spend that time with. Of course you will feel that no one understands you if you don't bother to make time for building a relationship with them because you are too busy being 'productive'. We prioritize our work over our friends, resulting in loneliness. I ask myself: who and what am I actually being busy for if I cannot enjoy it with others?

The New Method here is to understand that your loneliness is a direct result of modern capitalism, and a solution is to forge deeper friendships as a priority for your well-being. Adult friendships. Ones with intention. But making friends is hard, I hear you say! I tried to make friends, but it didn't work out. But did you try to make friends, or did you try to build your network? Because the two things are very different.

Communities, networks and now friendships have been at the forefront of my thinking in terms of women and equality. They are essential for us to thrive. Your community takes you from −5 to zero. Your network takes you from zero to +10, and your friendships? Well, they make the whole thing fun and pleasurable. Friends bring joy and play.

But how do you go from meeting someone at a party to making them your friend? I've tried many, many methods, and fundamentally you need to ask them out. You are essentially asking them, 'Will you go on a (play) date with me?' Understand you have to date friends, just like you have to date to find a partner. Reach out to someone you would like to become closer to and suggest a 'play date', not a coffee or a Zoom. This is not a network. I used to often suggest a fancy lunch for new friends, but it is far too formal. Make it a local café or a greasy spoon. Grab your lunch and walk and talk together. Walking together is singlehandedly the most popular way for me to form new friendships. I like to take new comrades down to the river, stopping occasionally to sit on a bench and admire the view. Eventually travelling together for a weekend away cements this friendship. Travelling unites people deeply. Walking is a mini form of that.

Fun and joy and fresh air are important to feeling alive with a new friend. Think about what you would do if you were thirteen. Walk around the park, go to a museum, go to the cinema. A date. Accept that if you don't vibe, it's not the end of the world. You've learned something about yourself and your needs. Make another date with someone else. You'll find your crew. I always say that ignorance is bliss and smart girls especially feel lonely. Mission-driven women like our Stack World community can experience the feeling of both wanting more time with our childhood or familial friends and also potentially outgrowing them as we explore our identities and our place in the world. The more you begin to understand the way the world works, and how systems of oppression work, the more frustrated you are with it and the more you want to withdraw from the system. The feeling can lead to tension – between wanting to discuss and analyse the ways Black femme bodies are historically devalued on reality TV, while also just wanting to just enjoy the memes and the gossip. We can get torn between our anger at the global war on women and sometimes just wanting to zone out and read trash. It's OK to have conflicting opinions internally. You are a vibrant work in progress. And you can satisfy all versions of yourself, just not always with the same person.

Don't expect one friend to meet all your needs – whether they are old or new. Your childhood friends will forever see you as that thirteen-year-old girl, and that may be what you need in order to stay grounded. Your new friends might not be able to immediately understand how your childhood has shaped your actions, and that too is OK, as they will get to know you over time.

Start thinking about a spectrum of friends to meet your various emotional needs, especially you folk who say, 'I don't have time for new friends.' In fact, I've said this many times myself. When I reflect on where I am putting my time, it goes back to work. I work anything from ten to sixteen hours a day in the endless pursuit of growth and achieving more. What would it mean to actually be content with where I am and what I have and build a sustainable life that is regenerative for me and my family? Is it OK to work just enough to maintain the life we already have, or must we fulfil the social contract of performative and economic self-actualization to keep the entire system afloat? After all, if we women aren't consuming, then who is?

More and more I'm hearing of young women who

are opting out. Spending three months of the year working and nine months vacationing with their best friends as they do the bare minimum to meet their financial obligations. Social media trends of 'enjoyment' and 'soft life' are daughters of this revolutionary act. Creating and building friendships may mean that you finish a project a little later or you don't respond to that email as quickly, but in quality of life terms, I believe the return on investment is much higher.

These new friendships are your Chosen Family – a term the queer community use to describe non-biological kinship bonds, whether legally recognized or not, deliberately selected for the purpose of mutual support and love. Coach Hannah Rankine calls this your A-Team. She lists the six people you need in your family:

- MENTOR: Who can you check in with along the way to share your progress with? They must be credible within the field to truly validate your journey.
- COLLEAGUE: Do you have someone who has a similar goal to yours? You're going to hit road bumps and experience failures along the way, and having someone else hitting their hurdles in a similar field will stop you feeling alone and disheartened. Together you can also collaborate and recalibrate.
- CHEERLEADER: Who is going to support you and lift you up? Whatever your love language, we all need words of affirmation. Find those friends that will high-five you at every juncture.

- ACCOUNTANT: Who are you accountable to? You have to have people that will make sure you show up – they are very different to a cheerleader but are supportive nonetheless. Their support looks like making sure you deliver where you said you would. And that is powerful. This could well be your life coach that you work with on a long-term basis.
- CHALLENGERS: Who is calling you out? Who is giving honest feedback? They have to help you rise, not cut you down. Ultimately you can take their advice or leave it, but it is good to have this constructive criticism. It might be hard to swallow at first, but don't take it personally, and you will soon see the benefit of such honesty.
- COMMUNITY: Your people! They are so important. Your community is built of people whom you know, love and admire. Communities support your growth and offer inspiration through stimulation and providing outside opinions when you can't see the wood for the trees. Your tribe will pick you up when you're on your knees, pour you a cup of tea when you're fed up and high-five you even for the smallest of bite-size wins.

I am sometimes excluded by my friends from certain activities. They correctly say it's because they know I wouldn't enjoy them (I'd rather be home watching movies than at another pointless party), but like a true Gemini, I still want the invite so that I can decide! That said, I've accepted that I play a role in their lives, as they do in mine. If you feel left out, have you verbalized it? Have you indicated your needs? Whatever facet of yourself you want your various friends to satisfy, be prepared to find that they'll be doing that to you too.

Depth, not breadth, is important with friends. You may not actually need new friends as you already have many friends in your life that you haven't invested enough time in. British anthropologist Robin Dunbar theorized that humans couldn't manage more than 150 meaningful relationships, a figure that became known as Dunbar's Number. His recent book, *Friends: Understanding the Power of Our Most Important Relationships*, maps out the circles of friendships. Dunbar explains in an interview with the *Atlantic*: 'The innermost layer of 1.5 is [the most intimate]; clearly that has to do with your romantic relationships. The next layer of five is your shoulders-to-cry-on friendships. They are the ones who will drop everything to support us when our world falls apart. The 15 layer includes the previous five, and your core social partners. They are our main social companions, so they provide the context for having fun times. They also provide the main circle for exchange of child care. We trust them enough to leave our children with them. The next layer up, at 50, is your big-weekend-barbecue people. And the 150 layer is your weddings and funerals group who would come to your once-in-a-lifetime event.'

Finding your circle of 150 requires consistent action and participation. In 2018, for an entire year, I held a dinner party at my house called Friday Fam and sent a booking link to 150 people I already knew but wanted to hang with. It was at my house intentionally because people act differently when they are in your kitchen and take their shoes off to sit on your sofa, and the results were amazing. Even if that was the only time I saw them for the entire year, we bonded deeply over homemade spaghetti bolognese or sometimes even takeout, and that time investment was enough.

Friendships don't always work out, but a pause is not a rejection. Because of my codependency issues in my twenties, I thrived on intense relationships and would be devastated if I felt betrayed or abandoned in any way. Sometimes I would be the punisher and withdraw my friendship, but it would not always mean the end. Humans are not static creatures, and as we constantly evolve and develop there are some points when we meet people on our exact vibration and times when we don't. Everyone is going through their private pain, and your friendship dynamic may add to it, rather than take it away. If you avoid making new friends to avoid getting hurt because the pain of early toxic friendships was too great, then I urge you to take a macro view. Some friends are right for right now. Some friends you instinctively know you're going to be hanging with when you're seventy years old. Most of the people I have in my life today I feel will be my friends for life. And they are also the same people I've taken pauses with – anything from a few months to a year of not speaking. Each friendship was unhappy in its own way. The vibe was off. But when the time came to reunite, it would take a little nurturing and then be as if we had never been apart at all. Best Friends Forever.

Zoom out on your relationships and assume that anyone you are going to know for three or more decades will invariably have some ups and downs. Don't avoid making new friends for fear of rejection. You will eventually be on the same vibration. Adulthood is the biggest scam around, but choosing who you are friends with is one of the redeeming features. You can lose those default friendships such as the same church/school/neighbours that no longer serve you and instead invest in friendships that nourish your soul.

One of the reasons I love business is that it is a theory in practice. Sure I can sit here rambling and writing about my ideas on women, work and equality, but I can also put some of my thoughts into action. Many of our Stack World members joined our community for professional reasons and were surprised to make actual friends in the network. They go on holiday, they have sleepovers, and they attend each other's weddings. It's a bond. So go forth and make new friends. Go and explore your city together.

My business is called the Stack World for a reason. Work may have become the defining feature of our life to date, but how can we redefine our environments, our cities, our houses, and our private and public world? It starts with you and how you're willing to spend your time. Making friends is never a waste of it.

PART THREE

Applying

With the beginnings of your wisdom forming, you can now begin the task of applying your New Methods to control and design your environment. You'll need to take to the task with great enthusiasm, as an electric shock to your old self. It is easy at this point to dismiss your self-knowledge and slip back into misery. That too is part of the process. You are being asked to make a decision on how much you actually want to be your most authentic self and how much power you truly want. How will you know unless you relapse and are reminded of what it feels like to be powerless? Unless you create dynamic application, you will be stagnant and revert back to type. To apply is to use force and to move things. To apply is to take action. Your chief aim is to be like a social scientist, running experiments from the first two sections and gathering data to refine what works for you. You are writing your own bible. Your own New Methods. This is a rigorous process of training and developing your muscle memory so that actions and feelings become autonomous. They settle as a natural part of who you are. The old version is no longer compatible.

New Method 20
Make Data-driven Decisions

With newfound intel about our every being, we start to make better decisions using our data. We make choices that keep us in high vibration and turn away from the options that are going to hold us back. We start a process of inquiry about all major decisions. We know that it does not nourish us to make the same mistake over and over again, so we test, experiment and double down on the things that are working, so we can get the best out of our actions.

One of the best parts of getting older is learning from your mistakes and growing as a person. Albert Einstein's definition of insanity is doing the same thing over and over and expecting different results, so by approaching your decision-making using the data you've collected throughout your life to date, you can avoid this and begin making smarter decisions.

Your twenties and early thirties are your prime data-gathering years. During these periods, don't be afraid of making mistakes. George Bernard Shaw once said: 'A life spent making mistakes is not only more honourable but more useful than a life spent doing nothing.' If we're learning, failing and perhaps failing again, we're collecting invaluable information to help guide us in the right direction. Making mistakes isn't a bad thing. Failing to take relevant lessons from them is.

So far, you have actively focused on understanding yourself and gathering all sorts of data so that you can recognize which decisions are immaterial and which warrant more careful consideration. You don't need to do an intense analysis of what to eat for lunch every single day. But you might need to be rigorous about it when dealing with a health condition or if you have an important meeting straight after that you need to be sharp for.

The very process of paying attention, of being observant of my body and mind, helps me make better decisions. Everything from where to live to where to work can be fast-tracked with some form of analysis and self-questioning on what you like and don't like, what keeps you moving forward and what holds you back. I lived in my London neighbourhood of Clerkenwell three different times over two decades before realizing that it was my favourite place to be because of the central location and relative anonymity. Now I'll remain in this area happily for the foreseeable future.

At work, I know what sort of people fit within the company. When hiring roles close to me, I know from experience that I can't hire people who will see me as a mother figure or people who want to be my friend. Dynamics like that tend to end negatively. I only know this because I've had many years of experience and hours spent working through team issues due to this unique relationship dynamic. If a potential employee has strong relationships with their parents, I know it'll be a different sort of working relationship, as they won't be subconsciously looking for a parental figure in their life. This is something I've learnt and can now take action on in the hiring process. I focus instead on their obsession with the company mission and their ability to deliver results.

Along a similar vein, I know the main personality traits that work or don't work in my colleagues. I work best with those who are less negative, have emotional stability and are not prone to gossiping. The way I know this is by having our team do personality tests and regular performance reviews. By using this data, I can make better decisions on who manages who and how the team is built. I like to connect certain people with complementary skills to work together, as I know they'll be more efficient. Office politics is my least favourite trait. It is so pointless and hampers productivity. I thrive in relatively flat systems where we can all have a sense of shared achievement and responsibility.

Dating is a huge area in our lives where data is critical. When we are looking to fill a position in our business, we will consider many candidates and interview a select number before narrowing it down and hiring someone. But when it comes to dating, we do the complete opposite! We might happily settle with the first person who shows interest. But imagine how much more successful our dating lives could be if we applied the same principle.

Over the years, I've come to know what does and doesn't work for me in a partner. I like to do a post-mortem on each relationship and reflect on where it broke down. Were they judgemental? Were they ambitious? Did they love forty-eight-hour trips like I do? Did they bring out my best qualities? Did they give me joy? Make me feel safe? Did I make them feel safe? Writing my reflections out clearly on paper helps me calibrate future compatibility.

The New Method here is to get into the habit of analysing all the data you've gathered up to this point before making important decisions. You're simply looking for patterns. Often, instead of making smart choices, we make fast decisions based on our impulses and short-term desires. This is about combining your gut feelings with all the cold-hard data that's surrounding you, creating a toolkit for yourself to make the best possible moves in life.

It sounds like a lot of work, but becoming a New Method woman requires you to think smarter. Over time, this will become second nature as you develop the muscle memory of what works for you, and you can communicate with conviction about where you want to go next.

New Method 21
Practise Non-binary Thinking

We recognize that by being predictable women, we are easier to control. By ticking a box, by clicking an ad, by submitting a like, we are saying: this is all we stand for. So, we scramble the algorithm and slide along a spectrum of our beliefs. We do not put ourselves in either/or scenarios, we are flexible and mutable and we explore the facts of a story, seeking all points of view to support us in formulating our own. We won't be drawn into simplistic mind games of a forced and safe decision for acceptance. We won't be backed into a corner of narrow-minded beliefs. We feel into the grey, seeking the space between.

I have never been able to fit neatly into a category and because of that, I have always been an outsider. Even as a child, my mixed Jamaican and Indian heritage meant there was never a tick box on the form for my Caribbean-Asian ethnicity. I came from a low-income household, yet I bucked government data trends as my literacy was high. I had devoured every book on the reading shelves as I entered my final year of primary school but also sat open-mouthed in front of the TV for hours. I wore pigtails, but I played football. The first two cassette tapes I ever owned were Notorious B.I.G. and Gustav Holst's *The Planets Suite*. I never had a single crew at school, preferring instead to table-hop in the cafeteria. It made it difficult for people to figure me out, as I always seemed to lie outside the edges. Sometimes it delighted them. Sometimes it frustrated them. But why?

Zeros and ones, zeros and ones. Humans like pattern and order, they like boxes and pigeonholes and things that make it easy for their brains to recognize what is in front of them. You can be a mom but you can't be successful at work. You can be frigid or promiscuous. You can be ambitious or an introvert, but you can't be both. But what about the space between?

As a child, it was fun to shapeshift and take on different roles, but as I got older and especially as I got into relationships, there was an expectation to conform. Women are often expected to fit into narrow and predefined roles, behaviours and beliefs that limit our ability to fully express ourselves and explore our potential. These expectations are like a straitjacket that can create a kind of binary thinking, where we are forced to choose between two opposing options that are presented to us.

Binary thinking is a mindset that is characterized by a rigid and limiting view of the world. It involves firmly held beliefs on what is right/wrong, good/bad or male/female. This kind of thinking can be useful in certain situations, such as when making quick decisions or solving problems that have clear-cut solutions. However, when applied to complex issues or human behaviour, binary thinking can be limiting and can lead to narrow and simplistic viewpoints.

Your belief in a 'right' and a 'wrong' is set very early.

Mine was set by Jamaican parenting and by my family church. From small things, such as it's wrong as a woman to sit with your legs wide open, all the way to, we don't eat pork as it's unclean meat, I've been culturally guided by my caregivers as to the either/or options for group acceptance.

It was around the age of thirteen that I started to question these binaries. My flexible belief system couldn't comprehend an Us vs Them. I couldn't figure out why some religions were bad and some were good, if we are all meant to show compassion and love. I couldn't make sense of why I wasn't allowed to do technology and study art at school, I had to choose. It seemed nonsensical to me that I couldn't play football with my male friends and be seen as a feminine figure. In addition to this, as I was coming into my womanhood, the most damning judgement of all was around being a sexual woman. It was seemingly impossible for me to enjoy sex and be seen as a moral woman. As I dove deeper and deeper into some of these tenets set by the world around me I realized that I do have the option of opting out. Of choosing the grey area.

I have always found gender roles limiting. When I have tried to play a pure 'female' part as designated by my culture, I simply feel trapped. The most basic trap is to either be 'a good wife and mother' or pursue a career, rather than being encouraged to find a balance between these roles or to design our own unique path. I adore being a mother, and I adored my career. While I never got it perfect, I am proud of the way I made it work. But there are many times when I was put into a box through criticism and it was hard for me to fight my way out. Similarly, I've always found the role of being aesthetically driven and intellectually curious a difficult one to play. I've been in rooms of technologists who can't place me because my eyeliner was done to perfection. I didn't fit their framework. Times are changing. Similarly for men, overtly masculine stereotypes can be limiting, and deny them the full range of their emotional spectrum. Patriarchal systems harm the majority of men too, as they are designed to protect a very small set of ruling elites.

Eventually, I realized that a binary identity can bring a lot of confusion and shame. The criticisms I have received from others may have been their unresolved shame at being forced to play a dutiful feminine role. My ambiguous identity was a muddy mirror to their standards. My own self-criticisms playing in my head were also the same voice. When we don't deal with this shame internally, we direct that shame outward. And then you begin calling women sluts. Or deriding working mothers. Or being disgusted with someone who displays their naked body proudly. Or cancelling or trolling someone online. It results in a warped, hateful and predictable sense of what is right and wrong, instead of fully embracing the complexity of the human condition.

The binary identity is also easily manipulated. Binary thinking suits advertisers, media and politicians by creating a world in which they can sort you and predict your choices. They can sell to you with ease. They know your insecurities because, in part, they manufactured them.

They know what to say to you to swing your vote. And they double down on the issues that are most divisive, instead of designing policies that work for us all. We are living in polarizing and disturbing times and non-binary thinking can help limit their control.

This doesn't mean that you stand for nothing. Technology forecaster and Stanford professor Paul Saffo developed an ideology he refers to as 'strong opinions, weakly held'. This means you can argue your point, while also being flexible. Trust your intuition, while also challenging it. Non-binary thinking involves questioning the 'either/or' thinking that is so prevalent in our society and recognizing that there are often more than two options in any given situation. Ask yourself why you feel so strongly about something, particularly if it has zero impact on you. Seek out diverse perspectives on any given issue and challenge your own assumptions. Be comfortable with uncertainty. You may not receive any concrete answers, and for a non-philosophical mind, this can feel unresolved and irritating. But what would it mean to be fluid, nebulous and operate in the space between? Rather than choosing a side, have you ever thought about the power that comes from being a free agent?

Practising non-binary thinking can help us break free from these constraints and develop a more open-minded and authentic approach to life. We become powerful by developing a more nuanced and sophisticated understanding of the world around us. We can learn to see beyond dichotomies, not be swayed by media or a political agenda. We recognize the many shades of grey that exist in any given situation. Begin to research, fact-check and see all sides to a story. We don't believe the first thing we see, we enquire about it. We get curious about it.

By avoiding binary thinking, you control your own narrative. Wherever your life is right now, you can call the shots and live authentically as you please. Ask, 'What's right for me right now?' rather than, 'What's right and what's wrong?' Your views are liable to change over time as your own circumstances do. The grey is not a cop out position, on a fence, or in Switzerland, but the choice to evaluate your own beliefs at any given time. At first, the grey can be lonely. Not falling into line makes it harder for you to be part of a group. But eventually, you may find that you attract others who share your open-mindedness and willingness to embrace the messy without causing unnecessary stress and conflict. By focusing on what's right for you at the moment rather than trying to fit into a particular mould or follow a specific set of rules, you can make choices that align with your own values and priorities, despite what anyone else thinks.

New Method 22
Train Your Internal Autocorrect

We commit to reprogramming our mental autocorrect with positive statements and inputs, repeating them obsessively until they become muscle memory for self-compassion and loving kindness. Inside us all, a war is waging between our higher and lower selves, and our internal monologue of negativity is where it takes root. We do not prevent our path to growth by echoing the barrier phrases we hear around us of 'I can't', 'I won't', 'I don't'. No one is born telling themselves they can't. Your internal autocorrect was not initially programmed by you. But now we're an adult and so by retraining our autocorrect, we can rebuild our confidence.

One of the earliest recordings of predictive text is the Ming Kwai typewriter. Invented in China in the 1940s, this electromechanical typewriter would suggest the next keys to press after you'd made your first stroke, making you work faster and more efficiently. Since then, predictive text has permeated just about every form of writing technology, from early SMS to smartphones to the software I'm writing this book with.

Predictive text birthed autocorrect, invented by Dean Hachamovitch, an engineer at Microsoft Word, in the 1990s. In an article in *Wired* on the history of autocorrect, Gideon Lewis-Kraus writes:

The notion of autocorrect was born when Hachamov-itch began thinking about a functionality that already existed in Word . . . He drew up a little code that would allow you to press the left arrow and F3 at any time and immediately replace teh with the. His 'aha' moment came when he realized that, because English words are space-delimited, the space bar itself could trigger the replacement, to make correction . . . automatic! Hacha-movitch drew up a list of common errors, and over the next years he and his team went on to solve many of the thorniest. Seperate would automatically change to separate. Accidental cap locks would adjust immedi-ately (making dEAR grEG into Dear Greg).

Autocorrect is the great machine, tidying up your errors as you go and making sure that your minor mis-takes disappear. Autocorrect will instantly revert to the right word so that no one ever needs to know that you wrote 'abs' when you really meant 'and'.

As well as replacing common grammatical errors, your phone will use an AI combination of predictive text and autocorrect to *learn from you*. The words you use the most are at your fingertips. Names, places and words I use daily appear on my phone as I'm typing the first letter of the word. I once typed my son's name in capi-tals as ROMAN and now every time I write his name, it appears in full caps. This doesn't happen on your phone. My autocorrect is different from yours.

In the same way that your phone is programmed for you, your brain is programmed only for you. So the question is, which version of you is programming your autocorrect? Who is the engineer behind your predictive text?

Think of it like this – if you start to write with good intentions, you write from your Higher Self. But your phone – with its autocorrect function battling against what you actually want to say – can act as your Lower Self, especially from your inner critic.

When you metaphorically start typing, your Higher Self is saying the things it wants to say; it's speaking its truth. Your autocorrect – your Lower Self – says, 'No, this is what I know based on previous data you yourself have told me and this is what I think we should do instead.' This might show up by switching out 'I'm going to' with 'I can't', or 'I need' with 'I don't deserve'. If you've only ever typed negativity into your personal keyboard, well, guess what, when you start typing, it's going to autocorrect negatively.

Your phone might be delivered with a fresh programme using the right language, and it understands the basics of grammar, spelling and your personal typing habits, but that doesn't mean it always gets it right. As people, there's a constant war between our lower and higher selves, just like you're at war with your phone and its autocorrect (I have never ever wanted to type 'ducking hell'!) If you don't catch this disconnect, and you hit enter too fast, the results can be harmful to your mindset.

The New Method here is to rebuild or reconfigure your internal autocorrect in a way that best serves you. When we aren't paying attention, we slip into our lower selves and autocorrect takes over. We act first and think later. The most annoying thing about negative self-talk is that your brain doesn't know the difference. It will take what you say as gospel and believe when you tell yourself you're unworthy.

To change this, you need to start reprogramming, just like Dean Hachamovitch and his team. They actively went through common English language mistakes and put mechanisms in place to eradicate them. Can you do the same for your thoughts?

While it's not something that happens overnight, you can start thinking differently, have an impact on your neuroplasticity (the flexible nature of how our brain works) and build new neural pathways, shortcuts to the way we think and act. We need to be an active participant to correct our autocorrect.

Start by writing down common thoughts and responses you have, e.g.:

'I don't know enough about that.'
'They won't want me.'
'I can't do that.'
'What if they reject me?'

And reprogramme it with opposing phrases, e.g.

'I know this.'
'They want me.'
'I can do that.'
'They love me.'

While in previous chapters we have looked at where these thoughts may come from, this New Method is about applying that knowledge with repetition and building muscle memory for positive responses. Growing confidence requires work, and by thinking about your internal autocorrect you're able to instantly swerve to a statement that serves you.

You may want to get lined sheets of A4 paper, and like Bart Simpson in detention write out lines and lines of positive statements, repeated like protective soldiers. You may want to record yourself on your phone and listen to it while you sleep. Either way, it needs to be positive and repetitive, so that when you start typing, your autocorrect is coming from a good place, not a critical one. It's time to be your own engineer and rebuild your internal autocorrect with loving kindness.

New Method 23
Separate Constructive Criticism from Personal Attacks

We have been in a state of perpetual victimhood for thousands of years, and sometimes we like to keep ourselves there by taking external verbal attacks as gospel. Instead, we turn away from the trolls and move towards constructive criticism from valued sources. We learn how to sort this criticism from personal attacks and use active listening to get to the root of what someone is trying to say about our person. Criticism can be a blessing if we use it wisely.

Rethinking how we take criticism can unlock exponential growth both personally and professionally, but we can often take everything said to us as a personal attack. Sure, sometimes unkind people are just trying to put you down, but an immediate run to hypersensitivity isn't your only option. Just because a comment isn't sparkly or positive doesn't make it a personal attack on you. Try to find the kernel of truth in the statement – the constructive criticism that will help you improve.

If you find yourself immediately feeling defensive or angry in response to something someone has said, it's a good indication that something may resonate but you're not ready to hear it. Instead of biting back to protect yourself, try leaning into the words to uncover an opportunity to learn and grow. Ask yourself why the words have struck a chord. Conversations can be about gaining new information and uncovering truths. But always making it a personal attack means you'll just be closed off to potential feedback loops. Why would people want to tell you anything if they always fear you'll take things the wrong way?

The New Method here is to separate constructive criticism – or even just plain, unloaded communication – from personal attacks. You do this by looking past the surface level of the words and uncovering the truth in what's being said. It's worth noting that it never gets easier; criticism will always hurt. We're human, after all. The pain comes from the elements of self-doubt and a feeling of truth in what's been said. Remember this truth is relative. This could be a perceived truth that comes from your inner critic and from self-hatred. A 'truth' that has no evidential basis. Always check on your truth.

I'm no exception to this. A friend of mine gave me some pretty critical feedback about my leadership style and it hurt. First of all, she was my friend, so it was hard for me to separate our friendship from the criticism of my working practices. That was the first step. I've also got my own traumas that I'm battling against that tell me I'm not good enough. It would have been easy for me to get caught up in the emotion and either believe it, letting it tear me down, or bottle up completely, and lash out defensively.

At this point, I took the words objectively and thought, where is the truth in their statement? I did an inventory of myself to question whether I attempted to be a great leader and maybe failed. Have I just outright been horrible at work? Upon analysis, I found that yes, I am a good leader for a *specific type of person* who works here successfully. If an individual has experience working directly with CEOs, I know they'll work well with me, but if a team player is used to layers of management and process, they tend to get anxious about upsetting the boss and therefore act from fear. That energy makes me doubt their capabilities and the cycle continues. That doesn't make me wrong, and it doesn't make my friend wrong either; instead, it's vital information that helps us decide who to hire in these early stages. In the end I looked at the team, working to understand who had thrived in the environment that I had created and taken themselves and their careers to new heights. I then asked for 360-degree feedback. The most useful piece of feedback was: 'We can't often tell what you're thinking, so we are on edge until you say what you're thinking and then when you do it's either extremely good news or extremely bad news.'

This was fantastic because it was a new piece of constructive criticism that I could work with. I'm instinctive, especially with design, so I either love something or hate something. But it's not nice for my team when I say I hate something in the first three seconds and they have been working on it for three days. So now I work on pausing before feedback, using more neutral phrases before offering useful insights to improve the work. I've watched some of my friends who are incredible managers sandwich their negative feedback with the positive and I've been inspired by that delivery style. It's helped me become better at how I deliver feedback.

When faced with a situation like this, gather information from the other person calmly and take some time to reflect. It could be that you didn't realize something about yourself, and this is an excellent opportunity to grow. Or perhaps it's something you've been avoiding doing the work on, and now is the perfect time to make some necessary changes. By handling it maturely, people won't feel like they have to walk on eggshells around you, afraid to speak their truths.

By taking the personal accusation out of the picture, I could get to the root of the problem. My friend had their own personal issues at work and home (remember it's not always about you), and at the time I felt like this feedback could have been delivered differently. But while the process was painful to hear (you're a bad leader), the outcome of it was good (learning how I can improve in meetings).

I find that personal attacks often contain ad hominems and are focused on your individual person rather than your role, problem or solution. For example, my friend's criticism could have been voiced as, 'The team is underperforming because they spend a lot of time worrying about your feedback rather than being creative', which is very different from, 'Your leadership style is terrible.' While both have the same output – an adjustment of leadership style because we all want to have a high-performance team – one statement focused on the individual rather than the greater goal. If your critic fails to deliver feedback in a way you're receptive to, it's fine, you can do it for yourself, with practice.

By focusing on the greater goal, you can avoid inviting your emotions to the party and leaving feeling attacked. We can recognize that we all want the same thing and we can make adjustments in our delivery style to get there. Being on the receiving end of criticism doesn't make you a bad person. If it's valid criticism, it can be useful for your personal growth. Take the truth – the little seed in the middle of the feedback – and act on it. Throw away the wrapper it came in and move on.

New Method 24
Create Your Big
Woman Energy Protocol

Understanding who we are has little value if we do not apply it to design our lives. So we diligently create our own personal handbook on how to live, based solely on what works for us. We acknowledge that almost all previous guidance for life was written from a patriarchal position, not an inclusive one. Even the greatest philosophers, storytellers and myth-makers spoke words of our diminishment. From them, we take what we like and we leave the rest. Using our own insights, we choose to write a new manual with new methods to help us step into our power.

I have done many workshops, many retreats, and many corporate exercises, but there are only three documents I return to again and again. These are the ones that remind me who I am, what my purpose is and how I want to move through the world.

The first document is fairly practical. Mundane even. It's called 'Guide to Working With Me'. This document gets out all the surface-level elements of your identity, your work, your motivations and your productivity. It's primarily designed for your co-workers, but the process of even asking the questions of yourself is useful for getting closer to what makes you happy and ensuring that the eight or more hours a day you spend on work are working for you.

The second document is a one-page 'Vision, Mission and Principles'. It outlines your life's work, your current work and how you want to show up in the world. This is the page I go to when I'm losing myself and getting distracted, or when I'm feeling overwhelmed. It's almost like a personal manifesto, written much like the introductions to these essays.

Our final document is our 'Vision Plan'. This is a series of prompts to help you write the story of your life. You can write it for one year, ten years or whatever timescale works for you. It's written in the present tense, with the intention of tricking your brain into thinking it's real right now. From this, you start to become that person immediately and act like your future self.

After many years of trial and error, these documents need to be done in the order listed above. It's easier to write your current mission when you've understood what motivates you. It's easier to create a plan for the next ten years of your life when you know what your life's work is.

All three documents should be reviewed annually. Perhaps in January, like me and my community. Or around your birthday, when your personal year around the sun begins again.

Regardless of the dates you choose, allocate at least two days in your calendar to this intense period of self-reflection, ideally a week. Maybe invite some friends for a working retreat and do it together.

Why is it called Big Woman Energy? Well, this work is about fullness, an expanding of space, a harnessing and then transference of energy. It's that feeling you get when you elongate your spine to hold your head high. It's walking with certainty. It's your own personal path to power.

New Method 25
Write a 'Guide to Working with Me'

We take the time to create a document of our operating style, setting clear boundaries for the way we like to work. It is our way of reflecting on the company environment that serves us best and is the first step to designing that environment explicitly. While not every desire will be in our reach from day one, the Guide is our compass, directing us towards our dream career and determining the people and activities that will help us reach our highest potential. Without our Guide, we and others around us are walking in the dark.

One of my favourite bits in Elad Gil's *High Growth Handbook* is 'Working with Claire: An Unauthorized Guide'. It was written when Claire Hughes Johnson joined Stripe as COO in 2014, and the company had just 165 employees. As the number swelled to over 1,000, she needed a shortcut for her new hires so that they could understand the way she worked, and so she wrote her guide.

As a new start-up CEO who was hiring rapidly, I was inspired to write my own guide and I rapidly wrote out on a sheet of A4 my ways of working, using Claire's format. My priority was to make sure everyone in the business understood what drives me, what motivates me and how to get the best work out of me. When am I least productive, when am I most productive? Knowing when I'm least likely to make a good decision, or the type of environment that demotivates me, helps me know when my behaviour is a result of external forces or otherwise. Sometimes it's as simple as the fact that I have to eat lunch around 12 p.m. each day. I have a high metabolism, so I don't schedule meetings then. When I'm hungry, my decision-making is cloudy. Other things are more complex, like how to balance intuition and data. Although I'm a highly logical person, some things just feel . . . right.

I presented my 'Guide to Working with Shar' to the company on a Friday afternoon, just before we all headed off for the weekend. For younger team members especially, it was like a window into my mind. No longer were they second-guessing my thought processes or unsure of my calendar structure. They had the document here right in front of them, and any new starters who joined the company didn't have to waste time getting to know me, they could get up to speed immediately and slot into the team. It also democratized access to my preferences. Now no one in the office could play politics by seemingly having private access to the way the boss liked to work and gatekeeping information.

It felt weirdly egotistical that everyone knew my mind but I didn't know theirs, so I made everyone else do it too. Everyone in the team found the exercise difficult initially, citing that they had never stopped to think about themselves in that way. This is common, especially in us Brits, and I find that most of my generation are self-critical rather than self-reflective. But like the entire Understanding section, I truly believe that you can only better yourself by knowing yourself. To stop and think about how you like to work is seen as a luxury. In the end, they found the exercise totally therapeutic.

We added it into our Weekly Meeting Cadence, whereby every Friday, after All Hands, we would do a 'Guide to Working with Me' session, usually on the sofa over drinks. All new hires present theirs within the first thirty days. It takes fifteen to thirty minutes for someone to present their Guide. Once they're done we all feed back as a team. One Guide unearthed that someone may be a better mentor than a manager, and another Guide explained how someone's childhood really shapes how they like to be spoken to.

Over time, they became more elaborate. The marketing team made slide presentations, saying they preferred a visual format. One designer made hers like a passport, with each page being a bit of her Guide. The engineers and introverts dreaded it, but once completed they loved the opportunity to share who they were behind a screen and also to find like-minded people in the most unlikely places. People would bond over all the classic identity markers: similar backgrounds, taste in movies or music, fears, ambitions, hopes. It has been the number one culture exercise we do to keep the team bonded and aligned.

A Guide can also show how someone doesn't fit into

your team. If you're shaping an attitude of intellectual curiosity, when someone doesn't display those characteristics in their Guide it can become clear that, in the long run, that hire may not last or that this company is not the right culture for you. Wouldn't you rather know sooner than later?

How does this work on an individual level? Regardless of your position in the workforce – student, stay-at-home parent or senior leader – documenting your style of labour is an invaluable resource for yourself and others. It might even be that you do not like labour and that the life of leisure is for you. Now that you've recognized it, write it down.

As a junior employee, do it under your own steam and give it to your boss with the note: it's important to me to do great work while under your supervision; here is a guide on how to get the best out of me. They may think you are utterly precocious or they might be impressed. Either way, they'll notice you and you'll learn if this is the right place for you to work. If you are a leader, use it to onboard your team and help them be most productive with you as their manager.

So what's in the Guide? First and foremost, do a free personality test online such as Human Design, Meyers Briggs, Enneagram or OCEAN to help stir your reflections. Then use some of the prompts below to get started. You don't have to answer them all, and you don't have to share your entire life history with your colleagues. Choose what is important to you. You can take a look at mine at: sharmadeanreid.com/guidetoworkingwithme

'Guide to working with . . .'

- **Who I am**
  - Name / age / DOB/ star sign / Personality Test Result
  - Where were you born?
  - What is your family like?
  - What were you like as a child?
  - Where and what did you study?
  - My family today.
  - Who I live with.
  - Where I live.
  - What I do with my free time.
  - What is important to me.
  - A skill I want to learn this year.
  - What type of work I'll be doing in 5 years' time.
  - The relationships I want to build.
  - The legacy I want to leave.
- **'Insert a quote you live by . . .'**
- **What I do**
  - My job title.
  - What I actually do.
  - What my perfect workday looks like.
  - My highest priority is . . .
  - How I add value to the company revenue.
  - How I add value to the company culture.
- **My productivity**
  - Locations where I am most productive.
  - Locations where I am least productive.
  - Time of day I am most productive.

- Time of day I am least productive.
- I get my best ideas when . . .
- **My operating style**
  - How I like to structure my time.
  - My ideal week in meetings.
  - How I treat meetings.
  - How I manage my calendar.
  - The company values that most reflect how I work.
- **How I communicate**
  - What method of communication I prefer.
  - For feedback.
  - For updates on projects.
  - For ideas.
  - For bad news.
  - My general style of communication.
  - My intention with my communication.
- **How my mind works**
  - My brain is best described as . . .
  - I process new information best when . . .
  - I learn by . . .
  - The information I will be biased towards is . . .
  - I make decisions based on . . .
  - After I've made a decision, my brain . . .
- **What motivates me**
  - I am motivated by . . .
  - My reward system is activated by . . .
  - A time I was incredibly motivated was . . .
- **What demotivates me**
  - I am demotivated by . . .

- ◦ I become disengaged when . . .
- ◦ A time I was incredibly demotivated was . . .
- **How my body works**
  - ◦ I have [genetic/chronic/neurodiverse/hormonal] . . .
  - ◦ It means I . . .
  - ◦ I manage it best when . . .
  - ◦ It gets worse when . . .
  - ◦ I work to keep my body in optimal condition by . . .
  - ◦ I rest my body by . . .
  - ◦ I love how my body . . .
- **How you can help me be better**
  - ◦ What you do that affects me positively . . .
  - ◦ How I want to show up for my team . . .
- **I am also . . .**
  - ◦ 4 positive words.
  - ◦ 4 negative words.

Once completed, sit with it for a while. Come back to it in a week and see if it rings true. I hardly edit my 'Guide to Working with Me' any more, as it really is my dyed-in-the-wool habits, but I do read it annually to ask myself if my day-to-day schedule is really aligned with what I know I like for myself.

I've often thought about doing other Guides for better communication, such as a 'Guide to Dating Me' or a 'Guide to How I Manage Friendships'. I could see a Guide working especially well in the home, whether it's with your family or new roommates, to assign division of labour. I especially want to do a 'Guide for Vacationing with Me', as I've had plenty of holidays where everyone has been on completely different vibrations. It may seem like overkill, but in today's world where so much communication is digital and we are not picking up on the non-verbal cues of human relationships, it's nice to have a clear and concise document that helps nip any miscommunications in the bud. Of course, the Guide is not the answer to all conflict resolutions. Nothing beats a face-to-face conversation or shared experience in order to get to know someone better. But whenever I am concerned or confused by my teammates, before I make any rash decisions, I will first consult their Guide.

New Method 26
Define Your Personal Vision, Mission and Principles

A manifesto is a rallying cry to the world, and our personal Vision, Mission and Principles is a rallying cry to the self. We document our own manifesto to declare our intentions, align our actions, and pursue a purposeful life. Our personal vision encapsulates the world we want to live in and create for the next generation. Our mission states how we will make that impact. It serves as a guiding star, inspiring us to reach for the extraordinary. With our principles, we articulate actions. If we stand for nothing, we will fall for anything, so we create our own doctrine to define us.

Just like the 'Guide to Working with Me', I feel that corporate exercises should not be the sole preserve of big companies, and there is much to benefit from applying those methodologies to yourself as an individual. Organizations are allowed to have big lofty goals for themselves. They have inspiring mission statements and guiding values and principles, and you can too.

The second document in your Big Woman Energy Protocol is a one-page Vision, Mission and Principles (VMP). It outlines your life's work, your current work and how you want to show up in the world. This is the page I go to when I'm losing myself and getting distracted or when I'm feeling overwhelmed. It's your personal manifesto.

Creating a VMP document for yourself encourages you to connect your life's work with your daily work with your vibe work, cascading down and ensuring you don't get distracted or out of focus with what is important to you. I also believe that doing this work will help you connect more deeply with yourself and with others, as you meet people with whom your mission and principles align.

When designing profiles for the Stack World app, we wanted to avoid the social anxiety one gets from not being cool enough, or aesthetically pleasing enough. Thus we eliminated all the fluff from a social profile and focused on three core elements: your mission, what you want to talk about and what your favourite quote is. Whether it's Epictetus or Maya Angelou, we can tell a lot about someone from this section of the app. Some people get intimidated or feel they don't know what their VMP is. Don't worry about it being perfect yet. Just get something down on paper and tweak as you go.

Vision and mission

Some people use the words vision and mission interchangeably, but in my approach, I try for very clear differences. For me, your vision is a short sharp statement of how you want the world to look. It lasts at least thirty years or is your life's work, and it's ideally written in the present tense as if it already exists. Some famous examples are;

Microsoft: 'A computer on every desk and in every home.'

Alzheimer's Association: 'A world without Alzheimer's disease.'

Oxfam: 'A just world without poverty.'

The formula I often use in the beginning while I'm still fine-tuning the statement is:

You + verb + outcome + customer + market = vision

So for example:

The Stack World + fosters + equality + for women + globally = vision

Which drills down to:

Gender Equity for Women

Your mission statement is what you are going to do to make that world a reality. In a company, this may only be for a decade or two. For you as an individual, I'd give it three to five years. So if Netflix's vision forever is 'Entertain the World', that would ring true for a mission statement pertaining to DVD rentals (1997–2006), streaming services (2007 onwards) or development of original programming (2013 onwards). I don't know what Netflix's mission statement was during those years, but I bet they all led directly to the overall vision of the company, 'Entertain the World'. Some more famous Mission examples:

Slack: 'Make work life simpler, more pleasant, and more productive.'
Google: 'Organize the world's information and make it universally accessible and useful.'
Nike: 'Do everything possible to expand human potential.'

These statements aren't literal and they don't explain the product. They explain a state of *doing* that will lead to a vision state of *being*. They tend to have verbs in them and to still be rather ambiguous and noble.

For us our current mission is Content and Community for Women at Work. In another ten years it may be through education or policy-making or film-making. Your mission is your current iteration of your vision.

I didn't happen upon my personal vision until my early thirties. I had to look back on my work and draw a line from the first personal project I ever created – my *WAH* magazine – past my present self and look to the future. I realized that people always said I empowered women, that I had an amazing network of women, and they would tell me their personal stories of how I helped increase their earnings or gave them more confidence through my work. I can see now, through my first foray into equality with a scrappy magazine about women and hip-hop when I was twenty-one, that I had always cared about women having money and power. I feel strongly that these two things lead to our autonomy and freedom. I can also see that media (content) and technology (community) were always a big part of this problem-solving process.

Every business I start or project that I found is just another mission working towards the same vision. As I said earlier, for you, this might change every three to five years. Your education might be a mission. Your own personal growth might be a priority in one period. Don't worry if any of this isn't fully clear to you yet – you can now start collecting the data to apply it when you are ready.

Principles

Once you have your Vision and Mission, you can now move on to your Principles. These are rules by which I operate, some of which have a moral justification for them. These Principles are your guardrails for decision-making. They help remind you of who you are and who you want to be. Like most exercises, I write these in the future tense as if they are already real. Some of them are way off the mark. I am terrible at replying to emails, so my Principle of Connection and timely communication is an aspirational statement that I find myself repeating quietly as a motivator rather than a self-criticism.

How do you find your Principles? The same as you would in a company. In the early days of founding my start-up, I would find myself repeating certain phrases over and over again, so I started to keep them in a little list on my phone. These might be in relation to how we build features, how we decide what to work on, or how we treat each other as a team. Over time I had around thirty of these mantras, so I looked for patterns and consolidated them into our 7 Company Principles. We use them each week to give shout-outs to our teammates in All Hands for representing those Principles at work.

For your personal ones, I would reflect on when you felt your highest. Think about the positive words that you regularly hear people say about you. Think about when you did your best work, or when you were most of service. Write down eight to ten words and then follow the tone below to create a personal manifesto. What do you want people to say when you are not in the room?

If you are a founder, it can be hard to untangle your Business VMP from your Personal one. That's natural. Most founders start companies based on their own challenges and are deeply passionate about what they do. I've found that my current Business Vision is simply my 3–5-year Personal Mission. So my Personal Mission changes each time I start a new business endeavour.

A final note on Vision Mission Principles: while the Stack World attracts some of the most intelligent, ambitious women out there, not every VMP needs to be some huge lofty planet-saving goal. There is a lot to be said about a Vision as pure as 'A world where everyone can live the most authentic version of themselves.' A Mission where you 'make people smile each day' and Principles that make you and others around you feel absolutely loved. Once you have your IMP, print them out and keep them close.

SR Vision Mission Principles

Vision

Gender Equity for Women.

Mission → 2025

Content and Community for Women at Work.

Values and Principles

Authenticity

I stay true to who I am and don't get distracted by what others are doing. I operate wholly from my Vision, Mission and Principles. All anyone ever wants is for me to be me.

Thinker

I am an infinite learner and continually improve my understanding of the world to advance my own intellectual satisfaction and also to share it with others.

Integrity

I operate from a place of justice, ethics and morals. I don't compromise my integrity in any part of my world, from my personal actions to my business ones. I do the right thing.

Focus

I say no to things that are irrelevant to my mission and don't feel obligated into taking on work that is not directly going to impact my long-term vision.

Abundance

I come from an abundant mindset and act without fear of scarcity. There is an outpouring of love and generosity from me because I know that I can always generate more.

Optimism

I am always hopeful and I can always find a way to thrive. Problems don't faze me as I know I always have the power and the intelligence to break through.

Connection

I create connections among others and use my network to strengthen my mission. I maintain timely and meaningful communications with others and am respected for this.

Innovation

I operate in the near and long-term future. Just because things have always been a certain way doesn't mean they cannot be changed. I see opportunities where others do not and break the rules to achieve them.

Creativity

Everything I do has a sense of flair and style. I am experimental in both my thinking and my output and create a world that is aesthetically pleasing.

Distribution

I primarily work with, hire and spend my money on women and excluded communities. Every consumption decision I have has an impact, so I distribute my wealth wisely.

Fun

My life is filled with fun and warmth. Nothing is more important than my happiness and well-being, or of those around me. I have an energy that is magnetic to others because they know they will have a good time.

New Method 27
Hold a Clear Vision for Your Future

We visualize an ambitious, powerful and even incredulous future for ourselves. We start young and we start early – some call it daydreaming. We form pictures in our minds of how we look, feel and act on our highest vibration. It feels good. We then transfer this image into words and cultivate a vision plan that aligns our actions with our aspirations, fuelling our journey with purpose and intention. Together, we break through societal norms and rewrite the narrative, leaving a legacy that inspires generations. We design our future selves with clarity and confidence, removing the fear and blockers that stop us from planning ahead. Without a vision for our future, we will always return to our past.

The final document of our Big Woman Energy Protocol is our Vision Plan. This is a series of prompts to help you write the story of your life. You can write it for one year, ten years or whatever timescale works for you. It's written in the present tense, with the intention of tricking your brain into thinking it's real right now. From this, you start to become that person immediately and act like your future self now.

I've always straddled the lines between fantasist, daydreamer and actual planner. Even as a young child, I would be able to hold strong visions in my mind of who

I wanted to be and the life I wanted to lead. I would formulate clear pictures, as clear as a movie, of my future world garnered from hours and hours of watching TV.

Athough we didn't have much money, we had Cable TV from when I was five years old, which exploded my worldview of what was possible. My schoolfriends were watching *EastEnders*, *Brookside* and *Coronation Street*. Grey, glum English telly, with long-suffering protagonists sucking on cigarettes, wearing drab clothes. I was watching *The Bold and the Beautiful*, *The Young and the Restless* and *Dynasty*, where the women were powerful, glamorous and always had the next move up their sleeve. I had MTV, Sky Movies and Oprah. Everything I consumed was much bigger and shinier than what was on terrestrial TV. It was the 1980s and it was all about the American Dream. Anyone could win. Even me, just a little girl in Wolverhampton.

I became adept at lucid dreaming, tucking myself into bed while planning what scenarios I would see inside my mind that night. I would repeat certain images as a self-soothing mechanism. Almost like a drug, I would use my vision for my future self as a relaxation exercise – everything's going to be OK because I can see it will be.

But at this age, I wasn't actively linking my daydreaming with my future. Like most ambitious little girls, I had a Filofax as a teenager and instead I would write long goals in its wirebound pages, a never-ending list of all the things I wanted to accomplish. It was only in my late twenties, while working with coach Cheryl Clements, that I encountered a more powerful way to plan my future. One that

I had actually been preparing for since I was a child. Here's how it goes.

You're going to write a narrative of your life down to the last detail. From your bedsheets, to how you feel in your body, to your relationships, everything. And then you are going to picture it in your head. It is really as basic as that. But you are going to write that narrative in the present tense. This is the hurdle at which everyone falls. You'll feel compelled to write the words *will, should, want* and others. These words remind you that you do not have them yet. They create a gulf between you and your future self. Instead use present-tense language as if it's already your real life, so words like *me, I am, I have*. Your brain can't really differentiate between the truth or lies, so why not paint a rosy picture? Don't write figures, numbers or deadlines, just write the feeling, the outcome as if you have it today.

So instead of writing:

'I want a $5 million house in New York.'

You can say:

'I have a big, beautiful home that makes me feel proud of my work and achievements. It is in a vibrant area of my favourite city and when I look around, it really represents who I am.'

This fundamental difference between goal-setting (lists and wants) and vision-setting (narrative and haves) has been powerful for me over the years. This exercise is the last piece in the puzzle of your Big Woman Energy Protocol. You've self-reflected, you've set your principles and you know what drives you, so now you can put the outcome down on paper.

Your Vision isn't a list of proposed achievements. This is a story, written about the future but in the present tense, of how your life will look and feel. It can be difficult at first to know how you want to feel. That's understandable, given that you may have learned to suppress your emotions. But you can reach for what you want with storytelling. It's important that your Vision is a narrative story rather than a list, as stories are how we learn and make sense of the world. A story of pure achievements would not make a good story. Bring the human element to your desires and write a story of your life that you would be proud to tell others.

When I work with my community to help them create a Vision Plan, I often hear a lot of fear: 'I can't write that I want to earn £100k. I only earned £30k last year . . .' but your Vision Plan has to be allowed to be completely bonkers and your imagination has to have free rein. You have to scare yourself a little for this work. As we mentioned, you wouldn't list the number metric of £100k anyway – this isn't about SMART goals or OKRs (Objective Key Results); you would list the *feeling* and the outcome – of what £100k will get you or how it will support you. You might find that £70k will suffice to satisfy your feelings and £100k actually gives you more problems. Either way, do not hold back on your Vision for yourself and make sure it is in a beautiful story format.

The Stack World community perform this exercise together as a retreat twice a year – in January and then on the Summer Solstice of 21 June. Writing together, knowing that you are all focused on your futures, creates an electrifying energy. Before we start, members stand up and reflect on their last year's Vision Plan and typically so much of it has come to fruition, making them confident to get even more clear on what they want.

If you find your inner critic rears its ugly head, reminding you that you cannot do something, write it down on a separate sheet of paper or a post-it note so that it's off your mind, then go back to your main Vision Plan with your wonderful future. At the end of the session, burn the critic's notes. They don't serve you.

Here's a list of categories you can break your ten-year plan down into, which are commonly known as the Wheel of Life.

- Money and finances
- Career and work
- Health and fitness
- Fun and recreation
- Environment (home/work)
- Community
- Family and friends
- Partner and love
- Personal growth and learning
- Spirituality

Take these sections and start by writing a paragraph for each. Do this task with friends so that the Big Woman Energy compounds and you can hold each other accountable. Remember, creating a clear vision for your future is a dynamic process that requires self-reflection, planning and ongoing effort. Stay focused, adaptable and persistent as you work towards your desired future. When I first completed my ten-year Vision Plan, I was so excited by the incredible life of the woman on the page that I decided to work to become her today.

Your Big Woman Energy Protocol is now complete. All three documents (your Guide, VMP and Vision Plan) should be reviewed annually. You are rewriting your narrative, one page at a time.

PART FOUR
Accumulating

It's now time to reap what we have sown. If you've been following your inner compass, trusting yourself and sticking to your methods, you will start accumulating. Things will start coming to you, slowly at first, but then the opportunities will be plentiful. Often, you will need to over-index for greed to make up for lost time and be firm in your boundaries and value. Think of it as reparations. You are ready for this inbound goodness, and you welcome it. You don't deflect the wealth or deny yourself. For me, wealth does not just look like material things. It could be a rich friendship circle or perhaps you've amassed some elite thoughts. Either way, you start to lean into abundance and when you exist with this mindset, a great power grows within you and around you. Accumulation requires concentration, as you must focus to triage this new wealth. As things start coming to you, figure out whether to hold, sell, buy or gift. You're merely a vessel for this newfound energy. Don't get suffocated by the weight of it. It will move and flow eternally.

New Method 28
Cultivate Abundance

By acknowledging that women have always had fewer resources, we can understand why a scarcity mindset may develop among us. The scarcity mindset is the zero-sum paradigm of life. Those with a scarcity mentality have a very difficult time sharing recognition and credit, power or profit. They can be critical of their fellow women. This mindset harms ourselves and our collective progress. Instead, we strive to cultivate an abundant mindset, knowing that we have endless resources and we can always generate more. There are always more opportunities, more money and more seats at the table – indeed, there are newer and better tables to be part of that we have the ability to build ourselves. We know that others' success does not take away anything from our own. In fact, genuine praise, appreciation and generosity towards others will only increase our bonds with our community and network, which will be reciprocated when the time calls.

An abundance mindset refers to the paradigm that there is plenty out there for everybody. Stephen Covey initially coined the term in his best-selling book *The 7 Habits of Highly Effective People,* along with its nemesis, scarcity mindset.

People with a scarcity mindset struggle to share. They can't give praise and they can't be happy for others' success. They only think of themselves in a zero-sum game. If others are winning, then they must be losing. They're stingy, with likes, compliments and credit.

Abundant people are my favourite. They have a deep sense of self-worth, knowing they can always generate more. More jobs, more energy, more money. They believe there is plenty out there for everyone and by working together, we can all succeed. They are generous with their spirit. Giving comes easy to them.

I understand why some women have a scarcity mind-set. The numbers around gender equality reinforce the notion that there is simply not enough to go around. If you knew that only 9 per cent of students on your university course were women, it's understandable that you would want to fight other women for your place. Think of Ruth Bader Ginsburg, the American lawyer and jurist who served as an associate justice of the Supreme Court of the United States from 1993 until her death in September 2020. Her class at Harvard Law School had 552 men but just nine women. In 1956, just six years after the law school even started admitting women, the school's then dean, Erwin Griswold, had a dinner party at his home. He asked each of the women in the class – all nine of them, including Ginsburg – to stand up and explain why she was at Harvard and how she justified taking a place that would have gone to a man. This could have made Ruth competitive with her fellow female class-mates. Instead she worked tirelessly for women's rights.

Ask yourself – does someone have to lose in order for you to win? A common anxiety I hear from the women in my life is that so and so is copying them. For example, 'I'm a mindfulness influencer and this other mindfulness influencer is taking my audience. They're posting the same content as me, writing the same captions and everything I do, they do too.' In my younger days, I felt the same. I would feel deeply wronged if I thought my friends were stealing my style because to me, my style was critical to my income and it was uniquely mine. If they bought the same brands and handbags as me it made me feel angry and like they were taking away my ability to earn. That's how insecure and strong my scarcity mindset was.

This also filtered through to my business. Having a scarcity mindset could be holding you back in more ways than you know. When it comes to making decisions, you will either be contemplating them from a position of scarcity or abundance. When I started my first business, WAH Nails, I would get upset when my employees moved on. When someone wanted to leave, it felt like a personal affront. I kept thinking that I had invested so much in their training and they would take the skills we had taught them to a competitor. It caused me so much stress that I realized I needed a New Method. I did nothing more than simply change my mindset on this. I made a declarative statement to myself:

When I hire someone within my company, I don't expect them to be with us for longer than two years. This is the amount of time I will feel satisfied that I have been able to teach and coach them, that they have upskilled themselves and it will look good on their CV. I don't own my team, I am merely a custodian of a small part of their career journey. My only role is to ensure that they're better than when they started. Because of this, more people will be inspired to work for the company, as our alumni become rockstars in their field. There will always be more team members available to train, hire and develop. There is enough for everybody.

This was a game changer for me. My possessive hold on the team loosened and I changed our employee handbook to reflect this, tagged them in our social media pages so that they could build their own audiences on the back of ours, and generally gave them more freedom. I abolished uniforms, thanks to feedback from one of our nail artists that it suppressed her individuality, and let them play whatever music made them most productive. What is your declarative statement?

Developing my abundant mindset was an ongoing process. This did not happen overnight, and there were many casualties – including myself – on the way. Unnecessary tears, frustration, anger and jealousy in the early years of business, and all it took for me to change was within me. WAH Nails never ran out of applicants and I love hearing the stories of how our little nail salon in Hackney inspired people to start their own beauty careers all over the world. There are enough fingers and toes in the world to paint. There is enough for everybody.

Believe that there is always enough to go around. The shift to an abundant mentality requires you to change your perception of life. With a scarcity mindset, you're likely to keep opportunities – good or bad – close to you out of desperation or fear. You question when the next paycheck, partner, friend or job will come your way, and hold on to all you can.

With an abundant mentality, however, you're confident of the fact that there's enough of everything to go around. You can say no to things that don't set your soul on fire because you know there will be more opportunities. You don't have to cling to whatever comes your way, because it's not going to be your only shot. You know there will always be more money to make, more people to fall in love with, and more opportunities just around the corner.

Have faith that there is enough to go around. Abundant thinking is not a privilege, anyone can practise it. I've met many wealthy people who are stingy with their resources, and many people in poverty who are generous with what little they have. Family wealth to fall back on does not necessarily make someone have an abundant mindset. It comes from within, when you are confident in your self-worth, your skills and capabilities. By creating your declarative statement around business, food, money, partners and opportunities and much more, you can start to change your belief system around ownership. When you let go of the notion that they'll never be enough, you'll start to see and attract more.

New Method 29
Play Games You Can Win

We eradicate the notion that life must always be hard for women. We move towards pleasure, towards ease and towards joy. We don't feel guilty if we worked for something and got it, even if we didn't work 'that hard'. We are totally fine with receiving things because of our mere existence, not because of what we have done in addition to our baseline productivity. We choose paths that are smooth, we curate our lives around our true selves, and we don't exhaust ourselves. We don't spend the eternity of our careers outside our comfort zones. We choose games we can win, and if we are focused, we design our own.

One of the most pervasive myths that allow the patriarchy to function is that women must struggle. Things must be hard for us because we sinned and we deserve it. They say it's human nature, it's just the way it's meant to be. And so, in a self-reinforcing way, we move towards the pain and away from the pleasure and joy. We feel guilty if we achieve something without struggling for it. We can make life so hard for ourselves with our poor choices. This could be your career, dating life, financial situation, friendships – the list goes on. Throughout my life, I work to improve my chances of success and pleasure by identifying and making the most of the games I can win, or, as renowned author Robert Greene calls it in his book *Mastery* – play to your strengths. He says: 'There are many paths to mastery . . . But a key component is determining your mental and psychological strengths and working with them.'

I see many decisions – especially when it comes to your career – as a tournament. There will be many teams, each with their own eager players, just waiting for their *opportunity to play*. They're standing on the sidelines, shivering and jumping to keep warm until they get their turn. Think of any job with a low acceptance rate – working at MI 5 or applying to Google. The starting line is packed, but have you considered why you even want to play? Why do you want to work there? Does the company match your values? Do you like the people? Will you be doing your best work?

If the reasons are sincere, there are two methods you can take to try and get on the pitch. The first is to try to find shortcuts. Ways to skip the queue and get on to the pitch first – an introduction via a family friend, for example. But taking shortcuts can sometimes leave you open and exposed when you finally do get on the pitch. You won't have put in all the time and developed all the skills to succeed. You're not ready yet. So, why not instead look to put yourself in the position to play the games you know you can win?

Let's apply this to my own career. When I was twelve years old, I was at my cousin's house. She was five years older than me and preparing for university. While I was waiting for her to get dressed one day, I noticed a pile of prospectuses in her room. Looking at the pile, there was one that stood out from the rest. It was long, thin, bottle green, and the paper was made to look like linen. It was beautifully embossed with the name of the London College of Fashion. I grew up loving fashion. At the time, I remember thinking, 'Wow! You can go to university for fashion?' I read the prospectus cover to cover and loved it. It piqued my interest and I started reading *Vogue* religiously. *Vogue* would always write about new designers, and each and every one of them seemed to graduate from Central St Martins. So that's where I set my sights. Every year from age twelve to eighteen, I got a CSM prospectus sent to my grandma's house in Wolverhampton. Over that time period, I finally settled on a Fashion, Communication and Promotion degree. Notice how I narrowed down my interests to a specific course. To get there, I looked at my skillset.

I loved fashion and culture, but within that, there were so many more specific tournaments (degrees) to choose from. I looked at Film, Photography, Design and more. But I selected one that I had a higher probability of winning because of my skills. I knew I was good at writing, and image-making, crap at craft detail, and I loved clothes but hated making them. Instead of inspecting and comparing fabrics, I would be digging through clothing rails and deciding what outfit would look good on a model. I turned away from the game of Fashion Design at CSM, which was the hardest degree to get on. Instead, my tournament became Fashion Communication, a game I knew I could win based on my existing teenage skills. When applying via the Universities and Colleges Admissions Service, commonly known as UCAS, you had the choice of three universities. I only put one down – Central St Martins – as I was so sure that I would get a place (and I only had the £5 required for one application). At my interview I was accepted on the spot.

When I started my degree, I found it quite easy. I was frustrated. I wanted to be challenged. I had been training myself for so long to get there, that when I got there, I knew a lot. I tried to switch degrees to Fashion History, I tried to make it hard for myself. But my tutor knew better. Judith Watt advised me to stay on this course, to enjoy it and go out and work. Hone my style of play, if you will.

So I did. In my first year, I went to work. I realized that, although I loved the glamour of *Vogue* and *Elle* I was also attracted to the grittiness of *Dazed & Confused*. The work I loved was always down to a particular stylist. I always read the credits of the shoots. This was the list of people who had worked on the images. Reading these magazines cover to cover, I'm looking at all the players and thinking, who's the coach? Who's the referee? What's their success rate? How are they building on previous wins? When you know who creates or wins the games, you can watch and learn what they do to be successful.

I realized one name kept coming up, Nicola Formichetti – the incredibly talented Italian-Japanese creative. He was the first person I'd seen who combined streetwear and high fashion. He was pioneering a new style in the early 2000s and I wanted in. I wanted him as my coach.

Now I had nailed my future down to a specific pitch within the wider tournament. I transformed my thinking from 'I want to be a designer' to 'I want to be a stylist.' And then, further still, 'I want to work with Nicola Formichetti.'

I applied for a job with Nicola. I only wanted to work for him, so I didn't apply to the magazine – that would be way too broad, given that fashion magazines get thousands of intern requests and my chances of success would have been low. I applied directly to the coach. Using all the research I had gathered, I photocopied all his photoshoots and transformed them into a pop-up book to send him. I created a focused application that only he would understand. He called me the next day and said, 'Come into the office and let's chat.'

I arrived at the *Dazed & Confused* offices for my interview aged nineteen, finally about to meet my style hero who I'd been studying for so long – who understood how this game works and, in my opinion, was writing a new playbook. I thought I was just going for an interview and he said – are you ready to start today? Fifteen minutes after meeting him, I had to rush across town to Chelsea to pick out some cowboy boots for a shoot. There were no iPhones or Google Maps in 2003, so I pulled out my trusty *A–Z* and lugged the empty case he had given me on the tube. It was nerve-racking, but I was prepared. I had been reading magazines religiously for the last seven years and studying his shoots for at least five of them. This is the point where if you'd pushed your way to the front of the queue without enough training or practice, you would have choked on the pitch. With all my swotting up, I knew his taste, so when I got to the store he had dispatched me to, I chose the things I knew he would love.

It's important to point out that I'm still not actually playing my game yet. I'm still in the scout camp being tested. I'm heading to the junior squad, doing my degree.

I continued working for Nicola Formichetti and fashion designer Kim Jones throughout my degree, while most of my classmates weren't working. I had no wealthy family, no fallback plan, so I had to work and build my network. I was studying and working constantly for my entire four-year degree, and it enabled me to be the strongest player possible when it was my time to head on to the pitch. After we all graduated, many of my classmates were still building their network a few years later, and some were starting out as interns while I was immediately being paid for my work.

During my degree, I'd also spend all my free time in the Central St Martins library. It was legendary. The archive was insane. It had bound issues of every *Vogue*, *Guardian*, *Times* – every resource you could need. Even today, it's better than the internet. I would flip through a magazine and put a post-it note on every page I liked. This wasn't strictly editorial. It could be a Snoop Dogg interview, a Ralph Lauren advert, a still-life article from the 60s, or anything else. Once I had finished a volume, I would take it to the photocopy machine and copy everything I liked. I'd print them (in black and white, I couldn't afford colour), put them into plastic wallets, and organize them into folders, building my own personal image library. These folders would be titled niche things like Tool Photography, WASP Sports, 90s Gangsta Rap and Leopards in Culture. I was logging everything I liked and subconsciously connecting the cultural dots. On each printout, I wrote which magazine and what specific page, so if I ever had to go back, I had my reference point. Not only was I training my stamina and body to be the best player ever, but I was also training my eye.

I ended up being one of two people in the class graduating with a first-class degree, and it felt pretty good. I don't remember university being stressful or taxing. Just tiring because of all the jobs I was doing. I just got my results and shrugged. I wasn't going to feel guilty about that easy win because I had been in training for so long. All the hours in Wolverhampton, all the hours assisting, all the hours in the library. I won this game of education and I won it painlessly.

I remember my first solo work game: Nicola had a small job for a global retailer that he was unable to do, so he subbed me in. He did a bigger job that day and I did this mini one. I was the only stylist on set and I loved it! I realized I could continue to carve out my niche by only doing this type of work. Instead of being a junior stylist doing all types of fashion, I did exclusively youth street fashion and men's streetwear and sportswear. Through Nicola I also got a job at *Arena Homme Plus*, working for the brilliant editor-in-chief, Jo-Ann Furniss, who taught me so much about commissioning and working with talent. I'd narrowed my game down to a point where it was just me and a few other stylists playing. I'd taken the time to find my niche and boost my chances of success. I won my first Nike job at twenty-three. My goal was that when any client thought, 'We need someone good at fashion sportswear,' they would think of me. That's when you know you're winning. During this period of my life, I don't remember any hardcore pitching or being scared of losing a job. My abundant mindset combined with focus and preparation meant that work flowed easily to me. This is the path I was on because I had created a game I could win, and I did so much work before I even got on the pitch.

Playing games you can win is one of the biggest secrets to success. The same level of work ethic can be applied anywhere, so if you are going to apply it, make it more effective by applying it to something comfortable that will reap the greatest rewards. Choosing an easy path didn't mean I didn't work hard. It just meant that my shots were mostly on target because I knew exactly how to kick the ball. I made key choices, practised a lot, and refined my likes and passions. If I'd showed up to university thinking 'I want to be in fashion', how on earth would I have got started? I'd have been in a massive pool of people, all after the same limited opportunities.

The New Method here is to apply the tournament analogy to your life and discover how you can start playing games you can win. How can you maximize your chance for success and pleasure? You may need to divert your path entirely.

You'll have spent your twenties playing a lot of different games. Reflect on that. Were you successful? Did you enjoy them? What games were easy? Which were traumatic? In reality, the rules of the game will change every five years or so as you move from high school to college to work. So perhaps you're in a transition period and you need to recalibrate what game you are playing. Don't stay stuck in a game that feels like an uphill battle.

There's this weird sense of achievement that women have from making life as hard as possible. It's as if we like to relish a struggle story. To be in victim energy. We bond over the pains of our life. A game worth winning doesn't have to feel like an impossible battle. The time and energy you save from not making your life difficult frees you up for other meaningful pursuits.

So let's define your game, understand exactly what it is you're reaching for and be specific.

- What is the game? What industry do you want to be in?
- What are the rules? What are the typical attributes for success?
- Can you train for this game? What education/ experience do you need?
- Who could be your coach? Who would be your ideal mentor?

- Where is it? What is the physical or digital location? Can you reside there?
- How long does it last? How much of your career will this take?
- Who are the other players on your team? Who will you be working with? Do you like these people?
- How often do you play? What does your work week look like?
- What is the prize? What is success as they define it? What is success as you define it?

The Holy Grail of playing games you can win is creating a new game entirely. What knowledge and skills can you apply to change the rules and make your own game? To move past everyone else and find the less concentrated spaces where you can thrive?

If you can design your own game; you can guarantee your win. And I've spoken about careers a lot here because that's where the analogy works best; but this also works for any aspect of life we tend to make harder for ourselves – such as trying to make toxic relationships work. Don't make your life any harder than it has to be. Play games you can win.

New Method 30
Understand Your
Relationship to Money

We recognize that financial security provides us with the freedom to pursue our dreams, support our loved ones, and make a positive impact on our communities. Therefore, we commit to educating ourselves about personal finance, so we have the knowledge and skills necessary to navigate the world of money. We reject the notion that women are destined to be dependent or financially vulnerable. We were not born to be the poorer sex. We strive to break the chains of financial inequality and practise prudent money management, saving, investing and smart financial decision-making. We harness the strength within us to shape our world through wealth and pave the way for a future where our economic independence is not a privilege but a universal reality.

So much of my attitude to money was shaped by my childhood. My mother had me at sixteen and we lived on alimony from my father and government benefits. On top of this she worked as a talented interior designer, hair braider and in sales. She did the best with what she had and I never went hungry, or felt poor. Our house was always cosy and clean and there was always music playing and the lights were on. That said, there were four of us siblings, and things were tight. I distinctly remember taking a PE kit from the lost property bin at school as I didn't have a set that fitted me. One of my earliest thoughts as a new mother to my son, Roman, was: I can't believe my mom kept me fed and clothed from just sixteen years old. I became intensely empathetic and compassionate to her experience as a young mother, while also recognizing how it shaped how I saw the world.

Even though we grew up with very little, instead of having a scarcity mindset I adopted an attitude of independence. I need to work to make my own money. Logical, right? So I got my first job aged fourteen as a waitress at a local bed and breakfast and I've worked constantly ever since. That first feeling of earning money was so sweet. I received £20 a week from my job, which I folded neatly and carefully into a tiny plastic pink Hello Kitty purse, and when I went to school, I felt rich! I was on free school meals, so now I could afford extra food, stationery and books. What joy!

So much of our relationship to money is instilled early on, and I inherited my family's lack of savings and generational wealth. We simply didn't have enough disposable income to save, and it is this experience that has really helped me understand how people from lower socioeconomic backgrounds, like myself, can get into a cycle of living hand to mouth. But even when I could begin to save, it wasn't a mindset that was natural to me. From my first £20 to the first twenty years of my earnings, I didn't save *any* of it. Even writing this down makes me feel icky. I have never ever been raised or been in an environment where someone said to me, you're making a lot of money, what are you doing with it? I never had those kindly middle-class parents you see in TV shows who at the dinner table tell me they are casually gifting me a deposit for a house. An important part of understanding why I had a non-saving attitude was reflecting on some of the reasons I got here.

I do believe we inherit our relationship with money from our parents, but my life choices also played a part. I always knew I would be in fashion, a typically freelance career of feast and famine, so I never had this monthly cadence of income. Up until my start-up, I had never even had a salary. Since graduating, I've always earned large lump sums of cash through styling and consulting, and I've paid for my basic expenses in big sums too. I would pay my rent for six months at a time and pay my phone for the year outright. I had zero concept of saving for the future. Feast and famine.

Another problem I had was that I was good at making money, so I always knew I could get more. I saw it as an energy and if I wanted to make more, I would literally just think about it and muster it, like mustering the energy for a run. Before money manifestation was popular, I was visualizing the results of my hard work. I never feared being broke, because I knew I had prospects. As a student, if I was low on cash, I would lie in bed and think, what can I sell today? I would buy shoes from Wolverhampton charity shops for 20p and sell them in London for £25, then spend it on food and bills. Feast and famine.

While I was young, I was sort of OK with that. Even before I knew what Stoicism was, I had a mentality that as much as I loved nice things, I could also do without them. I never feared being poor, because I was poor before, and I was happy. This gave me a really strong position in my personal freedom, because I would quit terrible jobs even if I didn't have a safety net – I was OK with having nothing as long as I was happy. I would regularly read *Down and Out in Paris and London* by George Orwell and find comfort in the idea of rubbing garlic over my bread to make the taste last just a little bit longer in my mouth. The famine, before the feast.

But now things are different. I have a son, and I want to do bigger things and be financially secure. I want to remove the financial worries for those around me and allow them to focus on being the best humans they can be. I want to build generational wealth and be the first in my matrilineal line to do so. Securing your financial future means removing anxiety about how you will pay for your existence in the world. My ability to hustle is good, but I would rather use that brainspace on new ideas than the stressed feeling I would have about paying my rent. The best time to start working on your finances is yesterday, so here are a few things I wish I'd done from age twenty-three, when I graduated, and some things I am doing today.

Write a short personal statement on money

Answer these questions: what are the money habits you inherited from your childhood? Are you comfortable with those habits? If not, what does good look like? What are the promises you are going to make to yourself to keep them?

Budgeting

Upon finding my teenage diary from when I was sixteen years old, I was elated to see that I used a very simple Incomings/Outgoings sheet to track my expenditure. Stick to this each week or month. Make it a group exercise with your friends if you need to. These days, most apps will have the data, but there is nothing like writing it out by hand or organizing it on a spreadsheet yourself for you to truly understand where your money is going. Two columns will do.

Live within your means

Don't exceed your expenditure, and if you find yourself going over budget, rein it in or figure out what your side hustles are to make more money. You don't need more stuff, truly. Being sustainable by consuming less is chic. The more you heal emotionally, the less you buy.

Pay your bills on time

I once had a friend who never opened his letters. He would have bin bags full of them. Bills from everywhere. He never paid his speeding tickets and eventually his car was impounded by the bailiffs. Again, just use a simple spreadsheet with your bills, your account numbers and your payment dates. Don't overthink it with fancy software. Just get manual and organized. The time you pay affects your credit rating. The two bills you must pay immediately are parking tickets (because the price goes up) and council tax.

Credit cards for credit rating

Only get a credit card to build your credit rating. Don't get it to buy things you can't afford. Pay 95 per cent of your credit card bill five days before it's due. Then your credit report will show low utilization and good credit. Don't ever, ever extend your credit card limit. Banks will want to give you more money. Politely write to them to decline, because if you don't write they will do it automatically. Think of them as casinos. The house always wins.

Negotiate everything

From your rent, to your phone bill, to your insurance, ask them – is that the best price you can do for me today?

That one hour of phone calls and emails will save you from the financial drip taps that drain your resources. Every year I call the phone company and ask them to review my data usage and give me the cheapest tariff possible, and they do.

Have a savings account

Start early, because this is where the concept of compound interest has its strongest effect. If you're a student, start with 5 per cent of your income and build up to 25 per cent as you get older. For your first savings account, choose a stable interest rate with no instant access. You don't want to treat it as a place you can spend from.

Buy a small house early

So much of generational wealth in the feudal-inspired West comes from land and property ownership. I had a mental block around buying a home, because frankly, I moved house every three years as a child and probably felt I didn't deserve one. What I wish I had done was buy a small home early and then moved according to my family's growth. My smart friends bought new-build flats cheaply and then sold them on to get their dream homes.

Pay into your pension

The current Gender Pension Gap is 39 per cent in the UK, meaning women are significantly poorer in old age. Make sure you have a centralized pension account that is easily movable from job to job. If you can, top it up or ask your employer to increase the monthly payments.

Understand good debt and bad debt

Debt is OK, when it's good. Good debt is when you borrow money for investments or assets that have the potential to increase in value over time or to generate income, such as education, mortgage or a business loan. Bad debt is characterized by high interest rates, lack of long-term value, and the potential to totally disorder your financial well-being. These are consumer loans, payday loans, store cards, etc. Try not to get into the cycle of bad debt. If you have, reduce your expenses and pay off in even the tiniest increments.

Educate yourself

Depending on your needs, it will be worth having some level of understanding of your country's financial system. Get to know loans, equities, derivatives, base rates, mortgage rates and other bits of financial jargon if you are so inclined. Subscribe to newsletters, financial newspapers and other specialist titles like the *Financial Times*. Get a few books that cover the topics you are interested in. Unless you plan on a career path in finance, you just need to understand the broad picture, so that when the next financial crisis happens you are not in the dark.

Start investing

When you reach a baseline of personal financial stability, now is the time to accumulate wealth by investing. Whether you've received a bonus at work or your side hustle is reaping rewards, use those lump sums of cash to increase your net worth. When you have excess cash, find the right advisors to help you manage it. There are plenty of women financial advisors, tax planners and wealth managers who will speak to you with empathy. They will work with you to understand your desired level of risk and create a diversified portfolio that will reflect your changing circumstances.

Update your electoral roll details

Not only does this improve your credit rating, but it ensures that all your bills are sent to the right place. Keep good records and stay up to date. I once had a court order because a bill was being sent to an address I'd lived at seven years before that I had no idea about. What a way to ruin your rating!

Change your passwords

Online safety is key if you want to protect all your hard work to be financially independent. Make sure your banking passwords are strong and completely different to your shopping or email passwords. Avoid phishing scams, double-check email addresses and URLs (look for the padlock logo in your address bar). Financial crime is always on the rise.

Eat the frog

Whether you are still a student or a CEO, sometimes it can be scary to look at your finances and take some action. Eat the frog and start with the hardest, biggest, most expensive task. Tackle the biggest debt, cut off the biggest financial drain. Be compassionate to yourself while also being objective. There's no point beating yourself up about the past. It's what you do from today that counts.

This is a simplified overview of what you need to get to basecamp, so go deep by DYOR – doing your own research. Why does it matter? Financial freedom is just that – it's freedom. Having security gives you the power to make the choices you want and design your life how you want. I knew money was important to my power when I was able to leave a bad vibes holiday by booking myself a new flight home and exiting an uncomfortable situation. Money allowed me to move out when I didn't feel safe in shared student accommodation. Wealth allows me to be confident in co-parenting, as I'm not relying on my son's father for income and so money cannot be used as a negotiating tactic.

The steps you take now to secure yourself will compound and significantly impact your future as well as that of others. Whether you're planning for two, five, or ten years, it's time to get the ball rolling on your autonomy. Everything you do for your own economic independence will contribute to the collective work to increase the global women's GDP. Do your part to move the needle.

New Method 31
Negotiate Everything

Women cede control in microdecisions throughout their lives. It may be as insignificant as where we eat dinner tonight. It may be larger, such as the price of a home. We have been socialized to be more accommodating and less assertive when it comes to saying what we want, but things are different now. We no longer allow ourselves to be the losing party. We say what we want and what we are willing to exchange for it. Some of us may require constant practice to feel comfortable expressing our desires. We begin to negotiate everything in order to build up our boundaries around what we are and are not willing to concede. We negotiate to get what we deserve.

Understanding how to negotiate effectively has been a defining characteristic of my growth. Despite the fact that humans are negotiating from when they are small babies, I had no idea how to do it assertively. My negotiation journey began in earnest, not around money, but around a relationship. I felt engulfed by this relationship and I could not say what I wanted during the moment. He would run rings around me with his eloquent language and before I knew it, I was accepting defeat.

Over the years, I've made many mistakes where I didn't negotiate properly, didn't stand my ground, and it cost me mentally and financially. I've worked hard to make this a tool in my Swiss army knife through reading, watching and practising with the best negotiators I know.

I was recommended Chris Voss's book *Never Split the Difference*, and I read it for four hours straight. I realized that purely through language and without force, I could regain control. The foundational principle I took from this book is that the other person is not an adversary. The situation is your adversary, and the best outcome is one within which all parties are happy. Seeing it this way was a big eye-opener for me. What is the shared goal and how can we both achieve it?

Negotiation is so much more than trying to haggle with someone for a bargain. Often confused with being a hustler or a salesperson, negotiating is one of the most vital skills you will develop, and it's critical to restoring your power. I find negotiation one of the most fascinating elements of human behaviour. It's something that gets you closer to living the life you want, on your own terms. It's not just about bartering down for the sake of a low price. It's everything. Your friendships, your relationships, any deals you go for – it needs to be fair for you. If any areas of your life are unbalanced, you aren't getting your fair share and over time, resentment and bitterness builds.

Reading Voss's book, I realized negotiation is something we do all across our lives. You're negotiating while you're driving, while you're ordering food, with yourself over having a treat – everything in your life is a negotiation.

The New Method here is to understand some basic

negotiation techniques and apply them in situations across your life – not to become manipulative, but to give you more control. Here are some starting points for negotiating well.

Be prepared

Preparation is the first step to negotiating well, so do your homework. This means taking the time to understand your goals and priorities, as well as the goals and priorities of the other party. Make a simple list of your goals and their goals. Where are you matched and where are you misaligned? Research the other party and develop a strategy for the negotiation. They may have just invested heavily in a merger, made lay-offs and company morale is low. This will give you a good starting point if you are negotiating the price of employee happiness software. Think about what you want to achieve and what you are willing to compromise on. Perhaps the deal is a three-year contract, with concessions in the first year to account for declining budgets. Write down your key points and practise articulating them clearly and confidently, showing knowledge of the other party's priorities.

Create a vibe

Building a vibe is a major key, as negotiation is a people-based process and people like to be appreciated. Building rapport with the other party can help create a positive and productive atmosphere for the negotiation. Find common ground with the other party, demonstrate empathy, and show a willingness to listen and understand their perspective. I always find it beneficial to learn personal details of the other party to show that you know where they're coming from. That you see them for who they are, as well as who they want to be. Start the conversation with some small talk to build a connection. A well-meaning and genuine compliment never goes amiss. This can help establish trust and make the negotiation process more comfortable for everyone involved. An atmosphere and a dynamic is set from the first interaction, so make sure it is a positive one.

Be clear on your position

To negotiate effectively, you need to be clear about your position and the reasons for it. This can include things like your ideal outcome, your bottom line, and any other key factors that are important to you. Why do you want this deal to happen? Communicate what you are willing to share from your goals and priorities list, then ask the other party to do the same so that you can check it against your assumptions. Make sure you understand the other party's position and ask clarifying questions if necessary. The reason it is so important to ensure that the other party knows where you are coming from is that they may be used to working with one type of person over and over, and they may not understand why you do not have the same goals and priorities as them. Make sure they understand. I found in tech that many investors are so used to working with single, very young white men that they couldn't comprehend why I needed a competitive salary as a breadwinner, a mother and someone in their mid-thirties. I had to spell out the cost of my life to them. Supporting a growing boy while running a company is like paying for a whole other adult in the house. I did a lot of 'help me understand' and 'how can I do that?' as outlined in Voss's book.

Learn to listen

When it comes to understanding the other party's position, active listening is key. Ask open-ended questions to get them talking and encourage them to share their perspective. Be sure to listen actively, meaning that you focus on what they are saying and avoid interrupting or getting defensive. Staying quiet is important to give breathing room to the discussion.

Once you have a clear understanding of both your own and the other party's position, you can begin to explore areas of common ground and areas of disagreement. Note all their actual priorities down next to your assumptions. This is where negotiation can really begin to happen, as you work to find a solution that addresses both parties' needs and interests.

It's important to keep in mind that clarification of

positions is an ongoing process throughout the negotiation, not just a one-time step. As the negotiation evolves and new information is revealed, be prepared to adjust your position and seek clarification on the other party's as needed. It's just dancing with a partner; you need to read their moves and adjust constantly.

The best negotiations are win-win situations, where both parties feel that their needs and interests have been addressed. Brainstorm creative solutions that address both parties' needs and interests. Creativity is important here. I'm a big believer that there is always a solution that works for both parties, and sometimes it may seem unconventional. Don't be afraid to put forward something radical and perhaps even personal. That's why active listening is an important prior step. For someone who is negotiating on behalf of a larger entity, try to discover what is the most important outcome for their ego. They need to look good to their bosses. What can you throw in to help them achieve that? Think two or three steps beyond the deal closing. How can we ensure that everyone will think that was a great deal, long after the papers have been signed? I have a founder friend who was hammered on his equity points during a funding round, and while he eventually signed the papers, he became incredibly unmotivated to work. He vowed never to work with those investors again.

Negotiation is about give and take and sometimes you don't hold all the cards. Be willing to make concessions in order to reach a mutually beneficial agreement. Identify areas where you are willing to compromise, and be clear about what you are and are not willing to give up. Write it down and draw a line under it. Be strategic in your concessions and don't give away more than you need to. I have watched women negotiate *against themselves* due to imposter syndrome, or perceived lack of self-worth. Negotiating against yourself goes hand in hand with the Method of Use Less Words. A friend of mine was asked to submit a quote for a job. Because she didn't hear back immediately, she started to panic that her price was too high. She sent another email saying she was available for a lower price, and at the exact same time, the client had sent an email accepting her first quote. Negotiating against yourself is when you are lowering the price over and over without the other party saying anything.

With all your preparation notes in front of you, you can remind yourself what your boundary is. Do not move from your baseline. People will try to push back, but stand firm. Many women think asking for what they want is greedy and self-interested, instead of viewing it as creating a fair compromise. Just because you're asking for what you want doesn't make you selfish or narcissistic. You're entering the conversation considering what both people want from the situation, so if the other person is going to leave happy, why not allow yourself to, too?

Once an agreement has been reached, formalize it in writing to ensure that both parties fully understand the terms. For something casual, this may just be a follow-up text or email such as, 'Confirming that we are splitting the cost of the hotel, 60 per cent me and 40 per cent you, and the budget is up to £500.' But for anything involving large sums of money, send a letter. When I first borrowed a larger sum of money from a friend, I was impressed, not offended, that she sent me a short legal letter outlining the terms of repayment. That way, we are all on the same page. Writing it down means you can be clear about the expectations and responsibilities of each party, and if there are any misunderstandings, they will be there in black and white. If necessary, seek legal advice to ensure that the agreement is legally binding and enforceable. Remember that a well-written agreement can prevent misunderstandings and disputes down the road.

After the negotiation, take the time to evaluate the outcome and reflect on what worked well and what could be improved in future negotiations. Continuously develop your negotiation skills and strategies over time. Seek feedback from others and be open to learning from your experiences. Remember that negotiation is a skill that can be learned and improved over time until it becomes second nature. My most recent negotiation was with a mobile phone repair shop. A simple service costing £59.99 found an error requiring an additional £69.99. 'Is that the best price you can do?' I said down the phone, while chomping on my lunch sandwich. He mistook my swallowing for silence and like most humans, he needed to fill the silence. 'I can do it for £100 all in.' A simple, yet delightful win.

No matter how tense a negotiation might get, recognize that the person in front of you is not an adversary.

If you want to reach an agreement, move from a competitive mindset to a cooperative one. Most people avoid negotiation, as they mistake it for an argument and most people don't like to argue, so they allow other people to take advantage as a way of keeping the peace; especially in interpersonal relationships. This stems back to our most basic human desire to get along with other members of the tribe. Get over it. The tribes have been negotiating for millennia and you can too.

Don't be too hard on yourself if, after reading this, you've realized you're currently stuck in a bad deal. I screwed up so many times and had many people take advantage of me before I got good at negotiating. It actually made me afraid to do bigger deals and kept me closed off from others. I'm a WIP too. Without negotiation, we can't grow. Effective negotiation is an important skill for anyone looking to achieve contentment in their personal or professional life. You don't want to be resentful and bitter, stuck in a bad job, bad relationship or bad contract. Take control, negotiate the terms and fight for what is fair.

New Method 32
Start with 50/50

We refuse to be the one who is always giving more, and we start from a place of equality until we have accumulated enough wealth and boundaries to be able to give our excess. Without the starting point of equality, we cannot work towards equity. 50/50 should be the baseline, and then we work to seek what is individually fair for us. We do not want to remain the poorer sex because of our unpaid domestic labour acting as a negative compounding factor in our lives. Whether it is time, money or attention, if we feel we are being treated unfairly within a relationship, we speak up, voice our concern and maintain the equilibrium.

There are three areas in relationships where I strive for 50/50 wherever possible: childcare, domestic labour and money. This has been born from a gut feeling of what feels right, as well as observing the older women around me who emitted a deep sense of anger and frustration about their free labour. This was long before I understood how important this policy is to gender equity.

Going 50/50 is about acknowledging that no progress can be made without equal contribution, and standing firm in your decisions about how you want to live. But in some cases there needs to be an equitable arrangement, not an equal one. So what's the difference?

Equality means providing everyone with the same resources and opportunities. It assumes that everyone starts from an equal position. However, this approach fails to account for the systemic disadvantages and barriers that certain groups face. As an example, it means giving Black mothers and white mothers the same amount of maternal care in hospitals, in regard to time and attention. It means treating everyone the same.

Equity, on the other hand, acknowledges and addresses that not everyone is on the same starting line. It recognizes that in order to achieve true equality, we must provide the necessary resources to those who have historically been marginalized and bring them from a negative balance to zero. If we continue our example, it means acknowledging that Black women are four times more likely to die in childbirth, and therefore giving them *extra* attention, maternal care and checking biases with the hospital staff. The marginalized need more.

Women bearing children is a significant contributor to gender inequity. It grossly affects our earnings curve and impacts our pension, with the stunted compound interest resulting in a gulf-wide Gender Pension Gap. By the time a woman is aged sixty-five to sixty-nine, her average pension wealth is roughly one-fifth of that of a man her age. Let this not be you.

In order for this particular New Method to work, you have to start it early. In fact, it is absolutely critical that you start it early and that you have firm boundaries. I learned this as a child when tasked with my first Make a Cup of Tea for the Grown Ups. My brother and I would be engrossed in cartoons when one of us would be called to make tea and I felt it was important that we take it in turns. Fairness and justice were top of my mind even back then, and what I can see now is that I didn't want the trap of domestic duties always falling to the little girl in the household and not the boy. In my observations of relationships, I've noticed that the power dynamic established between two individuals in the early stages tends to persist throughout their relationship, so set your boundaries from the start.

When Roman was around six months old, our family exhibited a fair 50/50 split with duties. His father cooked and cleaned and changed nappies just as I did. We roughly split the week so that I would not be the first port of call if Roman cried on a Sunday to Wednesday, which is typical of female caregivers. Instead his father would stop whatever he was doing and lovingly attend to him. This was possible because we were both entrepreneurs and could decide on our own parental leave. Still, it's why parental leave policy must include all caregivers – men, same-sex, non-binary, non-birth-giving. Raising a newborn in that first year of life should not be a solitary endeavour.

When we separated, we carried on with this routine. It was uncomfortable at first and certainly had some teething problems along the way, but our 50/50 split is something we've stuck to rigidly. It's hands down been one of the most self-defining things in my life. Now, over a decade later, our son continues to spend half the week at my house, and half the week at his father's, and we do many FaceTimes and phone calls on both sides in between. It works for us and is absolutely critical for me being able to pursue the things I want, whether that's in business, a relationship or a hobby. Most importantly, I have time to just think.

Humans are not rigid, and every week, month and year my feelings about our 50/50 split would change. When Roman was a baby, on Day 1 I would be elated with the free time and a lie in bed! By Day 2, mutterings of 'Where's my baby?' would surface. By Day 3, I would be utterly depressed, feeling like a limb had been removed from me. I knew I would not change the cadence because (1) I believed Roman needed some form of consistency and my entrepreneurial life was chaotic, and (2) I grew up not knowing my father at all and it haunted me deeply. I knew I could never do that to my child and that the bond needed to be formed early. Where I could not change the routine, I drew on my Stoic methods and changed my perception of events. I started to fill the days with meetings, self-care and friends. I filled my calendar so that I wouldn't be filled with longing for my precious son. Over many years, the feeling of being untethered from my son faded and part of the true equality we have today is emotional. I don't even feel I ought to have him more than I do, and Roman shows no indication today of preferring either home.

In terms of the money, because our time spent was 50/50 we would have equal living costs, so we never had any financial arrangement for our legal shared residence. This was logical to me. Even though my earnings at the time of separation were fairly low, I made a choice on how I wanted to live with Roman, which over the years would include travel, schooling, clothes, books, toys, so I paid for my choices as my wealth grew. People's circumstances change over time, and you may eventually need a more equitable arrangement, but for us it was not necessary and still isn't. If you have your child the majority of the time, calculate the cost and invoice the other parent accordingly.

When I'm dating, I don't keep strict tallies on who paid for what, but I work to distribute finances evenly. Concert tickets are rewarded with dinner. Flights bought for a trip mean the other person might pay for the hotel. I am yet to live with a man long-term, but I picture a world where I have a property and he has his, and we may buy a new one equally together.

For those of you who don't have dependants or are simply living in a shared house, domestic labour is a major form of uneven distribution, with the brunt of the work falling on women. A Jamaican family work ethic was imbued into me early, but I also knew my school work, reading time and play were important. My most precious commodity is time to think. In a typical Jamaican household, a big house-clean is all done on a Saturday or Sunday, usually to the tunes of Lover's Rock music while dinner would be on the stove.

Although like most people I like a clean and tidy home, domesticity wasn't something I ever got overly obsessed with as a personal responsibility; it was a shared responsibility. Everyone who knew me or lived with me as an adult knew that I was often engrossed in my work, and as soon as I had my first non-student home, I paid for a cleaner for two hours a week. This wasn't a privilege, it was a personal choice. Other friends may have spent the equivalent on wine, magazines and tanning beds. A set of lashes, even. I chose early to outsource my domestic labour and pay a fair wage. I've dated messy guys, OCD cleaning guys and everything in between, and my attitude to domestic labour stays consistent. I refuse to lean in to accommodate someone else's shortfall in these specific matters, only to be worse off in time, money and my thinking space. British sociologist Ann Oakley wrote in her book *Woman's Work: The housewife past and present* (1974), 'Housework is work directly opposed to the possibility of human self-actualization.' This may well be one of the mantras of my life.

There are many dynamics in the home that will not be equal and it's up to you to decide if it works for you. You may earn more. Your partner may earn more. You may be required to check your privilege and consider if your contribution is fair and equal. It is not always monetary but it also includes time and attention. If you are in a shared household, in a relationship or have children, make a list of your time expenditure and your financial expenditure in relation to your family unit. You might love cleaning, for example, but not want to pay for the expensive food your partner likes. You might want to buy cheap school supplies for your children because vacations are really important to you. You might be livid that you are always the one who has to arrange doctor's appointments for the family, taking away precious time from your reading and writing.

Professor Brené Brown believes that 50/50 in long-term marriage is a myth:

> Strong, lasting relationships are rarely 50–50, because life does not work that way. Strong, lasting relationships happen when your partner or friend or whoever you're in relationship with, can pony up that 80 per cent when you are down to 20, and that your partner also knows that when things fall apart for her, and she only has 10 per cent to give, you can show up with your 90, even if it's for a limited amount of time.

As life progresses, there is a push and pull dynamic between people, and the deeper you are in a relationship, the more trust can develop for you to honour each other and do the right thing at the right time. You may soon find that it is no longer 50/50, but as long as it adds up to 100 and that works for you as a family, that's all that matters.

List out your time and money spent, then rate each one from 1–5 on how OK you are with it. 1 for not OK and 5 for this works for me. Then in the next column, rate how much this affects the power dynamic. 1 – you feel powerless and 5 – you feel powerful. In the final column, write a short note on how you might get all the numbers to 5. It may feel transactional to list out your time and money in relation to the home, but without it, you won't truly see what gendered stereotypes in relation to family contribution are costing you. Once your list is complete, discuss it with your family. I have friends who think that in order to be equitable, men must pay more. They see it as reparation for millennia of gender inequities. For some this is empowering – you are living your best life on someone else's dime – and for others, taking money from their partners puts them in a place of disempowerment.

The reason for this essay is because I have heard far too many horror stories of supportive loving wives and mothers who devoted their entire lives to the noble labour of raising a family, only to be left completely destitute when there is a separation or death. Unable to claim insurance because it was in the husband's name. Not able to claim full income in a divorce settlement. And worst of all, unable to be recruited because of long gaps in work history. Raising the next generation of humanity is one of the most precious jobs anyone can do. I just want to make sure you are paid for it and that you have a pot of money that is all your own.

My childhood schema of 'I can only rely on myself' has put me in an obsessive position to be able to support myself and my family, alone. There has only been one instance where I was unable to support myself financially in a relationship and the lack of freedom choked me. I wasn't living authentically because this financial leash was on me. I vowed I would never be in that position again.

It's a simple fact that you can't have true gender equality without the power of a 50/50 split. We are still the global poorer sex, yet we continue to give away what we don't have. Money and time. Imagine the difference a woman could make with extra money to invest in themselves, their businesses, their passions and their causes. Yet, despite having less to start with, we still end up giving away more than we can afford.

Without my son's father sharing half the childcare load, I wouldn't have the headspace to come up with innovative ideas and work on my business. If you're stuck between work, raising your children, spending hours choosing school shoes, tidying the house, shopping, cooking and cleaning, where are you leaving time for yourself to have creative thoughts?

I call this domestic cognitive load. When your brain is so full of chores that you can't focus on the next big idea.

This is not a luxury. When people question 50/50 anything, I simply stand my ground and say – but this is fair and this is equal. Nothing else supersedes that. To me, true, equal co-parenting is the epitome of gender equality. When women are free of unpaid labour in the home, we open up the potential to what they can achieve.

Imagine if every woman had reduced unpaid labour. How many new businesses would spring up? How many technological innovations would we have? How many more women would have senior positions in great jobs?

And if you're a full-time parent, there's still an essential balance to maintain – work is not the only reason why 50/50 parenting is essential. Regardless of what you choose to do with your free time, you should be granted it. Professor Linda Scott wrote in *The Double X Economy*:

> [There must be] new protections for stay-at-home wives and mothers. I list this idea last only because it will probably take research to figure out how best to do it before legislation can be drafted. I am unconvinced that higher alimony payments are either the best or the only way to get this done. Our collective emphasis on working women has overshadowed the personal risk taken by women who are dependent on their husbands for income. Women's advocates inevitably cite the higher number of women who leave work to care for children as a cause of unequal pay and advancement. It is hypocritical not to have a platform for protecting these women.

Like her I believe that stay-at-home work is work. It is the work that keeps the world turning. It needs to be valued too.

The New Method here is to start with 50/50 and stop giving away what you don't have until you can build up the boundaries and the excess to give more. When you give to others, you only want to be giving away your compound interest. You need to protect the principal. You cannot freely give something away unless you're accumulating it in abundance first.

Think about how much you're giving the following away to others:

- Time
- Attention
- Money
- Effort
- Affection
- Resources

Now ask yourself, are you giving yourself enough of these things? Enough to grow, develop, succeed, and be in a position to help even more people later down the line?

If you often find yourself feeling like you're always the one giving, there's likely an imbalance in what you give away and keep for yourself. Give your half and then stop. Be comfortable with doing that, it is more than enough.

New Method 33
But Take As Much As You Can

We demand the highest price possible and don't feel guilty when we get it. We have been robbed over and over again. Through primogeniture, unpaid labour, common law and especially through discrimination. When the opportunity comes for us to over-index on what we are owed, we take it. We take as much as we can and consider it reparation for the generational wealth which evades us. We have not been primed to develop greed in our nature, so at first it will feel uncomfortable. But we continue to stockpile and accumulate, knowing that this wealth is powering our economic independence.

We live in a world where women are often undervalued and underpaid, but it's time for us to take control of our worth and ask for more. We deserve to be paid fairly for our work, and we should never feel guilty when our requests are granted.

Recognize that what you accept in life sets the pace for how other people and society perceive you and your value. By allowing this habit of accepting scraps, you're not only reinforcing your value to yourself but across society too. If enough women stand up and set new expectations for their true value, a real movement begins. Asking for more serves as reparation for the entire history of women receiving less. It's time to teach society the true value of women's work.

The first step to asking for more is to know your worth. Take the time to research the industry standards for your job and your level of experience and demand the highest salary for minimum qualifications. Don't settle for less than you deserve just because you think it's all you can get. Know your strengths and what you bring to the table, and highlight them when negotiating.

Don't apologize for asking for more, and don't be afraid to make a strong case for yourself. Apologizing, 'I'm sorry to ask but . . .', immediately sets the tone that you don't feel it's deserved but circumstances outside your control mean you must ask. Instead, use specific examples of your accomplishments and the value you have brought to your employer. Practise your negotiation skills with a friend or mentor, and be prepared to counter any objections or pushback you may receive.

In the UK, regulations introduced in 2017 require public, private and voluntary sector organizations with 250 or more employees to report annually on their gender pay gap, and where possible to close it, leading to a monumental shift in salaries. In the first year of reporting, my friend's sister got a £25,000 pay rise. She didn't have to ask for it – the company gave it automatically because they knew she was being paid less than her male colleagues and they didn't want it becoming public. Only then did she realize that everybody in the company was getting paid more than her, simply because she was a woman. What if she took it further? All the years she was a dedicated, underpaid employee would have had a negative effect on her compounded wealth, resulting in potential poverty in old age. If you can calculate the years she was underpaid, maybe it's about asking for an additional £25,000 bonus as compensation which she can use to top up her pension pot. That's not greedy. She's due the money she got denied because of their gender discrimination. Her co-workers were living comfortably on twice the salary without having to do twice the work.

As always, it's also crucial to be willing to walk away if necessary. If your employer is not willing to pay you what you deserve, it may be time to look for other opportunities. Don't be afraid to explore other job options and consider the full compensation package, including benefits, work-life balance, and career advancement opportunities. Asking for more may not always be about money, it may be about equity, time, or whatever has value to you.

Have a clear plan for what you will do with the additional compensation. Whether it's paying off debt, saving for a down payment on a home, or investing in your education, having a clear goal will give you the motivation to ask for more. It's a lot easier to stand your ground when you have a strong vision for what you want to do with the additional income.

Remember, asking for more is not about being greedy or entitled. It's about recognizing your worth and demanding to be treated fairly. By asking for more you have pinned a figure in someone's mind of what your expectations are. You have moved their perception of you towards a higher number. The worst they can do is say no, and you move on.

Money is freedom. We have not been trained to develop a mindset that we deserve more, so at first it may feel uncomfortable. But what does it cost you not to ask? It costs you your independence. It's time for us to take control of our financial futures and demand the highest price possible for our work.

New Method 34
Compound Money and Actions

We start small and we start frequently, knowing that by investing in ourselves, the results will compound. Just as in financial investments, where consistent contributions over time yield substantial returns, the same concept applies to our self-development. We make a daily commitment that may seem inconsequential in the short term. But over time we are confident that these small acts accumulate, deepening our understanding and expanding our capacity. Each new piece of information, each new idea grasped, serves as a building block upon which our further knowledge is constructed. The compounding effect of consistent growth enables us to amass a wealth of wisdom that far surpasses our initial efforts.

Power and opportunity don't come easily, and results don't come overnight. But when they do come, you can build results on top of results. The faster you understand the concept of compound interest, the better.

The phrase compound interest is a financial concept that refers to the interest earned or charged on an initial amount of money, called the principal, as well as on any accumulated interest from previous periods. In simple terms, it is interest on top of interest.

When you invest or borrow money with compound

interest, the interest you earn or owe is added to the principal amount. In subsequent periods, the interest is calculated based on the increased principal, including the accumulated interest from previous periods. You're making money from the money you made from your money. This compounding effect leads to exponential growth over time.

Compound interest can work for or against you, depending on whether you are investing or borrowing. When investing, compound interest allows your money to grow faster because the interest earned in each period contributes to the total principal for the next period. Over time, this compounding effect can result in significant growth of your investment.

Conversely, when borrowing with compound interest, the amount you owe grows faster over time. The interest charged on the outstanding balance accumulates, increasing the total debt owed. The frequency of compounding plays a crucial role in determining the impact of compound interest. Compounding can occur annually, semi-annually, quarterly, monthly or even daily, depending on the terms of the investment. The more frequently the interest is compounded, the faster it grows.

Compound interest is a fundamental principle in finance and is often employed in various investment vehicles, such as savings accounts, certificates of deposit, bonds and other financial instruments. It is important to understand the power of compound interest when making financial decisions, as it can significantly affect long-term savings or debt repayment strategies.

COMPOUND INTEREST:
WHO WILL EARN MORE?

This example shows how the earlier person takes advantage of compound interest, the more time that money has to grow.

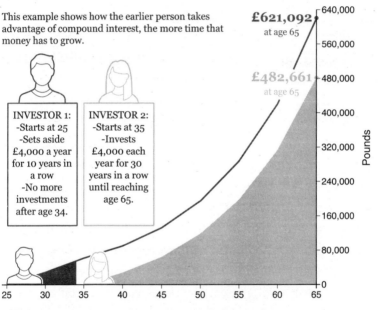

£621,092
at age 65

£482,661
at age 65

INVESTOR 1:
-Starts at 25
-Sets aside £4,000 a year for 10 years in a row
-No more investments after age 34.

INVESTOR 2:
-Starts at 35
-Invests £4,000 each year for 30 years in a row until reaching age 65.

NOTES: Assumes an 8 percent interest rate, compounded annually.
       Balances shown are approximate.

Compound interest embodies the concept of exponential growth, showing us how even small amounts of money, when allowed to compound over time, can lead to substantial returns. It is one of the reasons why we have intergenerational wealth and why the rich are able to get richer. Having good credit gives you better interest rates, enabling the rich to make more money from their money, while those with low incomes are unable to get on the accumulation ladder. The poet and novelist Katy Lederer once said, 'It should be everyone's right in a capitalist system to have some way to take advantage of compound interest.' And for women this is especially important, given the wealth gap later in life. We start later and we end up with much less.

There are many financial resources that can help you understand compound interest in more detail, but once I grasped the concept, I started to think about other places where compound interest was relevant in my life. Where, if I start making deposits in good habits early, will I be rewarded in the long term?

It was not difficult to see where practice in my early years resulted in compound interest in my favour. Exercise and diet was the most obvious one. As a teenager I played sports daily, meaning that even though I'm not at my optimum fitness level as an adult, it only takes me about a month or so of training to get fit again. My muscles remember what to do because of the early work I put in. My work ethic is derived from the practice of getting up at 6 a.m. from the age of eleven to go to school and not returning home until 5 p.m. and often later. Years of that daily grind mean I'm now built for long days of intense learning and work. At university, being forced each week by British etiquette writer Drusilla Beyfus to deliver a short essay in an hour meant that I can now sit in front of a blank page and get going with ease. Eating clean and researching nutrition in my mid-twenties while pregnant really helped give my gut a rest and laid the foundations for my long-term understanding of food as medicine. I think this knowledge of eating whole foods will help me live longer, naturally (fate willing).

And my favourite example: while it is often said that Black people having good skin is down to genetics and yes, melanin is a protective mechanism from the ageing effects of the sun, I also believe that the majority of it is the compound interest of having creams and oils applied to our faces since we were babies. Daily moisturizing from birth! When did you start moisturizing and does your skin today reflect your level of investment?

But there are other ones too. Imagine the compound effect of starting therapy at twenty-two instead of thirty-two, or communicating your needs with your partner from day one instead of waiting until year two of the relationship, when you're both frustrated.

Significant change doesn't always stem from big decisions and actions. Instead, smaller, consistent actions build up over time and if started early more effectively bring about the changes you want to see. We can so easily be put off by big goals and massive lifestyle changes when in actuality, the smaller, daily changes we make across our lives will often prove the most powerful. Good actions accumulate and compound too, just like money. What are you starting today for your future self?

In order to complete this book while running a business and being a mother, I had to channel the American science fiction author, Octavia Butler, who said, 'First forget inspiration. Habit is more dependable. Habit will sustain you whether you're inspired or not.' This resulted in me waking up at 5.30 a.m. several days a week so I could write in peace. Now I enjoy the morning routine and I get my deep work done in quiet.

Success doesn't always require us to go to extremes. It just requires consistency in our good choices, whether that's saving a small amount of our paycheck each month or setting aside one hour a week for our self-development. Start small and start early. The compound effect of whatever you did yesterday, will do today, and plan to do tomorrow can set the pace for your success.

Be patient with your results. Due to the nature of compounding, growth really starts to kick in around month 18, if you are investing monthly. Exponential change happens around month 27, and by month 31 there's been a massive impact. Give yourself time to let the compounding take off.

Just like with money, compounding can work against you. Investing in negative actions, things or people early on means that you are laying strong foundations for poor health and wealth in your later years. Take an inventory and trim whatever is increasing your negative balance.

The New Method here requires you to commit yourself to make simple positive deposits every day. You don't have to get your whole life sorted out overnight. Just wake up and do a little bit. Start with one or two growth habits and go from there. It might be setting aside thirty minutes each evening to learn something new, or ensuring you put the same amount of money into savings each month. The bestselling book *Atomic Habits* by James Clear provides a framework for building good habits and breaking bad ones. He says, 'Habits are the compound interest of self-improvement.' So create a system that ensures good, consistent practice.

One of my chosen deposits is meditation. It's taken me years to feel comfortable meditating, as at first I found it so hard to lie for twenty minutes and not do anything else. But the time to stop has proved so beneficial for my creativity, mental health and self-awareness. Now I meditate with ease and can fall into a deep state in a short period of time.

Once you find the deposits that work best for you, make them a non-negotiable part of your daily life. Little by little, putting one foot in front of the other, just keep on trucking. You'll start to see things grow.

New Method 35
Handle Competition Gracefully

As we come into our power and accumulate, some will try to take. This is a good thing. Competition is a natural phenomenon that signals our methods are working. We do not let competition frustrate us and we most certainly do not let it distract us. Time spent worrying about others is time wasted. We embrace competition and use our methods to tip the balance in our favour. Women competing against women is a complete and utter distraction from the fact that we already have so little. We don't fight over scraps. We stay in our lane and support each other where necessary.

The thing about creating a very cult-like team in any business that I start is that they feel super-protective over the brand and when they see anyone wade into our domain – whether that's from a visual aesthetic/industry/ambassadors, etc. – they get incredibly upset. But negative energy spent on the competition is positive energy not spent thinking about your business.

That said, our community is rapidly growing, and with thousands of members in their self-actualization era, it's only natural that there will be women among you who are working something similar, if not the exact same thing. So, let's talk about competition. I get it. Women have never had enough to go around. I totally understand where this paranoia comes from, but all it serves to do is stunt your growth and it's not going to get you to the next stage. Think about how to handle your competitors with grace using these New Methods.

Consider if you want a world with no problems to solve

Do you really want to wake up one day and have no new problems to solve? Nothing to do? No new challenges? If you're a New Methods woman, I can't imagine this is your bag. Try to see this competitor issue as an exciting new level to unlock in the game of business and life. If life was too easy, I'm sure you'd be somewhat bored. Embrace the problem.

Acknowledge that it proves your market is hot

Competition shows demand for your entire industry. There is no point in being too early in your industry because customers will not be ready. Many start-ups have failed by being the lone early launch. Customers start believing in a product when they see multiple offerings in the space and so competition legitimizes your work. You might see a crowded market, but I see an exciting growing space that will make customers believe it's real.

Use it as fuel, energy to burn on your rocket ship

Competition does keep you on your toes. The famous book by Andy Grove, *Only the Paranoid Survive* is slightly extreme in the title but an amazing treatise on using your fears as fuel. While I would advise against full-blown paranoia, I do understand that keeping abreast of what is going on in your industry is necessary if you are using that as a springboard for your next move. Sometimes I can get complacent and rest on my laurels, until I start to see that there are other people nipping at my heels doing the same thing. I like a healthy amount of competition to thrive, but just make sure it stays as fuel – underneath you, propelling you up, and it burns off – not your oxygen.

Look forward, keep innovating and stay one step ahead

Competition keeps you innovating and that fuel should take your rocket ship out of the atmosphere. If you create something and somebody replicates it in its entirety, the easiest way to remove any anxiety about competitors is by reinventing and reinventing and reinventing, over and over again. Launch and learn! You keep pressing forward and they have to keep catching up. What can you do today that will take your business out of the realm of average and supercharge it into an anomaly? Keep it moving.

Know what makes you special

If you want to keep moving forward you need to think strategically about what makes you special. List out your personal USP. Your fingerprint experiences of life that no one can replicate. Bake these into your product. It might be that you grew up in a small town, so you have unique knowledge of how to attract that particular audience to be your early customers. It might be that you had a former life as a DJ, meaning your branding will be inspired by rave culture instead of looking like the cookie cutter start-up logo. List what makes you, you, and play games you can win.

Now do the same for your work. One-liner answers for:

- Who is your customer?
- What do they believe in?
- What is the feature they'll use the most?
- How do you make money?

And now, the next time you encounter someone who THINKS that you're a competitor with something like, 'Oh wow we are doing really similar things, eh?' you can have the following conversation:

Oh amazing! Are you building a product for
    <insert your customer demographic>
Well, no . . .
Oh, are your users obsessed with <insert your
    customer beliefs and aims>

No, not quite . . .

Oh, can they <insert unique feature they'll use>

Well, no . . .

Oh, will you be monetizing through <insert your monetization strategy>

Well, no . . .

Oh! Maybe we have the same intention – and that's a good thing, right? Because we all want <insert company mission here> but we have a very different customer, business model and monetization strategy. It's so exciting that our industry is growing. We should stick together and share notes!

You'll soon find that when you break it down, most businesses win and lose on their distribution model, margins and monetization strategies, not their colour palette or social feed. However, if today, your business and your competitors' business IS doing the exact same four things, then now is the time to dig deep and think of ways to stand out from the crowd. Brainstorm how you can keep innovating.

Be gracious

Be the host. Invite, welcome and support your competitors. This is the easiest way to quell your competitor rage, and the first time you do it, it may be through gritted teeth, but trust me, it works. Invite them to dinner.

Ask them how you can collaborate. Send them kind notes and flowers when they win. This is not some slimy power play (we are over the aggressive way of building our empires), but a genuine New Method of calming your own anxieties and being the bigger person. The by-product of grace is that it does give you more power. Power over your emotions, as it makes you feel better to be kind than snide. Your competitors are expecting you to hate them. How classy of you to collaborate with and nurture them instead. You never know when you might need their support.

Being the host is now my default way of existing, but only because I have gone through the other New Methods and I know myself, I know my value and I know that I can always produce more. I know what makes me special and I have done research on how we can turn that into a commercial opportunity. When I first started this work, there was a big gap between me doing the right thing and me actually *wanting* to do the right thing, and there were times when I was petty. But now, my moves are transparent and genuine. If I give you work, it's because I think you're good at it; if I cut your work, it's because I can't afford it. If I invest in you, it's because I want to support you. If I cancel a meeting or keep you waiting it's because I really am running late or busy. If I'm uncommunicative, it's because I have higher priorities (and I need to do better in communicating that). It's not a power play, it is what it is.

Remember – no one is original, nothing is unique.

There's a reason the word Zeitgeist exists. There are only so many outputs when we are all currently consuming the same inputs. So just know your worth and enjoy the ride. The only person you should be competing with is your past self.

New Method 36
Act As an Alumna

Future generations of women will continue to be the poorer sex if we do not use our wealth to invest in them. As women we typically spend our money domestically and within our community, which has meaningful but short term gain. We start anew to direct our capital towards institutions that will use the money to grow and develop young women on a large scale and for longer periods. We act as alumnae by giving time and money to the schools, colleges and centres that helped us become the powerful women we are today. This is not about charity. This is an investment into future generations by giving them the tools and resources to win.

'Why are women poor?' asks Virginia Woolf in *A Room of One's Own*. One of my favourite parts of this seminal book is when she outlines, in her think-out-loud prose, how men graduate from their universities, enter the world of industry and become rich, then give back to the institutions that shaped them. They might give cash donations to their university or donate to a library, having their name immortalized in concrete and supporting the students attending. That's why you see classrooms, wings and sometimes even entire buildings named after the illustrious alumni that paid for them. In doing so, they make those elite universities better for the generations to follow and keep their 'illustrious', male names over the door.

They provide the means for better facilities, such as computer labs or swimming pools or sports halls which will then attract more privileged students and allow the cycle of wealth to continue. They make the path easier for those coming up behind them. And while this is also done by women, it's far less common. Keep your eye out for a university department or an art gallery named after an independently rich woman.

Power accumulates in the educational systems that birth them. Of the fifty-seven prime ministers we have had in Britain at the time of writing, thirty were educated at the University of Oxford (including thirteen at Christ Church), and fourteen at the University of Cambridge (including six at Trinity College). Silicon Valley's undisputed leading start-up accelerator, Y Combinator, invests heavily in Ivy-League-educated white male founders. In research, of 154 founders they invested in, 35 per cent of founders went to Harvard, Stanford, Yale, Princeton, MIT and UC Berkeley, while 45 per cent of co-founders went to an Ivy League school, Oxbridge, MIT, Stanford, Carnegie Mellon or USC.

In *A Room of One's Own*, Virginia and her friend Mary are at college, eating a substandard dinner, in an awful dining room and daydreaming about what the men's college dining rooms are serving. Virginia's eating soup, while the men are eating meat. She's not allowed to go into the university library unless accompanied by a male. Her physiological needs are below par and her self-actualized need for knowledge is completely out of her reach. Woolf imagines having access to a library, which was paid for by a rich and noble woman who mandated that the rules were changed. That if they wanted the benefactor's money for their library, well, they'd better let women students in.

Being an alumna of an institution should be about more than simply graduating and moving on. This New Method urges you to give back to your communities and all the helping hands you have had along the way, so that you have the power to make decisions within these institutions and young women can have the same opportunities you did. In fact, they should have more. Without giving back to the institutions and communities who helped us along the way, we aren't maintaining the economic investment necessary for gender equity to be possible. Men are excellent at forming their tightly-knit networks and support systems. They reinvest in their institutions and carry on the legacy of the powerful, successful men before them. In order for us to make an impact we need focused investment directly in other women's education.

Australian artist Wendy Whiteley was fifteen when she dropped out of high school to enrol in art college. More than six decades later, Whiteley has made a $500,000 promised bequest to her alma mater, now the National Art School (NAS) – among the largest gifts the institution has received. The money will be used to support female students and alumnae of NAS, including help with exhibitions, residencies and acquisitions of their work for the NAS Collection. Whiteley says she wants to encourage female creatives like herself who came to art school without financial support: 'I had to work at the same time as I went to art school. I worked at a coffee shop at night to earn the money because I didn't have parents who could pay for me. My mother was worried about me being a starving artist in the attic, that sort of thing, and not finishing high school properly. It was regarded as a tricky occupation being an artist, especially for a woman.'

If you are an artist, but not yet flush with cash, giving back might look like a donation of artwork to the community centre that helped unleash your creativity, or to the arts department at your school that taught you the discipline that's stayed with you to this day. This artwork will go on their balance sheet as an asset and increase the value of the institution.

While it's great to pay it forward once you've made it, you can also start acting as an alumna now with the resources you have. Money aside, there are plenty of other ways you can help, too. Such as telling your story to little girls who dream of what you have. Or even to those who can't comprehend that such a dream is possible yet. You can give with your time and your face. I regularly give talks in schools and will never hesitate to do anything educational. What I can't give with money right now, I can give with my image and my time. I can show up for young girls, to inspire, teach and lift them up. By saying, 'I've been where you are and now I am here. If you want this, it is possible.'

Institutions are competitive. They require applicants

and successful graduates to succeed. Here's what you can do for your institution:

- Recommend and recruit prospective students.
- Offer coaching to applicants.
- Provide jobs and internships to grads.
- Introduce students to others in your network.
- Help to raise funds.
- Advise students and/or fellow alumnae on career direction and opportunities.
- Provide advice to academic programmes and administrative offices.
- Advocate for the institution before governmental bodies.
- Help solicit gifts from alumnae and other potential donors.
- Serve on boards and committees.

We're not trying to get a seat at the table. It's about investing in the materials needed to build our own table. This is about giving back to the people who shaped us into who we are today, and lifting up the next generation to ensure that the legacy of dynamic women can continue. Even if you have not studied at a formal institution, there will be people following your footsteps in some way and a kind word of encouragement would not go amiss. You can act as an alumna to the little girl who grew up next door to you, in whom you see potential.

If you are occupying a position of privilege, through your race or class, it's important to ensure your alumna work does not simply perpetuate these systems of inequality. Invest intersectionally, so that all oppressed communities have opportunities to grow. Women's rights are here, but they're not evenly distributed. Being a woman alone does not automatically give you a complete, tightly bound, supportive network. We're still far too divided among ourselves. If we continue in this way, I cannot see how we can overcome our collective oppression. Don't just invest in the elite institutions where you may have studied. Support state and free education too.

Acting as an alumna is an investment in your world as well as theirs. As we grow into the latter years of our lives, it's imperative that we have an army of young women trained in thought to come behind us. This future generation will be building cities and roads, housing and schools. They will be the ones deciding on your pension and tax by designing economic policy. They will be making the decisions that affect us all. By investing in their education, we are investing in ourselves. I'll be happy on my deathbed if I know that my community are holding seats of power across the globe and spreading the message of equity for all. That is worth all the time and money I invest in them today.

New Method 37
Write Emotional Angel Cheques

Not everything in life is about a monetary transaction and the greatest gift you have is your time. Women disproportionately suffer from feelings of loneliness, which then impacts our ability to step into our power, with grace. While we are unable to manage hundreds of connections intimately, we are able to punctuate our relationships by depositing an emotional angel cheque – a selfless act of care towards another woman in her time of need. You may not even be close to this woman. You may not even remember what you did. But she will remember, and it will help lift her out of the darkness.

Everything in life is an energy exchange, and it's always honourable to pay things forward. The underlying principles of New Methods centre around taking back your power for yourself. However, there will be times in your life when you need to give away your power. At some point, someone will need your support and they'll be unable to give back in a way that makes the exchange 'fair' – you scratch my back, I'll scratch yours. And that's OK. In these instances, you can write an emotional angel cheque without the other party feeling they need to reciprocate in some way.

What is an emotional angel cheque? It comes from

the world of business and the term 'angel investor', which is an individual who provides capital for a business start-up, usually in exchange for convertible debt or ownership equity. Angel investors typically give support to start-ups in their initial stages, when most investors aren't prepared to back them.

Essentially, experienced angel investors invest knowing they may get nothing in return. There's no guarantee the business they're supporting will ever get off the ground. The odds are stacked against most start-ups, but angel investors are happy to have supported on the founder's journey. Maybe they will strike lucky and get something back. Maybe they won't. Emotional angel cheques operate by the very same principle.

I once met a girl at a dinner party who I couldn't quite connect with, so I took a step back and just listened. Our energies weren't compatible, so I practised some active listening and I left that night thinking nothing more of it. Until a few weeks later.

I don't know what came over me. I had the urge to reach out to her and ask what she was up to that night. The response surprised me. She was noticeably and understandably low; her friend had recently passed away. I told her not to worry, I'd be at her house in an hour. 'Get ready; I'm coming for you.'

The first thing I said to her when I got there was something along the lines of, 'I don't know you very well, so I'm not sure if what you need is a walk or to go out and party.' I ended up taking her to a restaurant. I was the shoulder she needed that night. I was a supportive friend — albeit one she didn't know very well. At that moment, I deposited an emotional angel cheque. I didn't expect anything from this exchange and I'm unsure if either of us thought this was the beginning of a blossoming friendship; she just needed someone to be there.

This Method is about being there in the moments when someone needs you the most, whether that's for advice, a way to release pressure or simply as a sounding board. Don't approach these moments as a 'fixer'. You can't always take on other people's problems as your own. Instead, your job in these instances is to be a source of support and guidance.

Move past the idea that interactions must always be reciprocal. All our interactions with other people are exchanges of energy, and be wary of being too much on the receiver end. Sometimes, people will need your help but won't be in a position to give anything in return, and that's OK. Someone within your network needs your support right now. Call them.

Sometimes you just have to show up. So much of life is about strategizing and calculating your next move. But now and then you have to put yourself to one side and help a sister out.

New Method 38
Take Your Wins

We no longer routinely downplay our wins as luck or an accident. We don't brush off compliments any more. Every victory, no matter how big or small, is a testament to our intelligence, strength and perseverance. We made it this far. We choose to break free from self-doubt and embrace the truth: we are deserving of recognition and celebration. We take all our wins, and honour our hard work. We stand tall and let our accomplishments shine. We own our triumphs, not as mere coincidences, but as proof of our capabilities. With our wins, we inspire others to follow their dreams and we demonstrate that success is attainable. When someone offers us a win, we take it, smile gently and say thank you. That is all.

In 2021 I won an award. The Veuve Clicquot Bold Future Award. One of the most prestigious awards for women in business, which has been running for forty-nine years in the spirit of the champagne house's leader, Madame Clicquot. What you may not know is that I had actually declined to be even nominated for this award in previous years. Why? At the time, I felt deeply in the pits. I felt a failure, I didn't know what was happening with my business, and I couldn't imagine standing up on stage and pretending I was a winner. Even though I was complimented for my work on a nearly daily basis, I felt like a fraud.

This is one of the key reasons women find it hard to accept compliments – it doesn't line up with our self-image. If you think you are not stylish and someone compliments your look, you feel compelled to diminish the fact, batting it away until it falls to the ground like a dazed butterfly. If your perception of self is based around you being an anxious person, when someone says you made a confident and decisive action you might try to reduce your stature by listing all the ways you had help, how it was a team effort, how you didn't really know what you were doing, and so forth.

How does this hold you back? Each time you deflect a compliment or minimize a win, you are minimizing yourself. You are saying – no, I don't want to be on the level you want to lift me to, I want to stay right down here, down at the depths of low self-worth.

Your self-worth and confidence are a muscle you need to nourish and train like anything else. You need to exercise your belief that you are worthy of everything that comes to you and you need to feed your healthy ego, by accepting your wins and accomplishments.

When I finally accepted the nomination for the Veuve Clicquot Award in January of that year, it was strategic. At that stage, I had made the decision to press forward with the Stack World and I knew that I would get good press from it which would bolster the success of this new project. As the ceremony got closer and closer, I started to reflect: 'Hell yeah, I deserve this nomination.'

I have been supporting women on their journeys since the publication of *WAH* zine in 2005 and our first-panel talk in 2008. That's sixteen years! Sixteen years of mentoring, hiring, paying, training and featuring women in my content. After raising $6.5m, that VC money is distributed among the salaries of women I hired, the women-founded companies we contracted as suppliers and so on. I have often been a new female founder's first client, and have helped them scale their business just by being an early customer and sharing it in my network. On top of this, I have raised a son, survived a pandemic and launched something entirely new that was growing. Hell yeah, I deserve it.

So I started to step into the compliment and walk into the win. I prepared for the ceremony and took my obligations seriously. I mentally stayed healthy, I didn't drink regularly for a few months before, I ate clean, exercised, planned my outfit so that I would feel great on the day and I brought my whole team along on the journey, knowing that seeing their faces in the crowd would also lift me higher.

As I graciously accepted the nomination, the judging committee were elated. This brings me to my second reason why you need to learn to accept your wins.

By not accepting a compliment you're also hurting the person who made it. You're making them wrong, or as if their opinion doesn't matter, or they're being insincere. Give people a chance to love and appreciate you. It makes them feel good to know they made you feel good. When you don't accept a compliment it's like someone just handed you their baby (their kind words and their heart) and you just took one disgusted look at it and handed it right back.

The New Method here is an easy one to practise. Assume that when someone gives you a compliment, they genuinely mean it, and accept it with grace and a smile. Hold that baby, stroke its cheek and show it love. Be present with it for a few moments. I want you to remember the last time someone complimented you and how you reacted. How would you do it differently next time?

It's as simple as saying: 'Thank you, that's really kind, it means a lot, I value your opinion.'

Take all your wins. Let kind words feed you and lift you higher. You've come a long way, baby, and you deserve it all.

PART FIVE
Trimming

You may well lose it all, and if you don't, now is the time to actively try to. Trim everything that does not concern you. Trim everyone that does not serve you. Cut it out! Get rid! Snip snip! As you ascend to reach your Higher Self, there is a point where you may think that getting more will help you rise, but much like an anchor holding down a hot-air balloon, you need to cut the dead weight to fly. In the existence of a scheduled busy life, consider if you are busy doing nothing. What would it look like to strip everything back to its purest essence so that your full attention is on your Important Work? How far could you go if you swept away the trash in your path? Trimming can hurt people. They'll be clinging on to your old self like a barnacle. But the ones that are meant to be will cross your path again. Trimming can also hurt you. Be cautious of denying yourself to the point of self-abandonment. Be aware of cutting things out as a form of self-punishment. First, aim to truly understand why the issue doesn't work for you, and decide whether to sit and solve the issue or stay firm in your boundaries and trim. Just as in nature, you trim at exactly the right place in the branch, in order to help it grow.

New Method 39
It's Not Always About You

We remove ourselves from the fantasy that we are centre of every-one else's world. No one's judgement, opinion or action is solely derived from our existence. They don't care about us. They bring their own issues to the table, which are theirs and theirs alone. Almost everyone is hurting in some way, and when that hurt is directed at us, we know that it's not just about us. Very few people actually know us, and everyone else is constructing an image that is not us. Only when we truly believe it is beneficial to our well-being do we take the time to rectify misjudgements and characterizations about our person. Otherwise, we thank them kindly and move on.

We all have a habit of taking things personally, especially public negativity. Let me paint a picture. I'm driving down the road in my car and someone is tailgating me and beeping for me to move faster. There are three ways I can react. I can panic, wondering what I did wrong. I can get angry, let the road rage begin and beep back. Or I can just accept that it most likely has absolutely noth-ing to do with me and continue driving at my own, legal, pace. This latter option is the focus of this New Method. I know I'm driving well and I don't assume that I am the centre of this person's world right now. I take a holistic view of everything that is happening and accept my role as a mere cameo in their daily drama.

What allows me to take this view is understanding the following: Someone who has spent zero time with you can't possibly know you. It takes roughly fifty hours with someone before they become an acquaintance, ninety hours to forge a genuine friendship, and 200 hours to establish a close relationship. Whether it's an angry driver on the road, someone being snotty in the super-market queue, or someone commenting on your social media, this person does not know you. Therefore, their negativity cannot be about you. You know who you are, so you're good.

By the same token, you have no idea about them. About their situation. They could just be a nasty person, but I tend to believe in the good in humans and give everyone the benefit of the doubt. Something else might be stopping them being their best selves at that moment. The person in the car could have a wife in labour or a hurt family member. The angry person in the line at the super-market might be caring for someone and rushing to get home and feed them in between balancing two jobs. You don't know what's happening behind closed doors.

The New Method here is to avoid the drama, by remembering that you're not that important to others, and most people don't truly know you. When you absorb the negative energy of others, you are holding their negative emotions in every fibre of your being. It's likely you'll repress it and it will come out at a later date, usually in the form of self-hatred or anger.

If you can shift your approach from meeting people at their negativity to instead understanding that there will be plenty of other forces at play, you'll save yourself a lot of headaches. Instead of a defensive approach, try being abundant with generous support. When someone cuts into you, you can ask them how they're doing, if they're OK and if there is anything you can do to help. By doing this we can disrupt the energy exchange. It completely changes the dynamic. By acknowledging your irrelevance you can stop someone in their tracks. By not stooping down to their level, you leave them alone down there. When they're not fuelled by you reflecting their behaviour, they're left only facing themselves.

If someone is adamant that you are the problem, I stand firm that their placement of you as a central figure in their life is wrong, and if they took you off the pedestal, they would be less impacted by your actions. Too many people give others their emotional basket to hold, expecting outside people to be responsible for their feelings. Don't make anyone else the centre of your world. You'll be sorely disappointed.

By adopting this New Method, you'll find a lot more peace and contentment. You only have so much energy inside you, so instead of wasting it on insignificant events and people's opinions, preserve it and use it for something that's going to propel you towards your economic and personal success. By not taking everything so personally, we clear away the mess of distractions and upset that typically stops women advancing both in life and in their careers. It's not always about you.

New Method 40
Use Less* Words

We use clear communication to be heard and understood. By using fewer words, but words with impact, clarity and simplicity, we are more effective and powerful. We control our 'ums' and 'ahs'; pause and reflect between sentences; breathe and talk lower and slower. We don't need to add more words to convince someone of what we're trying to say. Say less.

Think quality over quantity when it comes to your communication. We are living in a time of noise. The chatter on and off line is often deafening and it can take a lot – or rather a little – to cut through. How are we able to be heard when there is so much information to consume? Use less words.

The art of communication requires constant work, but for this method, rather than thinking of the quantity of your words, I'd like you to think of the quality. People love to chat. We make our point and then keep going. The problem is, the more we talk at people, the more we risk them zoning out. To get our points across in a more

---

* I know the correct style is 'use fewer words', but 'fewer' has two syllables and 'less' has one. So I've decided to practise what I preach irrespective of the grammatical error.

clear and engaging way, we need to be comfortable using less words.

A former partner once downloaded our WhatsApp conversation and ran a script to tell me he had typed 6,000 words over the course of our dating, while I had typed 11,000. His point was that women speak more than men, or at least they did in this case. There may be many reasons why women talk more than men (some say a protein called FOXP2: the 'language gene' that is 30 per cent more present in the female brain than the male), but I'm going to focus on just one – lack of confidence.

Feeling undermined in the room, feeling that no one is listening to you, respecting you, or interested in what you are saying is understandable when women have been silenced for thousands of years. This may cause you to reinforce your point, repeat yourself, over-explain, and when you're feeling really unheard, talk louder and lose your breath. As women, we feel the need to do the extra labour of showing our knowledge and credentials and making us believable to the person doubting us. We embellish, and repeat and work hard to make ourselves understood. Think back to Ruth Bader Ginsburg having to stand up in front of her classmates and explain why she deserved the place at Harvard Law School. We are used to having to explain ourselves.

But does talking more actually solve the problem and help you step into your power, or does it work against you? Why is it important to be understood? Because we are on a mission to change the way women move through the world. Changing culture and ideology is a source of power. Ideas cannot be shared if they are not understood. How can we launch key ideas if people have to battle their way through a convolution of words to get to what we mean? We can mistake more words for more truth, but the best ideas can be drowned in unnecessary side dishes and diminish the perception of the presenter. It's as if even you don't believe what you have to say, so you keep talking to convince yourself.

The New Method here is simply to use less words. The key to using less words is to know your audience and what's important to them. I know first-hand just how tempting it can be to fluff up what you're saying. Especially when you're nervous or uncomfortable. When I'm pitching, my concepts can be grand and abstract and I'm desperate to get them all out. I want them to know how clever I am and how much research I've poured into it. But if they cannot understand it, they don't care. My first pitch deck to potential investors was so long and had way too much text on it. The reality is they don't need to know all the micro details straight away – or perhaps ever. They want to make money. They just need to see the broad strokes and the profitability milestones we're looking to hit. That's it. So I gave them the bare minimum, bit my tongue, and shared all that extra energy and excitement that I was dying to get out with my team after. To this day, the best pitch deck I've ever done has so little text on it, just a single declarative statement on my intentions and subheadings with a little data on each page. That deck raised my first venture capital cheque.

As well as the basics, learn to love silence, just like I mentioned in Start Actually Listening; frequent pauses are powerful. They might make others feel uncomfortable, but by taking a breather you allow whatever you've just said to be heard.

Keeping your points to three takeaways is another great habit. I used to find myself making my arguments in such multilayered, roundabout ways. I have what investor Alex Dunsdon calls 'Linky Brain'. I can severely overcomplicate things, as I like to ponder and think out loud. But by selecting three core messages, I immediately elevate my impact. Once you have your three, don't deviate from them.

When you use less words, you show yourself as considerate of your listeners' time – as well as improving your own productivity and efficiency. At university, we were taught a brilliant exercise that shaped my now vital skill of communicating with as little information as possible. Our goal was to create a mood board for our idea with as many images as we liked, then from that we were allowed to pick only one picture to articulate the vision. It was such a challenging task. Narrowing everything down to a single image felt impossible when I had so much to say, but it inspired me to think about what's essential versus what is merely decoration. Only being allowed to share the bare minimum stopped me trying to go above and beyond to seem like the smartest person in the room.

Imagine applying the philosophy of my university task to a pitch. Imagine if, instead of reams of paper and death by PowerPoint, what you wanted to say was on a single sheet of paper. Just one sheet with a single picture, a single sentence, and a single data point. My picture might be an all-male boardroom. My words, 'You can't be what you can't see.' And 'Less than 10 per cent of CEOs are Women' as my data point. I hope you would understand in an instant why we need the Stack World platform as a way to bring content and community for young women at work in order to close the gender leadership gap.

The goal here is to show absolute confidence that your idea can be illustrated in a clear, succinct way. A real mic drop moment is to say a few sentences and get your point across with clarity.

Get what you want, by saying what you mean. And when you've said it, stop.

New Method 41
Prove Yourself Wrong

When we feel compelled to move towards the situation or person that helps affirm our core negative beliefs, we instead try to prove ourselves wrong. Moving towards the potential pain is a way we are trying to prove ourselves right. That our inner critic is right. This serves no purpose other than to hinder our growth and make us retreat into ourselves. We try new things, meet new people. We go towards the things that give us an opportunity to rewrite our internal inner critic. We stay open to learning. By consciously choosing to challenge our negative beliefs and seek experiences that contradict them, we break the cycle of self-sabotage. Instead of seeking satisfaction in proving ourselves right about our limitations, we strive to prove ourselves wrong by embracing growth and self-discovery.

If you have negative beliefs about yourself, you may be subconsciously drawn to situations that you know will have a negative outcome. This is commonly known as 'self-fulfilling prophecies', and it's a way of proving yourself right.

For example, if you have a deep-rooted belief that you are not worthy of love (a belief you may not even be consciously aware of), you will find yourself attracted to situations that prove that you are not worthy of love. Such as dating married people, or avoidant people, or people who live in another country – anything that creates a barrier between yourself and love. This is because our brains are constantly looking for evidence to support our subconscious negative beliefs about ourselves.

There are ways to break this cycle. One way is to become aware of your negative thoughts and biases. To move them into your conscious mind. Once you're aware of them, it's time to stop proving yourself right and jump off the cycle of negativity. Mindset and performance coach Polly Bateman taught me this in the summer of 2020. I had so many negative beliefs that I've had to work through, and with her support I became aware of what was happening and how I actually enabled my own misery. The simple act of awareness gave me the first step to solving this. So, let's talk through what was happening for most of my adult life.

I was constantly experiencing negative people and negative situations with my romantic partners, business partners and friends. They didn't start out negative, in fact, they were wildly attractive. The boyfriend I was obsessed with, the friend I idolized or the business deal that was going to change everything for me – they were all seductive, attractive and completely driven by my ego. My ego wanted so badly to be right about my negative beliefs – 'See, I told you so . . .' – that it would lure me into situations it knew would not work out.

The relationships would quickly turn sour as incompatibilities started to emerge. The red flags would come up and I would ignore them. Even when I voiced to a friend that she reminded me of another friendship that did not work out, I still went there and pursued the relationship! I was a total masochist in this way. In short, I had to figure out my belief cycle to reverse it. All variations of my negative thinking came back to this single statement – 'I can only rely on myself.'

How does this show up day to day? Here are some of my negative beliefs and the things I do to prove myself right.

- No one understands me = Hanging out with people from a different social circle who I can't identify with.
- I can't rely on anyone = Hiring underqualified people so that I'll be forced to micromanage and do the job myself.
- I'll never meet anyone interesting = Never going out socially or talking to strangers at parties.
- I don't fit in = Hanging out with people who are complete opposites to me, and aren't that nice.

How many times have you had a negative thought about yourself and then immediately attracted a negative situation to prove yourself right? By working through my negative beliefs, I was able to stop being drawn towards negative situations. We all have negative thoughts floating around in our brains, whether we know it or not. But neuroplasticity, the flexible nature of the wiring within the brain, means the brain can be reprogrammed, if you make a consistent effort. So now I try and approach things differently.

I try to move towards situations that are going to prove

my negative thoughts wrong, such as dating people I would never normally date, who look different and work in different industries to my former partners.

Proving yourself wrong is done through your inner critic. So I take the negative things I often say about myself, such as:

- I'm so bad with routine.
- I'm not good at saving.
- I'm not great at hiring.
- I'm inconsistent.
- I'll never be able to scale.

And I use these thoughts to create rituals, rules and situations that enable me to prove these statements wrong, instead of moving towards awful situations that allow my ego to keep saying these nasty things about myself. A significant routine I developed was holding a session for Stack World members each week to discuss the topics of this book. I was amazed that I held these conversations every single week for close to three years consistently, and it helped me rewrite the narrative that I am an inconsistent person.

I want you to think of the last time you were in a situation where you said, 'I knew it!' or, 'I told myself so,' or 'I had a feeling,' and think about whether it was your intuition protecting you or your ego pushing you into a negative situation so that you could prove yourself right. And for this year, please aim to prove yourself wrong.

New Method 42
Calculate the Cost of Your Visibility

My physical appearance has nothing to do with my success. My work and my personal growth can stand on merit alone. I protect my visibility and don't give it away freely. I don't use my image as a tool for growth because I know that relying on something which is in constant decay is not good for my mental health or my ability to focus. I can use my intellect to find a solution that has longevity, and in a world where trends and fashions are transient, I anchor my aspirations in the stability of knowledge, resilience and innovation. By cultivating a mindset that values substance over surface, I navigate the professional landscape with purpose and don't let others use me for tokenism or eye fodder. The normal rules don't apply to women. And so I don't engage unless they pay me for this additional labour.

Unpaid labour comes in many forms and one of the iterations is in our personal likeness and image, which has never before been so accessible to the wider world through social media. While visibility is important for our ability to see role models, it is also another way that women are at a loss, as the standard for this visual image of ourselves is unequal and is exploited for gain.

The unpaid labour of women is not new news. UN Women states: 'From cooking and cleaning . . . to taking care of children and the elderly, women carry out at least two and a half times more unpaid household and care work than men. As a result, they have less time to engage in . . . paid labour. Unpaid work is valued to be 10 and 39 per cent of the Gross Domestic Product and can contribute more to the economy than the manufacturing, commerce or transportation sectors.'

As a conscious woman, I've always assumed I had swerved the majority of activities that are typically defined as gendered unpaid labour. I share all responsibility for my son 50/50 with his father. I have a local cleaner once a week, and on the days I'm not with my son, I mostly cook and care for myself. But in my career journey, I've begun to reflect on a form of workplace unpaid labour that women endure, and one that puts them at relative risk. The labour of visibility.

For female founders in particular, this can be acute. Women starting companies today are often expected to play the additional and unpaid role of brand ambassador, CMO, DEI and company therapist. Where in larger organizations (just as in higher-income households) these roles would be split between several experts, early-stage female founders are expected to deliver on these skills and always be accessible to both their employees and their customers, in addition to learning how to be a CEO and build a company.

What does this look like in reality? Sharing your journey on social media and being visible can be inspiring, but it can also be a time suck. Male founders and investors just don't understand this huge time loss, but let me explain . . . No one takes a 'selfie' and posts it immediately. The 'Insta' in Instagram is a lie.

You take anything from 10 to 30 pictures
    (10 minutes)
Then use some editing tools (5 minutes)
Then spend time constructing a caption
    (5 minutes)
Then constantly refresh the post to see the likes
    (10+ minutes)
30 minutes lost in the day, minimum

Some people even send the caption to friends before posting, waiting for positive affirmation first. And it doesn't end there, as you lose micro minutes through the day when you constantly refresh your profile to get those dopamine hits of likes and comments. Not to mention that you'll probably get distracted and start scrolling.

Traditional media such as a magazine cover or interview is a whole different level of lost time and brainspace for women. Male founders can rock up to a shoot with a less than fresh T-shirt and a £10 haircut; meanwhile we need a two-hour session for hair, manicure and makeup. It wouldn't be OK for women to just turn up in 'civilian clothes' and be photographed, because as we have gathered from previous chapters, the societal expectations are different. Another day of work is lost every time I have to show up shiny. Could you imagine any of us being photographed for a magazine in a tracksuit, no makeup, no blow-dry? The vision of the male technical founder, wearing a nondescript shoe, a backpack, with unkempt hair and a slight musty smell, makes sense if you consider that they are working on their start-up, up to twenty hours a day head down and focused. So why can't it work for us?

I distinctly remember telling a board member that post fundraise I was going to get my head down and do fewer interviews, given that we didn't need to attract investors in the press, and he shook his head: 'No, no, no, you need to be out there!' Out there, I mused? But at what cost? Being a brand ambassador is an additional job that your company should pay for. Instead it becomes your unpaid labour. Do you know what else we could be doing in those precious hours? Working on our financial plan, building our strategic relationships, reading a book, speaking to a mentor, meeting with future investors, doing 1:1s with our teams, in fact ANYTHING to help us learn how to be a better CEO. Founders in general are often visionary, but inexperienced, and require time and support in order to gain the skills so that their business maturity can match their brilliance.

Most people who run companies with several hundred employees get decades to gain this experience. For a venture capital backed founder, you're automatically expected to know how to do this and are given just a few months and years to catch up to the level of an established CEO. We can't blame our rare female founders (the true unicorns) if they were handed millions of dollars overnight and were then unable to run their companies because of the demands we placed upon them to also spend time being influencers. We know that inexperienced leadership leads to dysfunctional companies. Some of the most incredible female founders I know had just one or two junior roles before deciding to become pioneers and go their own way.

Being an influencer is a full-time job. It's a fun and challenging job requiring varied skills. You become your own mini company. Sometimes a huge company. Being an influencer is an exciting career path. But by expecting female founders to take on the unpaid labour of brand ambassadors, etc., you're advocating for time spent NOT becoming a better CEO. Consider that the next time you're quietly judging a female founder on how she looks, lives, or in fact anything outside of her ability to scale a company. Consider that the next time you place expectations on a CEO to also be a brand ambassador or influencer. Consider that the next time you feel like you *ought to* post on social media for the sake of your company.

In addition to the time cost, the financial cost is huge. Because of that expectation to be 'always on', there is a requirement for hair, skin, nails and clothes to be of a certain standard. After a quick text to my founder friends on what they spend on grooming, here's what I found:

Hair – £100 to £600
Nails – £120
Facials – £150
Clothes – Varied, from £300 to £3,000
Lashes – £100
Tanning – £50

Waxing – £50, although many had invested in
    laser hair removal for efficiency
Miscellaneous beauty products and makeup –
    £100 to £800

PER MONTH! And these costs cannot be written off as a business expense, despite many of them being unwritten requirements of the business. You are paying for these yourself, meaning that at the end of the year, your personal wealth is down.

But by far the biggest cost to your visibility is the public flogging that is a very real and present danger the minute you make a rookie error. Consider the spate of female founder takedowns that were prevalent in the media between 2018 and 2022. Women who managed to collectively raise hundreds of millions in venture capital funding, despite the odds, were torn down on everything from what they fed their pets to their wedding registry lists. Some of them were cancelled and some lost their companies entirely. Alongside this, several male founders, who lost billions of dollars, committed fraud, sexually harassed their employees or simply permitted a toxic culture to thrive, were not only revered as heroes but given second and third chances and continued to raise funding. Some committed actual crimes and suffered little public recourse.

What's the difference? For the female founder, the blending of private and public means blurring the lines between sharing what you're building and sharing your very being. You become inspirational, aspirational and iconic. With each fundraise, each new office and each new hire, an army of strangers (not customers) is celebrating your every win. They put you on a pedestal, worshipping your every move and lifting you higher and higher, within a narrower and narrower framework, until one day you make one misstep and fall off. There isn't enough room for you to make mistakes, and the fall from grace is painful and indeed visible.

One of my good friends was cancelled online, and it cost her a year of her life in recovery, another year of self-doubt and a final year of starting again through the lens of fear, not passion and excitement. The cost of her very visible rise was a fall so deep, we were concerned she might never be the same again.

The media played a key role in her downfall. Ironically, it was female journalists who dissected her every move with a freakish obsession, with one even admitting her own insecurities around this founder. What this journalist probably didn't realize is that by taking down my friend because she felt a little bit envious, it caused a ripple impact on the female start-up community as a whole, generating mistrust in women by investors and contributing to a decline in funding. Bo Ren, a Silicon Valley-based product manager turned investor, stated on X, 'I hope we can stop attacking women founders, b/c when we take down one, we collectively condemn a whole group.'

In 2023, US start-ups with all-women teams received 1.9 per cent (or around $4.5 billion) out of the around $238.3 billion in venture capital allocated, according to

PitchBook data. That percentage is down from the already pathetic 2.4 per cent all-women teams raised in 2021. It has been on a steady decline since 2018. The media plays a role in trashing female founders. Women play a role by putting themselves in the firing line and being public personas. Investors play a role by expecting women to be free marketeers. The public plays a role by demanding that their business leaders become influencer icons, and on and on it goes.

The takedown of female founders stops other women wanting to start businesses – why knowingly put yourself through it? The assumption that by starting a company we'll be expected to become a public figure, and thus be exposed to the risk of cancel culture, may influence us in the decision to just not start a company, much like the way so few women run for public office because of the fear of online abuse. This is quite possibly the scariest and most disastrous result for tech and sets us back another fifty years. We must allow women to build companies, and fail quietly, with the same frequency and fervour as men.

So what is to be done? I've tried to quit social media over and over again, and it's only now that I find myself genuinely posting less and less. It took some time to get here. I would become an online recluse for a few months, then somehow get dragged back in, under the myth that it is essential for my business. But with that free time you can build up other sales channels. Repeatable and scalable ones that don't rely on your face. By getting off social, I soon realized that I had more time for generating other owned communication channels because I wasn't posting on a rented platform.

This has been difficult because I've always found joy in sharing random bits of my life. In 2006 I was uploading blurry BlackBerry phone pictures to Facebook as I travelled around the world. I was on Myspace and Tumblr and Blogspot and I loved to pour my thoughts out on to the internet to my community, but now times have changed. The purity of a visual diary has been polluted by Big Tech and the innocence of sharing your favourite things is now sullied by 'in partnership with'. For a brief moment, visibility was incredible for the first generation of this new wave of women-founded businesses. There is no way that my first business, WAH Nails, would have become so well-known had I not been very early on Tumblr and Instagram. But then the algorithm changed, we became the product, and as a business account we were expected to pay for attention and penalized when we didn't. If the business account is suffering, you merge your private life with this company asset in the hope that the halo effect of your personal 'likes' will result in business 'sales', and the cost of your visibility begins to rack up.

It is understandable why we get caught in the trap. The reason why female founders end up becoming brand ambassadors is because it's a really low-cost way to get your business off the ground, which makes sense if they don't receive funding. Start-up holy grail is spending as little money acquisition via Meta ads as possible, and instead getting 'free and organic' growth. But let's be real – it's not truly organic if I have to take several hours of my week to be a brand ambassador for my company, is it? What you're not paying Meta in ads, you're paying them with your time.

Personally I think relying on the CEO to be brand ambassador is a non-scalable acquisition channel which doesn't actually help you understand your customer, because you have no data or tracking on them. You just have some likes. So try a New Method and calculate (and cut) the cost of your visibility. There are so many other ways of early product adoption that don't involve seeing what you ate for breakfast, so work on developing your proper business hustle and experiment with them: WOM, referrals, content marketing, network sales, etc. If your board wants to wheel you out as brand ambassador (and if you enjoy it), you should ask for a pay rise to cover the unpaid labour (and the outfits and beauty treatments) that you're putting in on top of your additional job. Don't let it cost you your time, your money, or your passion.

New Method 43
Don't Let the Small Stuff Slide

We are the creators of culture, whether we realize it or not, and we collectively possess the power of our voices. We recognize those small moments that may cause harm, both to us and to others. It's the small, persistent actions that bring about significant change. With each word we speak and every action we take, we contribute to building a culture rooted in equality and respect. We are not alone in this journey. We have allies and supporters who share our vision of a more just world. Together, we will foster a society that values every individual, regardless of their background or identity. We acknowledge our power to challenge the status quo and confront uncomfortable situations. Each time we do so, we create ripples of change in the fabric of our society. We are dedicated to preventing death by a thousand papercuts, and we will continue to work towards a more inclusive and harmonious world.

Racism. Sexism. Any other -isms. Bullying. Microaggression. Injustice. Anything that labels a group of people and oppresses them unstopped, unchecked and unconfronted will grow like a mushroom cloud. When you let things slide, perhaps because you think they're small or insignificant, you're setting expectations. You're enforcing loose boundaries regardless of whether you want to or not. It's up to you to choose healthy expectations for yourself and others.

When I was younger, I was sometimes hesitant to speak up because of social expectations. Quite frankly, it's frightening. Speaking up means standing out, setting yourself apart and completely going against the human nature of being a social animal. We don't want to stand out. A few millennia ago, going against the tribe came with the risk of getting kicked out, and no one could survive the wolves and the bitter cold, but that fear no longer serves us. Staying within a tribe for the sake of it is no longer always a matter of life or death, but it *is* a case of integrity or inauthenticity.

Fast forward to now, and we also have the added pressure as women to live under the guise of sugar, spice and all things nice. Women are expected to be likeable and polite. Standing up against something that doesn't sit right with you isn't considered agreeable and goes against the idea of how one is supposed to act. Don't Let the Small Stuff Slide is about breaking through that fear, trusting your intuition and saying what we think anyway.

Perhaps someone in a meeting says something a little off-key and at the time it slips under your radar. It's not until you're home that night that you realize how inappropriate their statement was, but as you're no longer in the moment, you brush it off. To get out of this habit, address the issue as soon as possible. If you realize it after the fact, send a text to arrange a coffee with that colleague or actively try to bump into them the next day. If you'll never see this person again, chalk it up to experience and you'll be quick to pick up on it next time.

Eventually, you'll train yourself to listen out for certain signals and catch these moments in their tracks. It's much more impactful to speak sooner rather than later. Imagine being out with the girls and they leave you on your own. You wake up feeling uncomfortable, but don't say anything. You let it build up and annoy you. You continue to feel disrespected and after a year you have an outburst. They're rightly going to respond with: 'What are you talking about? What party?' The best time to have raised your grievance was when you woke up the next day and decided it didn't work for you. Resentment matures like a fine wine and it's under the duration of time that it develops. I've been on the receiving end of this, dumbfounded when someone raises something that I did months ago, that I didn't even realize I was doing. Not speaking up can leave everyone feeling confused, disrespected and at a loss as to what is actually going on.

Taking the approach of tackling the small stuff head on was key for me to feel like I was gaining authority in my personal affairs but also creating a company culture that I would be proud of.

In home life, this could be about domestic duties. Taking out the trash, booking family doctor's appointments, ordering toilet rolls. All these are gender neutral activities. So whether you live with a partner or in a shared home with friends, assigning these duties equally upfront is key. When you become the person who constantly removes used teabags from the worktop, you're setting expectations for how you want to be treated. That teabag is small, but letting it slide speaks volumes.

At work, I'm afraid the small stuff comes at you daily. Mansplaining, not being invited to work functions, asking the female colleagues to make the meeting tea. The list goes on . . . My golden, golden rule is NIP IT IN THE BUD immediately. Don't let it grow into a poisonous flower. In my early business experience with WAH Nails, it took me a while to realize how one toxic team member can affect the whole company. I distinctly remember the first time I had to let someone go because it wasn't the right cultural fit. A new nail artist had been making so many small snide comments to another, younger nail artist that I found her crying in the bathrooms. I was naïve in workplace bullying, but I understood that my mistake was not to have picked it up *the first time*; instead I let it get to a point when one team member was trauma-tized and another was now out of a job.

What could I have done differently to not let the small stuff slide, the first time I hear it? My initial strategy is to embarrass the perpetrator with kindness. Rather than get angry, defensive or accusatory, I simply talk to them as if they were a mean-spirited child (because to me, the unkindness is coming from their wounded inner child). Approach calling out from a place of constructive criti-cism with nothing but good intent.

> That's not a nice thing to say, is it?
> How do you think that makes her feel?
> Why would you say something like that?

I also use phrases that show that their normal is not my normal, thus recalibrating their world to fit in other viewpoints:

'What decision-making process did *you* take to come to this conclusion?'
'Is this a normal way of communicating for you?'
'Is this how your family and friends talk to each other?'

A good example of this is with a friend who comes from a dockyard working family. He frequently swore at me during conversations, adding extra wounds to an already heated moment, and I had to explain to him that in my Jamaican, church-going family we just didn't use profanity in that way. Of course I swear in casual conversation, but not as an insult and most definitely not to a partner or friend. To him, it was small and insignificant and just a normal way of communicating, but it made me feel deeply uncomfortable and I couldn't let it slide.

My final strategy is to show them how unscalable their microaggressions are – although this can sometimes feel patronizing and needs to be delivered in a considered tone. I want them to understand that small negativity only works in small situations. Early on at Beautystack, my first start-up, we had a tester who had to go through all the beauty professionals' pages and check them for quality. After a few hours she said: 'Oh my gosh, I don't know why people would do this to their face!' – referring to a Botox treatment. I knew this criticism of our users had to be dealt with immediately, otherwise it would become company culture to joke about our users in an Us vs Them scenario. I pulled her aside and explained that our users are free women who can do whatever they want without fear of our judgement. But that wasn't the main thing. This attitude doesn't help the company scale and she needs to think of the bigger picture. If she is judging our first 100 users, why would the first 100k join? At this point, I start to try to get the person to understand that what we all want is to be successful in our various ways. Growing our userbase will translate into more sales for the company. That means access to more funding, better access to hiring talent or a promotion to the next stage in her individual career. Will this small-minded approach get us there? Understanding people's motivations can help your argument. So I say:

> 'I know that this might be working for you now, but will this approach work to get us to the next stage?'
> 'I remember you saying that [insert topic] was important to you – do you think this is the best way to achieve that goal?'
> 'I understand that this might be OK now, in this small room and in this small world, but would you be OK with this being out publicly and in the bigger world?'

This also works in reverse if you are the one dishing out the small stuff. When I'm physically and emotionally drained I can also let my lower self take over. So how do I rectify it swiftly? When I act in an untoward way, or as what I know to be my worst self, I apologize immediately, sometimes right at the end of the meeting, in front of everyone. This breeds a culture of compassion and respect. Understand this is a two-way street. If you want to freely express your boundaries, when others cross them, be open to people doing the same back to you.

Over time, if you nip all the bad buds and don't let the small stuff slide, you'll be setting clear healthy boundaries and a thriving company culture. If it feels wrong in your belly, deal with it there and then. Neither you nor anyone else should have to hold those negative feelings or trauma. The phrase 'Revenge is a dish best served cold' comes from an aggressive, warring mentality. Switch it up and think about how you can create harmony from the get-go.

New Method 44
Pick Your Battles

In a world brimming with conflict, we embrace the wisdom of choosing our battles wisely. When we find ourselves entangled in a web of endless disputes, both trivial and substantial, they drain our energy and divert our attention from what truly matters. We embark on a path of discernment and deliberate action, understanding the significance of preserving our resources for battles that truly warrant our time and effort. Women's energy is already spread thinly. Let us not spread it across irrelevant issues.

Not every battle you come across will be worth your time, energy, or focus, but also understand that conflict, if well handled, can cause growth. As the philosopher emperor Marcus Aurelius said, it's also completely normal. If we are to exist in a social world and if we are to go outside our familiar networks and communities, misunderstandings will inevitably follow. Consider the opening lines of his famous journal, *Meditations*:

> Begin each day by telling yourself: Today I shall be meeting with interference, ingratitude, insolence, disloyalty, ill-will and selfishness – all of them due to the offender's ignorance of what is good or evil. But for my part I

have long perceived the nature of good and its nobility, the nature of evil and its meanness, and also the nature of the culprit himself, who is my brother (not in the physical sense, but as a fellow creature similarly endowed with reason and a share of the divine); therefore none of those things can injure me, for nobody can implicate me in what is degrading. Neither can I be angry with my brother or fall foul of him; for he and I were born to work together, like a man's two hands, feet or eyelids, or the upper and lower rows of his teeth. To obstruct each other is against Nature's law – and what is irritation or aversion but a form of obstruction.

So how do you differentiate between a battle and a war? By battles, I mean mild irritations, arguments and minor conflicts. The day-to-day annoyances. Because arguments are physically and emotionally draining, I have learned to apply the New Method of carefully choosing which ones are worth my time. I do this by asking myself a few questions:

1. Where are they coming from? Do we have the same values and ideals? Are we looking at the world from the same angle? Are we speaking the same 'language'?
2. If we are coming from the same place, what is their intention with their statement or behaviour? What are they trying to achieve here? What am I trying to achieve with my disagreement?

3. If we are not coming from the same place, will I learn something new? Will this insight or wildly differing point of view expand my knowledge of a subject or community?
4. What will this fight cost me?
5. How will this disagreement affect me in the long term? Will it genuinely have an impact on my life and the lives of others after me, or will it be irrelevant the minute I stop turning my attention to it?

I work through these questions to come to a decision on who I'm giving my time to. The last one is particularly important – will it be irrelevant the minute I stop turning my attention to it? So many times we give energy and fuel to a situation that has no real importance in the long game of our lives.

In addition to this decision-making framework, I also don't engage with anyone who doesn't have the ability to reason or be self-aware. Narcissists are a good example. They usually find it difficult to see another's point of view or to be reasonable within arguments. So I don't attempt to argue with them. I have a friend who is always getting involved in fights with strangers on Twitter. She gets really stressed and worked up, holding her phone until her knuckles turn white and furiously tapping every response to the point where I'm worried she might punch through the screen. My thoughts are always: 'Why are you bothered?' As my old Jamaican hairdresser used to say when people would discuss celebrity gossip, 'Me nuh kno dem and dem nuh kno me' (I don't know them and they don't know me).

The New Method here is simple. Don't allow yourself to march into every battle placed on your doorstep. There will always be people who disagree with you; you don't always have to be the educator, caretaker and activist. Sometimes you can just say – it is what it is. Pick your battles and think about attending them with loving disengagement versus fighting them.

So which ones are worth my time? Very few, to be honest. I'm too busy using that brainspace on myself, my family or my business. That said, given our current divisive and polarizing world, I often feel like I'm going to learn something from a conflict. I think it's important to learn and study alternative viewpoints, so even though I don't agree with far-right groups, I will often listen. I use these moments to build up my knowledge of an opposing argument, learn empathy and respect for others' views and practise my active listening, powers of persuasion, negotiation techniques or just compassion.

Buddist monk Thich Nhat Hanh founded the Plum Village Retreat, which aims to foster civil dialogue between two nations in a long-term conflict:

For the past few years, groups of Palestinians and Israelis have come to Plum Village to practise mindfulness. When they first come, they are often suspicious of each other. They can't look at each other with sympathetic eyes. But with practice and the support of the community, they are able to calm their suffering, their anger, their suspicion and their hate. After several days, they are able to see that the other group also suffers. It takes time. (Plumvillage.org)

Why is this battle (one of compassion and under-standing) an important one to attend? Because of numbers 4 and 5 – what it will cost the nations and who it will directly affect in the long term. The generational trauma of literal war. At Plum Village, it starts small. The battle of meeting your fellow man in the eye, cooking together and sharing stories. This is a battle of empathy worth attending to.

Which arguments are not worth fighting? Those with bigots, conspiracy theorists, internet trolls or people with bad manners. Spam calls. Anyone who has no actual power, but is determined to use their voice to do harm. Like Marcus Aurelius said, 'None of those things can injure me.'

Naturally, there will be times when the small stuff (see previous section) is worth fighting for because it's a microaggression that if left unchecked will develop into something more sinister and define the way we see the world. But do you really need to argue with your taxi driver? Or a stranger who bumped into you accidentally? Or trolls on the internet?

For the first time in my life, I recently met a climate change denier. I had just finished a shoot, and exhausted, I got into a private taxi. I had two hours to get home and get myself ready to do another event and shoot, which I was quite nervous about. The taxi driver began telling me how hot it was outside. 'Well, climate change ...' I shrugged before tapping at my emails, and he looked at me in the rearview mirror before telling me, 'Well ... I think it's all made up.' I stayed silent, allowing him to continue. 'When I was a boy at school, fifty years ago, they said, "The planet is heating up." They didn't say nothing about climate change and it's just natural that the planet is heating up. It's not our fault.'

So I am starting to calibrate quickly, working through my mental models. He was at school in the 1960s. He is British Asian. He is a cab driver. He believes this is a fifty-year-old conversation. What does all this mean?

The 1960s was a time of huge educational changes. Also, post-war, the country might not want another bogeyman. Being Asian in Britain in the 1960s may have given our man a desire to fit in. To agree with disagreeable arguments and seem like one of the lads. A cab driver. His work literally contributes to the emissions. Guilt? Shame? Denial? And finally, he remembers a conversation about climate half a century ago.

As everything else is very personal, I start with the last one: 'Well, you do know that the Industrial Revolution is around 250 years ago and prior to that, humans had never created such vast amounts of carbon emissions. You had the emergence of steam trains, aeroplanes, cars, all in quick succession. So yes, your teachers at school may have been discussing it fifty years ago, but there were warnings about greenhouse gases in 1896. We just didn't call it climate change.'

At this point, I can see he knows I vaguely know my stuff and that I'm also not going to let him continue.

So he tries a different tack. 'I just feel like they're charging us so much money to solve climate change and they aren't doing anything with it.' Ah, so now I can see it's about his livelihood and the cost of his work. Like most public aggression, it's about a personal fear of the threat to his way of life.

'I agree, public money is being wasted. I think it is always being wasted in every department. That said, climate change technology – such as carbon capture – is so new, we need to continually invest in it, to make it efficient. Just like we did with the steam trains, planes and cars too. I hate the additional cost today, but in reality, if we don't, our kids will suffer.'

At this point, I've stated some basic facts in a few sentences and I start making phone calls to establish that the conversation is over. This is not a battle worth continuing. He continues to grumble on but with less enthusiasm.

When would it have mattered to continue this fight? If he was in charge of legislation around climate change. If he was a teacher or in a position where he had to share his views at scale. Then it would matter, as his beliefs would influence policy.

Knowing when to fight your corner and when to let things go works wonders for protecting your peace. You're the one who's prioritized your own time and energy, so who's the real winner here?

New Method 45
How to Deal with a Narcissist

While we are doing this work on ourselves, and are likely at our most vulnerable, open and wounded, we unconsciously send signals to predators in the form of abusers and narcissists who meet us at our lowest common wound. Behind the façade of their self-assurance lies a fragile self-esteem that's easily damaged by the most minor criticism, and their abuse can have lasting effects. While doing the work, it can be very easy to self-soothe with a saviour-like relationship with a narcissist, someone who does and says what you need to hear. We remain disciplined, protecting ourselves by making good choices about who we allow into our lives and trusting our intuition.

Being in a relationship or friendship with a narcissist can be one of the most traumatic life experiences. The effects are wide-ranging and long-lasting, determining how you view yourself and others for many years to come.

Narcissistic personality disorder, or NPD, is a complex and dynamic set of traits that can show up in a variety of ways and degrees, making it challenging to diagnose and understand fully. The presentation of NPD can range from subtle narcissistic traits to more extreme and disruptive behaviour, with individual differences in how these traits manifest and evolve over time. The simplest sign I look out for, in others as well as in myself, is the ability to be charming and manipulative and suck people into a vortex, while also being insecure, full of distrust and completely jealous.

The Mayo Clinic states that people with narcissistic personality disorder can:

- Have an exaggerated sense of self-importance.
- Have a sense of entitlement and require constant, excessive admiration.
- Expect to be recognized as superior even without achievements that warrant it.
- Exaggerate achievements and talents.
- Be preoccupied with fantasies about success, power, brilliance, beauty or the perfect mate.
- Believe they are superior and can only associate with equally special people.
- Monopolize conversations and belittle or look down on people they perceive as inferior.
- Expect special favours and unquestioning compliance with their expectations.
- Take advantage of others to get what they want.
- Have an inability or unwillingness to recognize the needs and feelings of others.
- Be envious of others and believe others envy them.
- Behave in an arrogant or haughty manner, coming across as conceited, boastful and pretentious.
- Insist on having the best of everything – for instance, the best car or office.

At the same time, people with narcissistic personality disorder have trouble handling anything they perceive as criticism, and they can:

- Become impatient or angry when they don't receive special treatment.
- Have significant interpersonal problems and easily feel slighted.
- React with rage or contempt and try to belittle the other person to make themselves appear superior.
- Have difficulty regulating emotions and behaviour.
- Experience major problems dealing with stress and adapting to change.
- Feel depressed and moody because they fall short of perfection.
- Have secret feelings of insecurity, shame, vulnerability and humiliation.

Of all the information I found about those with NPD, I found this Mayo Clinic list to be the most accurate in reflecting my experience. The biggest realization? Narcissists are everywhere, and some elements are even within me. Their sense of entitlement means that they manage to climb to the upper echelons of society, which also reinforces their belief in their own self-importance. They are also highly visible, because of their hypnotic attractiveness. And they're notoriously difficult to get rid of. Once they've realized that they can feed off you, they won't want to let go of the power you give them. Because of this, it's worth understanding as much as you can about those with NPD, as it's likely they'll present themselves in a partner, boss or family member at some point in your life.

Once you've identified the narcissist in your life, you then have to make an essential New Methods decision – keep or cut. Sometimes I was able to trim, but sometimes I had to learn how to cope and deal with narcissists in my life rather than cut them off. My self-development was supercharged by needing regular protective mechanisms. I had to safeguard my sanity. If you haven't had a narcissist in your life, these suggestions may seem drastic. But if you have lived through this, or are currently living through this, you'll understand the need for concrete, high-walled boundaries. Here are some of the ways that I deal with narcissists.

Inventory: Narcissists are experts at gaslighting, making you repeatedly question yourself and 'what happened'. So I would regularly print off all messages and emails, and keep lists of the facts of how things *actually happened*. When I was vulnerable to gaslighting, I could refer to my record of reality.

Distance: If this is possible for you, move to another city or another part of town to create some physical distance. This is only a minor help, but it will give you new things to experience to supersede the trauma of your previous environmental situation. For every step we retread, we may be reliving the trauma.

Block: Typically, I try not to block people, but narcissists will try every single way of communicating with you and the minute you open a text or answer the phone, you become sucked into their black hole of back-and-forth messages. Nothing they have to say is going to affect you positively. Block them on all your standard messaging and create a completely separate email address or phone number for them only, if you have to, so that you can answer them in your own time.

Use the law: Whether it's for custody, harassment at work or a restraining order, use the law to create legal boundaries and exercise them the minute they are crossed. Get a court order if necessary.

Therapy: I didn't have therapy at the time for my traumatic experiences with narcissists, and even now, many roads of healing lead back to those experiences. I advise professional help for unbiased support. Your friends will be sick of hearing you talk about this person, as they'll consume your life and you do not want to pass on your trauma to those that you love.

Create time boundaries: I have realized that after one hour with a narcissist things will start to take a downward turn and begin to enter into the realm of rudeness, snideness and conflict, as we become comfortable enough in the conversation to say what we really think.

No matter how good a time you're having, set your alarm, make your excuses and leave.

Listen to your friends: One of my wake-up calls was when my friends said how stressful my relationship with narcissists was *for them*. This was before terms like gaslighting, codependency and narcissism were in the common vocabulary. They didn't know how to verbalize what was happening to me, and I didn't realize how much our ongoing drama was affecting them. I feel such sadness that this situation affected their well-being as well as my own. I remember one of my team gave me a postcard saying 'Play It Cool', which used to ring in my ears. Try to reflect on the impact this type of relationship might have on anyone who sees you as their role model. Their heroine is suffering and there is nothing they can do about it.

But ignore your parents: Narcissists are incredible guests – charming, sociable and confident – and they are often able to bamboozle your parents or elders as they know how to say and do the right thing. It can be frustrating when those who are supposed to be protecting you are able to be so easily fooled, but refer to your inventory and ignore your parents.

Forget mediators and meeting in the middle: For similar reasons, mediators or friends as

334

go-betweens don't work. Even some authorities are bamboozled by a narcissist's deception. Unless they're NPD specialists and have seen this behaviour before, they too get charmed. I've found that you cannot be neutral or equal to a narcissist. For them, their sense of self-importance means a neutral response is positive and means 'yes', so I would err on the side of negative to survive. You have to be colder than neutral to remain civil and not involve anyone else unless they are professionally trained and know the full story.

Learn the art of negotiation: I became interested in negotiation purely to be able to manage the many, many argumentative conversations without getting spun in circles. Narcissists try every angle of accusation or try to find ways to confuse you, discredit you or pick holes in what you said. Now I laugh when someone tries to do this, as I can read it a mile off.

Figure out why you: The more I learned about narcissistic personality disorder, and accepted it as a mental health issue, the more I realized that I cannot change this person. So after working on negotiation tactics so that I can manage them, I started to shift the focus to myself. I would stop saying – why are they like this? Instead, I would ask – what made me so susceptible to being coerced like this? Looking at my past, I realized that experiencing emotional neglect made me vulnerable to love bombing. I would feel proud to have someone who was obsessed with me. I wanted desperately to be loved, making me a ripe target for someone who could shower me with it. I realized that a narcissist was able to fill the void inside me. So I focused on filling it for myself.

Have compassion: Narcissists are made, not born. It's not known what causes narcissistic personality disorder. Like that of other mental illnesses, it is likely to be complicated, and studies claim it can be linked to the following factors:

- Environment – mismatches in parent–child relationships, with either excessive adoration or excessive criticism that is poorly attuned to the child's experience.
- Genetics – inherited characteristics.
- Neurobiology – the connection between the brain, behaviour and thinking.

I try to hold the two things in my head at the same time, to have compassion for their childhood experience while also knowing that their actions have been abusive and wrong.

Keep busy: The narcissist will absorb all your physical and mental energy if you let them. I found that by keeping extremely busy and making my life so full, I wasn't able to give any time or thought to it. It's pointless to say, 'Don't think about them,' because if they're a true narcissist they will consume your thoughts. But until you've worked through the deeper issues and can block them out with ease, keep busy. If you don't keep busy, they will keep *you* busy with their demands and self-imposed deadlines. 'If you don't text me back by tomorrow, I'm going to . . .'

Live well: Exist in love, not hate. Eat clean, don't drink. Keep your body pure and your mind will follow. Try various healing techniques and figure out what works for you. Smile as you walk. Bathe in nature. Learn from the ancients, read philosophy, and seek wisdom. Work on yourself. Looking back, I can see how angry and hateful I was back then. Revenge is being your best self, on your own terms.

Make money: One of the reasons I'm so passionate about women making money is because the increase in earnings can result in the biggest shift in dealing with a narcissist – the power of choice. Having the finances to fight and the independence not to allow anyone to control you is absolutely vital. Total independence infuriates a narcissist. They can no longer use their emotions or money to own you.

When I reflect on the above list, I mourn the time that was wholly and completely absorbed by my numerous experiences with narcissists. It still stifles me in relationships today, as I am unable to trust my own judgement and will often end good relationships the minute I fear I might be 'consumed' again. It has made me create barriers between people so that 'no one can ever hurt me again', and has raised my bar for relationships much higher, as I refuse to be with anyone who shows even the slightest tendency towards narcissism, even something as simple as someone who regularly cuts in front of people while driving!

Something else I have noticed is that I am often attracted to women who have also experienced parents or partners who are narcissists, and we subconsciously bond over our traumas. Over time, the friendships become toxic, as both of us take on the wound of our abuse and become abusers of each other, experiencing criticism, jealousy and nastiness. Not only do narcissists impact you directly, but they impact the way you move through the world and your future relationships.

I often wonder what would have happened if I had acted on the very first red flags, if I had just kept walking without looking back. My intuition with narcissists was active and I ignored it. I wonder for only a moment, because this experience has given me so many positive things and made my life infinitely richer in the long term. Narcissists have given me the ability to understand more about human nature and the skills to deal with difficult situations. They have shown me how resilient we truly can be.

New Method 46
Choose Your Front Row

The people we allow in the theatre of our lives have an impact on the way we deliver the performance, so we choose our front row wisely. Rather than cut off friends that no longer cheer us, we simply move them to the back row, understanding that when we cut a relationship, we are suppressing ourselves. We fill our audience with those who are rooting for us while giving us constructive criticism and feedback. We have the power and capacity to control who we share our innermost experiences with, deciding to stay with those who make us feel safe to perform and letting go of those who give us stage fright.

It can be easy to think that those who do you harm need to be entirely cut out of your life. Friends who betrayed you, lovers who cheated on you, colleagues who let you down – that sort of thing. You may say to yourself, 'I am never speaking to that person ever again!' and I'm certain you mean it. The issue is, when you cut someone out, you're only cutting yourself.

The act of cutting someone out requires you to emotionally disconnect from someone who you once had a great attraction to or affection for. To cut them off requires you to suppress the part of you that felt connected to them. You're suppressing a connection which can be damaging to yourself. A New Method I learned from my first-ever coach, Cheryl Clements, is to choose your front row. Reorganize your relationship circle and stretch that connection until it's just a loosely held, thin band that doesn't choke your emotions or control your mood. Be grateful for the time you spent with them and the lessons learned, but don't force yourself to wish it never happened.

Imagine your life is a theatre. When you are performing on stage, your front row gets to see the sweat, the spittle, the blood rushing to the veins in your temples and the imprints of your nails on your palm as you clench your fists. They may see that your knee is trembling, even as you deliver a stellar performance. Your front row gets to see the real, unabridged version of you. They are given access to your innermost thoughts and fears. They may be the people you talk on the phone to for an hour every evening or those who you turn to when you're in your most desperate hour. Your front row is your main crew.

If you feel that you need to cut someone out, try moving them back a few rows instead. Phase them out. They may move from being the person you go on holiday with to someone you see twice a year at drinks parties. Or perhaps they were the person you would always call when you were at rock bottom, and they move to become someone you only message on social media with clipped comments on how well you/they/the kids are doing. They're now a Level 2 acquaintance.

Some will demand an explanation as to why they're now in the cheap seats. Some will even ignore you and, much like the pompous theatre-goer waving their VIP ticket around, may continually sneak into the front row seats they believe they deserve. This is natural – if anything, it's bound to happen, because negative people like the power they hold over you. Don't worry, just stand your ground and gently usher them to the back. Remember, this is *your* theatre and *you* control the seating plan.

Some people acquire their front row seat by default. You went to the same school/lived near each other/ played on the same sports teams/your parents were friends – arbitrary details that bear no weight on how much you can trust them now. Your front row might have been filled easily with these default friends without thinking. It's OK if your front row is not strong yet, as you're learning who will best appreciate your performance.

During your twenties, your front row may seem like musical chairs, with friendships sparking high and fast, only to burn out before the first act is over. Don't berate yourself. This is the part of your life where you're figuring out who works for you, and in fact the quicker you downgrade those relationships, the faster you're learning. In my business, I've gone from taking six months to fire someone, to three months, to now recognizing within thirty days whether a team member will work out or not. Playing Jenga with the people in your life means you start to understand which of those smiling faces helps you give your best performance in life and which of them makes you a bit nervous to go full throttle. It's totally normal to enter your thirties thinking: 'I have no real friends,' because the constant movement makes you feel that those in your front row are transient. I got over this by saying to myself that I would rather perform to an empty theatre than have people pretending to like what they see, but secretly passing mean notes about the quality of my delivery. Waiting for your ideal audience is just as important as the performance itself.

How does someone lose their seat? Simple: you don't ever feel truly safe around them. The ones who do something really aggressive are easy to identify, it's the smaller and more frequent acts of betrayal that are harder to spot. It's the ones who are always rustling, giving you small frictions in your life, or whispering and gossiping about you, who need to be removed from your front row. Something inside makes you feel you cannot trust them.

In my early twenties, I was often magnetized to women who represented everything I thought was cool and chic. If they lived in the more upmarket side of town, drove a cool car, had an incredible body and all the other things that I wrongly valued as a vulnerable and inexperienced adult, I would be hooked. But a pattern would emerge. For the first few years the relationship would be fantastic, we would go on holidays, we looked good together (an important and stupid prerequisite for teen and twenties relationships) and for a moment in time, I would feel like I had a solid crew. But, over time, I realized that some of those relationships that I formed during my twenties were harmful to me.

Nothing actually changed during the relationships; however, I started to change as I began to understand my issues and listened to myself. My intuition told me that my performance was stilted, because the people occupying my front row were not rooting for me in the way I needed. By the time I was twenty-seven, I had achieved a lot but my life was also a mess. I was going through a separation, unsure about my business and moving to another city. I felt wholly inferior around some of my friends. I didn't feel graceful enough, accomplished enough or rich enough, as they were quietly discussing my performance with each other and I had no idea who to trust. I spent much time reflecting: what do I need right now to grow?

In my early years of motherhood, I found it difficult to connect with friends who had neither run a business nor had a child, and I would feel quite lonely as our life stages diverged. When I met women with similar experiences to me, I would feel instantly seen and understood. What I needed at that time were front-row occupants who would smile at me and nod encouragingly when I forgot my lines, and maybe even throw a shirt on stage if I couldn't find mine. I may have been all over the place in my performance during those years of my late twenties, but that particular front row didn't ask what I needed to be better. They didn't offer loving kindness and support, they just offered consistent negativity. I was hurting and I began to emotionally check out as a form of self-preservation, and this wasn't healthy. I would start to numb out. At the time, I cut those friends off.

Cutting people off was a regular tactic for me in my twenties, as I did not have the faculty to reorganize my relationships. It was born from repression – I would never be able to truly say what I was feeling or what

I wanted, so I said nothing. It also came from self-preservation. My life has been a series of moves towards pleasure and ease and away from pain. I would just block things in my brain and keep pushing forward. It was helpful in the short term, but in the long term I mourned those friendships because I loved all my friends and it made me mistrusting. I became scared of people engulfing me in a toxic relationship, and I would push good friends away as well as bad, unable to tell the difference. So now I practise a New Method – quietly and calmly identifying when people are no longer in my front row.

Moving this era of friendships to the back of the theatre took some time and you may experience similar binding ties. You might move in the same circles, live near each other and go to the same places, but in my case as my start-up journey started to take over, my life became full and exhausting, which made it easier to not hang out. You don't have to be a workaholic like me to move your front row, you can make other conscious efforts. I moved out of the area. I ate at different restaurants, went on holidays alone, and attempted to find replacements for the front row by making new adult friendships.

During this transition period, it can be very lonely. But, as I mentioned before, I am adamant that performing to an empty theatre is better than performing to hecklers. That's not to say that old friends won't attempt to slink back into their seats. Every now and then you might get a text asking you to meet up or bump into one of them and have an awkward 'Let's have lunch next week!' but it is best to be honest about what you are going through right now. Rather than ignore messages, be vulnerable and truthful. Tell them, with kindness, how you feel.

Unless you clearly explain why you have chosen a course of action, it can be natural for your counterpart to protest. I advise you to communicate clearly and without blame. State your emotions, don't seek understanding – your ego might want you to share how you feel hard done by, but this is unnecessary energy, just seek acceptance and acknowledgement of the boundaries you've set.

In some circumstances, it is of course necessary to eject someone from the theatre entirely, but this should be a rare occurrence. The further back you move your theatre attendees, the less harm they can inflict on you. When they throw a tomato, it doesn't make it to the stage. If they start talking mid-performance, you can't hear them anyway. The idea is to have a full and thriving audience whose energy lifts you up. Who give thoughtful and constructive criticism, because they want you to go out again the next night and give it your best shot. They are rooting for you, they're telling others about the great play they've seen, and they're ready to give you a standing ovation. Choose your front row wisely, they'll be the ones who determine the quality of your life's performance.

New Method 47
Cut the Noise

We create absolute silence, around us and within us, to be able to hear ourselves. The constant hum of life can be a distraction. These webs of information hold us back as we spend time and energy untangling each new thread. By cutting the noise we have the clarity to move forward. This may be as literal as silencing the group chat. Or cancelling a media subscription. Perhaps we leave a party early. But eventually, we will have to cut the noise entirely. We will have to go on a journey, alone, to be faced with the crushing noise of our own thoughts. Only then will we learn to silence them.

It is important that we create silence and remove distractions in order to access our True Self. In a world filled with constant noise and external demands, finding moments of stillness becomes essential for self-discovery and personal growth. Throughout history, great philosophers and thinkers have emphasized the significance of introspection and self-reflection in understanding our true nature. In an era where it seems we are not allowed to be unavailable, how do we embrace the power of silence and the journey to unveiling our authentic selves?

I've always spent a lot of time alone with my thoughts. I remember long stretches of playing alone as a child, just as equally as I remember the rooms filled with cousins and laughter. Being alone allowed my mind to rest, wander and space out. As I got older, the ability to be alone with my thoughts became less and less frequent. The social demands of being a student in London meant I had lost the capacity to be alone, and in my youth, I hadn't identified it as something that was essential to me.

It was only when I entered a relationship and had a baby in my mid-twenties that I felt the suffocation of being around people all the time. The incessant requests for my attention from others, whether that was from family, friends or my business, were unmanageable and I often felt like I was silently screaming from the inside. I still hadn't quite cultivated the ability to be alone. In fact, at this point, I was afraid of it and actively avoided it. Early in my healing journey, being alone meant dark intrusive thoughts reflecting on the perceived pitiful state of my life. Even though I hated the noise, I was scared of the silence.

Eventually, that changed, and I believe the desire for self-development and the ability to be silent are bound together. Many women feel that self-progress is available to them. There are endless courses, manifestation workshops and wellness activities you can do. But once you have started a family, silence and aloneness may not be something that you feel is available. American author Barbara De Angelis once said: 'Women need real moments of solitude and self-reflection to balance out how much of ourselves we give away.' At the time of writing, my son is twelve and this is the first year since he was born that I have seriously considered taking a trip longer than two weeks away from him. Over the last decade, I don't think my heart could have managed the anxiety of being separated from my child for that long, but as he begins to enter a new phase of his life, so can I.

One shouldn't have to desire to be separated from one's family in order to find some stillness in life, but it seems that this stillness is challenging in the modern world. We have to create it. Throughout history, we have been told stories of wandering men able to prise themselves away from society in order to seek wisdom. Men such as the American essayist, poet and philosopher Henry David Thoreau, renowned for his book *Walden*, which chronicles his experience living in solitude for two years in a cabin near Walden Pond. Thoreau's time in seclusion allowed him to muse on nature, society and the individual's place in the world, becoming a key figure in the transcendentalist movement and launching a million wandering walkers who hold him as a figurehead for quiet reflection.

Practices such as meditation and mindfulness have been utilized for centuries as powerful tools to achieve stillness and inner peace. These techniques encourage us to be fully present in the moment, cultivating a deep connection with our inner selves. Through meditation, we learn to observe our thoughts and emotions without judgement, gaining clarity and self-understanding. By cultivating stillness, we recognize that our thoughts and external circumstances do not define our essence. We are the sky. Women should not be excluded from this essential human experience that is a critical part of achieving and maintaining our Higher Self. Our busy work should not prevent us from finding deeper spiritual connection. This silence should be accessible to us, and created on our own terms.

In our history, women have often been silenced by force. Acting with agency and *creating silence*, both internally and externally, can serve as an act of power. Women have long sought and created spaces conducive to introspection, communion with like-minded women and self-discovery. From the monastic traditions of Hildegard von Bingen and Teresa of Ávila to the literary salons of the Enlightenment period, women have used private spaces to connect with their inner worlds. These gatherings provided an opportunity for women to engage in intellectual discourse, challenge societal norms, and nurture our spirit. Even in the face of adversity and suppression, women of the past have always found ways to cultivate inner silence and self-expression, and you can too.

This New Method is to start to cut the noise. A slow snipping at first before the big chop. The easiest way to start is with your communication. In today's fast-paced and digitally connected world, silence has become a precious commodity. Endless notifications, social media and external pressures can drown out our inner voice, so it is crucial for us to set boundaries with technology. You do not need to reply to every email, phone call or text message. You can mute the group chats. You do not need to comment on every social media post. Unless you are a world leader, the world will not end with you cutting the noise.

At the next level, you can cut the physical noise or your presence. Say no to non-essential social events, and the ones you do attend, leave early. Once you have gained what you need to gain – for me, it's as simple as one meaningful conversation – leave. I have become so adept at this that my friends have even coined it as me 'Doing the Dip'. For years I have dipped out of an event, a French exit if you will, once I am satisfied with my social interactions or learned what I needed to learn. Preserve your energy so that your mental battery is not drained.

Perhaps this is a sign of me getting older, but noise-cancelling headphones have become essential for being able to live in the city. When I am walking around London with headphones, I am oblivious to every argument, catcall or crying baby. In an airport or train station, the constant buzzing of information is overwhelming. My great life hack for a calmer journey is giant headphones from the minute I enter the airport to the minute I leave the airport at the other end. Eyes forward and in my own world, by cutting the noise I feel I am in a protective bubble. In the areas where I need to stay alert, I still maintain one earbud in to dampen the sound.

But even these small steps are not enough for you to build a deeper relationship with yourself. Carving out time and space for your Vision Quest – a term coined by nineteenth-century anthropologists – is key. A Vision Quest, or sacred journey, is a traditional practice that involves seeking spiritual guidance and self-discovery through solitude and connection with nature. It is commonly practised by indigenous cultures around the world and they each have their own names for this essential rite of passage. Call on your ancestors to find out what is true for your culture.

During a Vision Quest, you can be guided by an elder or spiritual mentor, and you withdraw from your everyday life, entering a period of seclusion in a remote and natural setting. This secluded space, such as a sacred mountain, forest or desert, will serve as the backdrop and supporting character for your journey.

Your quest will typically involve fasting, prayer, meditation and other rituals specific to the cultural tradition. The goal is to enter a state of heightened awareness and receptivity, so you can connect deeply with your inner self. With time, you may receive visions, insights and messages from the divine, and most importantly from within.

The purpose of your Vision Quest varies depending on your current circumstances and your cultural context. You can do it to seek clarity on life's purpose, receive guidance for important decisions, heal emotional or spiritual wounds, or gain a deeper understanding of yourself. A Vision Quest is never time wasted. It will be a leap forward in cutting the noise.

When I first read about the idea of a Vision Quest, it seemed completely out of my reach. If you are currently leading a full life, with many responsibilities, you may feel this too. But you can start small. Maybe it's a few hours' walk or a weekend away. Start building up comfort in silence. Upon reflection, I feel I had a mini Vision Quest when I took eighteen months out of London to move back to my home town of Wolverhampton. I completely took myself out of my daily grind. The backdrop was full of nature. My aunts were my spiritual healers, I ate mostly vegan food, and I began meditating and walking regularly. It was a transformative period for me to relax my nervous system and be receptive to new thinking. It is also where I got the idea to start a tech company, and I had the time and space to develop the idea further before moving back to London. Sometimes what you may need is just a long stretch of time out of your current situation or location.

When moving out of London I had a huge fear that I would be forgotten. That I would become irrelevant and no one would care about me. Well, no one did care, because I am not the centre of their world, and I learned to live with that. I didn't talk to friends for a long time and I got OK with being alone, or, as spiritual leader Ram Dass called it, All-One. When I was ready to come back, I picked up my social life and career like I had never left. The world will keep turning without you, and that's OK. Your healing is more important than your social relevance.

Even now, I am planning a longer journey when my son is thirteen, one I have been planning for years. If, like me, you didn't get the privilege of a gap year, don't worry, because the world will still be here for you in a decade or two's time when you are able to take that journey that you need. Maybe we need a new Grand

Tour – the lofty name for the rite-of-passage trip through Europe taken by privileged young men in the eighteenth century. We need a Goddess Trail. A global travel journey that is available to women to reconnect with themselves in sacred spaces within our earth where they can seek a higher consciousness.

The quest for self-discovery and self-understanding is both timeless and essential and I want you to know that it is available to you. By creating silence and removing distractions, we create opportunities to connect with ourselves. In a world that often tries to define us, embracing silence allows us to listen to that inner voice and live in alignment with our deepest values. So, begin to plan your solitude and remember, you are alone but you are not lonely.

New Method 48
Manage Your First Existential Crisis

As intelligent and introspective women, we are constantly searching for meaning in the world. Trying to make sense of it all. At various moments in our lives there will be no answers, pushing us to the edge of the abyss. We know that existential crises will come for us, and we know that with management, this too shall pass. We do not stand still and wallow in the melancholy for too long. We push forward, we stick to our methods, and we generate new purpose. By adopting strategies to manage our various existential crises, we can emerge whole, with a great sense of clarity about who we are and why we are here.

If you really knew me you would know that I have experienced sadness a lot. Long periods where I am disconnected and not acting in true purpose. I'm just very good at maintaining consistency in my output and very good at fulfilling my duties at work. I can be a high-functioning depressive person. But people can feel it. They can feel my quiet black hole energy. My son and I call this 'the Muffin'. When he was small, we watched the classic movie *The NeverEnding Story* and for years he thought the Nothing was called the Muffin, so we affectionately continue to call it that whenever we are sad.

What is the Nothing? In *The NeverEnding Story*, it was

the result of humans' inability to believe. As their busy working worlds took over, they forgot about Fantasia, the land in the story book, and so it started to disappear, swallowed up by a dark nothingness. That is what the Muffin is. It's an apathy about the world around me, which leads to me slowly starting to disappear. I had so successfully managed my emotions and anxiety, that sometimes I just felt nothing. And as someone who feels so deeply, with the full spectrum of her emotions, this was quite scary. Apathy protects you very well from anxiety, but I lost my heart and my drive within the process.

People, things, feelings, all matter. And when they stop mattering, that is when my existential Muffin begins. In the movie, there is a significant scene where the protagonist, Atreyu, is faced with a daunting decision. He must walk through twin Sphinx statues, towering on either side of him, which mark a grand entryway leading to an important destination. However, passing through the statues is not so simple an act – a failure to believe in oneself results in the Sphinxes opening their eyes and unleashing powerful lasers, destroying anyone who doubts themselves. We must walk through the valley, fearing no evil.

Doubt forms a big part of my existential crisis, not only in myself, but in the systems and institutions that are here to protect and serve us. When nothing is right in the world, how can I be expected to be right in myself? How can I stay in my tiny lane, working on what I'm meant to be working on, when all around me there are forces working against me? Against womenkind?

Existentialism, as understood through the work of philosophers such as Jean-Paul Sartre and Martin Heidegger, invites us to confront the realities of the human condition: our mortality, our freedom and our responsibility to create meaning in a world that can so often feel chaotic and uncertain. It asks us to grapple with the big questions of life, such as 'What is the meaning of existence?' and 'What is the purpose of my life?' and to find our own answers, rather than relying on external sources or societal norms.

There are many times in my life when I have desired to be more of a ripple on the surface of an ocean than a deep current at the bottom of an abyss. Thinking deeply and reflecting often makes you more attuned to the complexities of life and more prone to questioning your place in the world. Knowledge, in this regard, can sometimes come at a cost. Ignorance is bliss.

As is my usual perspective, pain is the lesson and so I believe that at its core, existentialism is a signal to take ownership of our lives and make choices that align with our deepest values and beliefs, even in the face of adversity or the unknown. It challenges us to embrace the discomfort that comes with being human, and to find meaning in the struggle. It encourages us to connect with others in a way that acknowledges our shared humanity. In short, existentialism asks us to live with awareness, intention and a willingness to embrace the full range of human experience – the joy, the pain, the love and the fear – in order to create a life that works for you.

But to do this is also a luxury. We have work, children,

lives, to get back to, so what can we do to move through the process more efficiently? There is a series of tasks that I now work through whenever these crises come, which they do with regularity, giving me a toolkit to manage them.

Firstly, I list some emotions and attempt to list the current issue that matches them. I don't always have answers at this point, but I write the words anyway.

- Sad – why?
- Angry – at who?
- Frustrated – at what?
- Annoyed – by what?

Then I zoom out and look at macro world events and my media diet and assess how that might affect my mood. Did someone declare war? Was another woman brutally murdered? Accept that you do not exist in a vacuum and that the content you consume will have an underlying impact on your mood.

Next, I look at my state of being. A key part of me slipping into crisis mode is the Upper Limit Problem – a concept, first explained to me by coach Jess Ratcliffe, that comes from Gay Hendricks's book *The Big Leap*. 'Here's how an upper limit problem works: We all have an inner "thermostat setting" that determines how much success we allow ourselves to enjoy in various areas of life. When we exceed our inner thermostat setting, we may do something to sabotage ourselves, causing us to drop back into the old, familiar zone where we feel secure.'

As I scale myself and my business, could my mind be

attacking itself to keep me at my safe level? Was I proving myself right? What was I afraid of? Furthermore, as I reflected on the book, I realized I was just hanging in my 'Zone of Excellence' with my work. This Zone is where you are already doing all the things you are good at, which can then make you apathetic.

'Most people build their careers in their zone of excellence, the area of life in which your skills are proficient. The problem with the zone of excellence – and the reason why so many people in it are most unhappy – is that it is the mastery of that which already exists. It is building out other people's preexisting needs and ideas. It is a fine line away from the zone of genius, the mental state in which you will actually thrive.'

This Upper Limit Problem is something I can crash into while Playing Games I Can Win. It's the result of doing 100 per cent of the things I already know how to do and being in too much pleasure and ease. The result means that I never get to my Zone of Genius. The tension between wanting to stay in my safe zone, while also not feeling like I was pushing myself to the next level, while also feeling a little bit angry and annoyed, was resulting in a very noisy head, which I couldn't seem to escape from. A swirling storm of feelings. I tried to tackle them one by one against my words.

- Sad – Upper Limit Problem.
- Frustrated – not achieving my Zone of Genius.
- Angry – what was I angry about?
- Annoyed – what exactly was I annoyed at?

One answer could be the suffering it took to get here.

It is at this point of the toolkit that I begin to have some compassion for my experience. I worked a lot, I sacrificed a lot. I did a lot alone. Would I have got here without the suffering? Why must I always suffer to create things that do well? This feeling – like clockwork – then leads to me being angry at the system that rewards a ridiculous amount of overworking, game playing and bullshit, and so I withdraw from the system and the Muffin begins.

OK, so I had some more answers:

- Sad/despondent – Upper Limit Problem.
- Frustrated – not achieving my Zone of Genius.
- Angry – a system of inequality and labour.
- Annoyed – the suffering to get to the wins.

So now I had some things to resolve to get me out of my crisis, but first I had to take care of the basics. One cannot be expected to work through these difficult mental challenges without first addressing our fundamental human needs.

1. Physiological: I took care of myself. I stopped drinking completely. I got enough sleep, I attempted 20 minutes cardio a day or 10k steps. This meant that my body could support my mind.
2. Spiritual: I went to yoga, I meditated, I chanted. I felt connected to something bigger than myself. What is your church?

3. Social: I joined several community events on the Stack and hosted many dinner parties. Social bonds are essential for humans to feel human. Hosting a dinner party gave me a micro sense of purpose and excitement at meaningful conversations.
4. Gratitude: I would look back at my life (especially at pictures of Baby Roman) and feel utterly grateful for the things I've seen, experienced and done.
5. Stopped watching the news: I listen to the morning news on my Alexa, and that's it. No papers, no TV, no social media news.
6. Made playlists of music I loved aged fifteen to twenty-five, aka the responsibility-free years. UK Garage, Grime, Dubstep and the Spice Girls.
7. I bathed in nature. Lots of long, wet walks in the English countryside.

These things are table stakes. The basics to get you prepared. Let's now go to the next level of optimism making. This requires active participation and work.

1. 12-Step Programs – I returned to my programmes to find communion in those also experiencing suffering.
2. I consumed stories of purpose in books, TV and film. Classic stories of people fighting for justice.
3. I reflected on Joseph Campbell's Hero's Journey theory, understanding that this was all just part of my cycle.

4. I listened to the usual motivational and
   philosophical podcasts, but also audiobooks,
   while walking.
5. I went back to my home town for a trip, to my
   siblings. I returned to my source. As soon as I
   was back in Wolverhampton I experienced such
   a positive energy shift! I love this place and it
   reminded me of how far I've come.

So after taking some action to consume content that
helped me understand the importance of meaning, I
now had to apply it. This is the hardest but most
rewarding part of finding my motivation again. All this
work was done through conversations with friends and
journaling.

1. I seriously started to question what I really
   wanted. Do I want to be on this growth
   trajectory and keep being included in start-ups?
   The answer is yes, but on my own terms. My
   life's work – equality for women – remains the
   same, but what exactly was my role in that? I
   know what I want to be doing at seventy, but is
   my work today going to get me there?
2. My current mission – the Stack World – how
   are we executing on the vision? Do I feel like
   we are really making an impact and difference?
   How can we make this difference at scale?
3. Does my role suit what I'm good at and suit my
   lifestyle? Where am I best supported and where
   are the gaps I need to fill?

4. Am I giving to myself what I'm giving to others? Being of service is my default state and it's now my job. Am I supporting myself the way I support our members?
5. How do I get to my Zone of Genius? What am I uniquely good at that means that without my contribution it wouldn't exist, or wouldn't exist at the level I could do it?
6. What actions can I take today to make progress rather than setting unachievable goals as a form of procrastination?
7. Learning Mode is critical for me. Am I actively learning in my role?

I rounded off these questions by actually updating my own Vision, Mission and Principles, the simple one-page document that reminds me who I am and what I stand for. I then completed my annual Vision Setting Document, creating a narrative for my future. It's at this point that I usually begin myself again. I am fired up, I'm excited about the future and I am full of my usual energy and optimism. My work and my purpose are aligned.

When this feeling returns and the Muffin is eaten, I then take the necessary steps to update our business goals, build a team who will get me there and let go of the people who won't. With each surge forward, there must be things, people and practices I leave behind. You'll notice that this essay is almost like a CliffsNotes to the whole book. It is indeed a summary of the jump-start

I need when I begin to lose way. Remember, we are works in progress and it is easy to go off the path you seek.

I understand now that the Work is never finished and I need to practise what I preach. These New Methods were started when I was twenty-eight, and a decade later it is easy to feel complacent, like I know it all. Only through consistent and concerted effort with my methods did I find my zest for life again. By understanding my role in this speck of humanity on the timeline of this universe, by designing products that give me something to look forward to and by finding a group of people to help me move towards that goal, I am myself once more.

Why is this essay titled Managing Your First Existential Crisis? Because as life continues, you will likely experience many more, but they'll require different tools and reflections to solve. With age and wisdom, new layers of self-revelation occur. Don't feel disheartened if your crises re-emerge, just know they have to be chipped away at, day by day.

New Method 49
Rip It Up and Start Again

We are not afraid to die and be reborn. We are not afraid to reject the life we currently have. We know that starting again is not a failure or a loss; it is a courageous act of self-discovery and growth. It is a declaration that we refuse to settle for mediocrity and that we demand more from life than mere existence. By rejecting the life we currently have, we create space for new experiences, new relationships, and new possibilities to enter our lives. The only thing that is truly constant in life is change. So we embrace it. We encourage it. We take on an abundant mindset and a punk attitude. We can, at any time we wish, rip it up and start again.

One might think that the path to wholeness is a clear and direct line, but it is almost always a series of conjoining circles looping up and hopefully to the right. With each loop, you must go down before ascending to greater heights. At the very bottom point of each loop is where you can decide to rip everything up and start again.

You have the choice. Burn it all down. Opt out. Smash it up. Don't be afraid of radical reinvention. It is only through something dying that we can be reborn anew. Kill your darlings and watch as fresh possibilities emerge from the ruins. In this chaotic act of destruction, we find the seeds of transformation, the fertile ground in which the purest version of ourselves can flourish.

I have ripped it all apart in big ways and small ways. I am not afraid to take an axe to my life and build again from the ground up. All the Methods in this book have given me the tools to have no fear, but it is especially my abundant mindset that gives me the reassurance to know I can always start again.

When you have that knowledge that you can always start again, destroying the familiar not only becomes something you are unafraid of but something you actually seek to do. Your life will have a series of chapters and you'll start to instinctively know when it's time to start a new one. You'll feel bored or depressed or anxious to go to work, or see a person. These are signals that you need a change.

When I closed my first business, WAH Nails, after ten years of operating, it was a shocking move. I knew I wanted to press forward with building software and at the time I didn't have the bandwidth or the team in place to manage two businesses, so on the advice of others I shut it down. This was a defiant and seemingly crazy act. Even today people will still talk about the salon or share a memory of it, and while I do miss being a shopkeeper, I knew I couldn't honour my goals by keeping it open. Ripping it all up meant that I no longer had that connection and domain authority in that world. I was no longer invited to beauty and fashion events, I was irrelevant in that domain. I had to start again. But that's OK because my loop was preparing for an upwards trajectory, and

I moved into technology and pressed forward with Beautystack.

After an exciting start, including becoming the first Black woman to raise millions in venture capital in the UK, the pandemic compelled me to rip up Beautystack. We had early customers, a working product and funding in the bank and then, like so many other businesses around the globe, we couldn't operate. For fourteen months, no one in the UK could book beauty treatments. At the time, our start-up mentality and my inexperience in major world events meant I was not primed for planning. We could have done many things to survive, such as introducing video therapy and coaching, but I was also in the midst of a collective trauma around race, gender and health. When we had our third lockdown announcement I decided to end Beautystack and start the Stack World. The stress of these years took its toll on my mood and my body. I didn't really want to rip it up but I also knew I had to act. It took me many, many months to be OK with the decision, but I went ahead anyway, knowing my enthusiasm would catch up.

The Stack World proved to be a wise move, as my business endeavours and my personal mission got closer together through building a company designed to give women the knowledge and the network to lead. Starting again was tough and there were many moments of doubt. With little capital left and scaled-back resources, we slowly crawled our way to product market fit, signing deals with some of the world's most innovative companies to provide content to their young women employees.

In just a few years in the life of the business, I feel we have made a significant impact in creating a brand and a community that is changing the perception of what a leader looks like. We now have users in thirty-two countries and are regularly described as 'life-changing' by our members. But the forward motion animal in me is already itchy – how can I achieve my mission at scale? What's the next chapter for me?

As I close this arc of my life, what I am ripping up is not totally external or visible, but it is a complete destruction of the role I play to myself and others, especially with regard to my work/life satisfaction. Like most humans, I want to be appreciated for my work, I want to be dutiful and I want to be successful. But now I see a duty to myself and my well-being. My current view of success is very different from just a few years ago, and is about putting my creativity – not my productivity – at the forefront of my life. This means a period of downsizing while I invest my time in seeking mastery. It takes time to turn what you love into a viable revenue stream so you downsize while you figure it out. This means not just downsizing in my material world but in my superficial power too. It might mean fewer fancy trips, fewer invitations, fewer accolades. It might mean getting off the start-up fundraising treadmill. It means that just because I *can* do many things, it doesn't mean I always *should*. All the things that suck your time and keep you away from your Important Work and True Self. Starting over means saying no to the demands of the outside world to say yes to myself and the work that I find meaningful.

To rip it all up and start again requires courage – a willingness to confront the familiar and question its validity. Why are you sticking to your current lifestyle choices? Are they actually working for you? What does it mean to shed your identity? Who are you without your current social circle? What do your material possessions do for your status?

Sometimes it's not that anything bad or uncomfortable is happening in our lives that requires us to rip it up, it's just we are travelling at a constant speed and so we need to reject complacency. To me, coasting through life is the equivalent of walking backwards on a travelator. You are expending energy and time but you aren't actually going anywhere. A rejection of complacency is a refusal to be confined by what feels safe. We must be unafraid to let go of the attachments that keep us in stasis, the beliefs that no longer propel us forward, and the relationships that allow us to fester.

In this process of radical reinvention, we continue to shed the last layers of societal expectations and external validations. We free ourselves from the weight of conformity and embrace the truth of our own desire. It is a reclaiming of our agency, a declaration that we are the architects of our own lives. You are designing your own life.

I'm under no illusion that the process is easy. Ripping it all up is not without pain, uncertainty and doubt. Ripping can sometimes leave scars. Ripping can hurt those around you. I have cried and cried at my choices, before realizing that the difficult path is the one that sends me to new heights. Doing this requires us to trust that something greater awaits us on the other side. It is a journey that demands unwavering determination. It requires unmovable boundaries.

When it is most painful is usually when it carries ego and shame and humiliation. You made a choice, you now want a different choice – what will everyone say? What will they think? As we tear down the structures that no longer serve us, we must also be willing to confront our own inner demons – the insecurities, the self-doubt and the limiting beliefs that whisper in our ears, attempting to hold us back. I have always felt that I didn't want to be labelled a failure. The word alone felt like a stink that I did not want attached to me. We must be brave enough to silence those voices. They're not the ones living your life, so why should their ten-second comment affect your next ten years?

In this process of destruction and rebirth, we discover our true power – the power to define ourselves, to create our own narrative and to live authentically. We do as we please. We realize that the external world does not hold the key to our happiness and fulfilment; they say self-development is an inside job.

The act of ripping it up and starting again, of letting go of what we once held dear, is a physical embodiment of our growth and evolution. It is a recognition that change is not only inevitable but necessary for our personal and spiritual development.

We learn to detach ourselves from the outcome, embrace the impermanence of life, and find beauty in the continuous cycle of creation and destruction. Louisa May Alcott said it beautifully: 'I make so many beginnings there never will be an end.' I created a family signet ring with exactly this sentiment. Under a leopard, holding the Jamaican flag no less, are the words REGENERATIO. Rebirth. A constant reminder of my ability to start again.

So, my New Methods women, do not be afraid to destroy it all and burn it all down. Give open arms to the chaos, the uncertainty and the discomfort that accompany this process. Trust in your own resilience, in your capacity to rebuild and redefine yourself. In the act of destruction, you will find liberation. In the ashes, you will discover the seeds of your own rebirth. And in embracing this transformative journey, you will get closer and closer to that elusive feeling of contentment that you have been seeking all along.

Epilogue

Waking up on my thirty-ninth birthday, I had never felt such peace, contentment and love. It was the first birthday in a long time when I hadn't cried due to feelings of intense loneliness or exhaustion. Even though I was single, I felt *loved*. I thought, well, something about my Methods must have worked. I felt *good*. I do hope that my words have helped you during that critical time in your late twenties when you might feel like you're never going to make it. I'm here to tell you, you absolutely will.

Of course, it's not all roses. How cruel the cycle of life can be! After a brief moment of bliss where it seemed as though all was right in my world, a few months later the cycle began again. The summer of 2023 was challenging to say the least. I scrambled for my Methods again, heading to the 'Manage Your First Existential Crisis' essay, which has always been my go-to in moments of need, and nothing was quite clicking into place for me. After slipping into a new set of feelings that summer, I suddenly realized that I was entering a new era of womanhood. I was going to be forty years old. Let's call it New Methods, Season 2.

My hormones were experiencing their first wildly fluctuating levels as my body prepared to shut down its reproductive system. Everything I worked for I was reassessing with a new lens. Everything felt out of my control. I started to question my choices once more. Was it all worth it? Seeking answers, I connected more with women who were fifty years and older, desperate for some recognition of what was happening to me. I started to understand why so many women in their later years had opted out. A few older women smiled at me knowingly, sort of in the same way I would smile at a teenager going through puberty. The smile that says – oh honey, there is so much more to come.

As I write this now, my first wave of this new season is over, I am feeling re-energized and motivated. I am making some drastic changes to my life to get closer and closer to what works for me. I continue to work to not abandon myself. While incremental steps are key when you are younger, I feel that for Season 2, I need to make big strides in order to get back to my purpose and calling in life. I recognize that what got me to here won't get me to there, and I know I need to start all over again.

Don't be afraid if the journey is not smooth. Don't be afraid if you feel like you're slipping back to the starting line. Honey, there is so much more to come.

References

p. 6 'The interlocking systems of . . .' *Feminist Theory: From Margin to Center,* bell hooks, (Pluto Press, 1984)

p. 7 'We'd all been thinking . . .' *Fix the System, Not the Women,* Laura Bates, (Simon & Schuster UK, 2022)

p. 11 'The "inner" books rarely . . .' *Revolution From Within: A Book of Self-esteem,* Gloria Steinem (Little, Brown and Co, 1992)

p. 49 'To exist, humanly, is . . .' *Pedagogy of the Oppressed,* Paulo Freire, (Continuum, 2000)

p. 56 *Attached: The New Science of Adult Attachment and How It Can Help You Find – and Keep – Love,* Dr Amir Levine and Rachel S. F. Heller (Bluebird, 2019)

p. 77 'This weaponization of White Womanhood . . .' *White Tears, Brown Scars,* Ruby Hamad (Trapeze, 2020)

p. 81 'Without confronting internalized sexism . . .' *Feminism is for Everybody,* bell hooks (Pluto Press, 2000)

p. 82 'I am not free . . .' 'The Uses of Anger: Women Responding to Racism', Audre Lorde, National Women's Studies Association Conference, Storrs, Connecticut, June 1981

p. 86 'Listen actively and acknowledge . . .', *Getting to Yes: Negotiating an Agreement Without Giving In,* Roger Fisher and William Ury, (Random House Business, 2012)

p. 105 'Every woman knows what . . .', *Men Explain Things to Me,* Rebecca Solnit (Haymarket Books, 2014)

p. 111 'When boys grow up . . .', *The Authority Gap: Why Women Are Still Taken Less Seriously Than Men, and What*

We Can Do About it, Mary Ann Sieghart (Doubleday, 2021)

p. 124 'Level 5 leaders display . . .' *Good to Great*, Jim Collins, (Random House Business, 2001)

p. 128 'The night before his enlightenment', *Radical Acceptance*, Tara Brach (Rider, 2003)

p. 135 'The first function of mythology . . .', *Pathways to Bliss*, Joseph Campbell (New World Library, 2004)

p. 136 'The state couldn't function without', *The Patriarchs: The Origins of Inequality*, Angela Saini (Beacon Press, 2023)

p. 142 'In the beginning . . .' *Moana,* dir. Ron Clements and John Musker (Walt Disney Studios Motion Pictures, 2016), written by Jared Bush, et al.

p. 145 'The story of the human race', *Women's History of the World*, Rosalind Miles (Harper Collins, 2010)

p. 147 'I am the Nala . . .' Beyonce Knowles-Carter, Donald Glover and Jay Z, 'Mood 4 Eva', *Black is King,* Columbia Records, 2019

p. 154 'The reality you experience . . .', *Rebuild: The Economy, Leadership, and You*, Graham Boyd and Jack Reardon, (Evolutesix Books, 2020)

p. 257 '[There must be] new . . .', *The Double X Economy: The Epic Potential of Empowering Women*, Professor Linda Scott (Faber & Faber, 2020)

p. 269 'Habits are the compound interest . . .' *Atomic Habits: tiny changes, remarkable results : an easy & proven way to build good habits & break bad ones,* James Clear (Cornerstone, 2018)

p. 277 'Why are women poor? . . .', *A Room of One's Own*, Virginia Woolf, (Penguin Books, 2004)

p. 357 'Here's how an upper limit problem', *The Big Leap: Conquer Your Hidden Fear And Take Life To The Next Level*, (HarperCollins, 2010)

Acknowledgements

This book started out as a series of newsletters for my Stack World community, so I first give my gratitude to the women who allowed me the space to turn over my ideas, get feedback and find communion. Some of the OG Members who came to those early sessions such as Nana, Dachinii, Marina, Anna, Jen, Viv, Scarlett, Ramat, Kim, Roshanne, Tiwalola, Joyann, Zuzanna, Jemma, Natasha, Aprileen, Paula, Polina, Teju, Natalie, Kate, Hannah, Rochelle, Romy, Róisín, and many more I will fail to name, kept reminding me that I was not alone in my thoughts.

That newsletter would not have been sent out if it were not for Lola Rose Wood's brilliant assistance, then picked up by the dear Erin McKee when Lola went to college. Both of you have given me great feedback, ideas and examples for the book. I thank Dan Woodbury and Ken Lalobo and the Stack World team for building the technology that allowed me to create what I consume and own our entire tech stack rather than living on a rented platform, an important Method for sure. And finally I am eternally grateful to my colleagues Bella Cary and Alice Finch, who through all the ups and downs of starting a start-up reminded me to take my own advice.

Those newsletters became a book through the tenacity of my agent Adrian Sington, who has continually supported and believed in me during this period of my life. Thank you for always pushing me to take my ideas public when I could easily have been comfortable in my small corner of the world. This book would never have made it if it was not for Emily Robertson being such an encouraging and patient editor. At each point of the journey that I found tough, you extended your generosity and support to get me to the finish line. Anya Hayes was instrumental in giving me the final push as I got closer and closer to the deadline. I must also give thanks to Alia Coster, who helped me get the first draft out of my head and on to paper.

The first conversation with Alia happened via Zoom while I sat at the kitchen table and the study of Barn House, the home of Alexandra Jackson and Philip Kay, where I did the bulk of the work on this book. I want to thank you for the gift of space, nature and silence to write. Alex Eagle and Mark Wadhwa have also been endlessly supportive and generous with space at Peanut Cottage, Oakley Court and 180 Strand – my triumvirate of homes from home. Your ability to support and nurture creative talent is inspiring and I am forever grateful. I wrote this book in many hotels and bed and breakfasts around the world, from Jamaica to Egypt and beyond but I would say Italy was the place where I headed many times to write and I thank Arthur Kay for his Umbria home during the final edits of this book. All of you have inspired me to create space for others to write. What a luxury and a gift!

In the final stretch, it was Kirsty Kenney, Steph Nicolaides and Sinead Reed who were kind enough to read this book and give their notes. Claire Barnett gave her expertise from her leadership at UN Women UK to take the time to talk through and give notes on New Method Nine. Not only was Dr Hannah Dawson's book, *The Penguin Book of Feminist Writing*, a bible for me during my research, but she also honoured me with her thoughts and feedback on my final drafts.

There were lots of conversations with friends about the topics in the book on long walks. Poppy Jamie, thank you for being a constant soundboard. My friends Emma Louise Boynton, Michelle Kennedy, Kharmel Cochrane, Phoebe Lovatt and Grace Ladoja all were gracious about me nattering on at them with these topics. I'm sorry to all those friends who told me their problems, only for me to annoyingly say. I've got an essay for that! (And to those in the future, to whom I will do the same.)

I wouldn't be where I am today without the professional support of so many experts. My coach Cheryl Clements was the first person to tell me to take care of myself. Polly Bateman pushed me through the pain to get to the other side. David Samson sealed all that knowledge into my subconscious with hypnotherapy. Manizeh Rimer made spiritual wisdom accessible to me through Jivamukti Yoga. All of them were teachers on my journey alongside so many strangers who taught me lessons without knowing it.

Thank you to my dear sisters, Shakira and Ashanti, the pure hearts who always had the wisest words when I was at my lowest. My aunties Esther and Ruthlyn, who gave me support as well as pivotal books in my time of need. Thank you to my mother and father for giving me the challenge and opportunity to grow and develop. Greg for giving me a reason to expand my emotional range and Roman for giving me a reason to live, to look ahead to the future and let go of my past.

While I acknowledge in the introduction that this book does not create a wholly new framework for equity, I have picked and chosen through existing works what suits me personally and professionally and thus I take full responsibility for what I have written at the time I have written it. Knowledge is forever layered and growing and I am excited for readers to challenge me and for my own journey to continue, going deeper on themes which will eventually form the next wave of feminism.

I believe women should treat all books like this one with a questioning tone. We are always taught that we must be the ones to change, to strive, to do better. But who for? If you read this book for anyone please read it for yourself, for your own wellbeing, irrespective of who capitalism or the patriarchy tells you you ought to be.